Al-Anbar Awakening
Volume I
American Perspectives
U.S. Marines and Counterinsurgency in Iraq, 2004-2009

Edited by
Chief Warrant Officer-4 Timothy S. McWilliams
Lieutenant Colonel Kurtis P. Wheeler

U.S. Marine Corps Reserve

Marine Corps University
United States Marine Corps
Quantico, Virginia
2009

Marine Corps University Press
3078 Upshur Avenue
Quantico, VA
22134

1st Printing, 2009

Al-Anbar Awakening

Volume I
American Perspectives

U.S. Marines and Counterinsurgency in Iraq 2004-2009

Edited by Chief Warrant Officer-4 Timothy S. McWilliams and Lieutenant Colonel Kurtis P. Wheeler

Foreword

by Lieutenant General John F. Kelly

Words like "won" or "victory" really do not apply when speaking of counterinsurgency operations. Insurgencies grow from problems and discontent within a given society. Solve the problems, and the insurgency goes away, as opposed to being defeated. The difficulty is that a government is not always willing to address the root causes of the insurgency because it is often the government itself that the insurgents want to eliminate.

In Iraq to a very large degree, we—the U.S. military and civilians—were the source of the insurgency. Honest men and women can argue the whys, what ifs, and what might have beens, but ultimately, it was mostly about unfulfilled promises and the heavy handed military approach taken by some over the summer of 2003 that caused events to spiral out of control. No doubt the insurgency radicalized over time with al Qaeda and Shi'a extremists playing a key role, but the insurgents did not initiate the war and only took advantage of the discontent.

If you asked Anbaris during my third tour in Iraq in 2008 why the insurgency began, most would look away and try to find a way not to answer. They would tell you that "we are friends now, and the causes are unimportant. It's all water under the bridge now." If pressed, they would talk about mutual misunderstandings and a lack of cultural awareness on both sides. They would say that expectations were too high on the part of the Iraqis about what America could do for them and how fast, but they seldom if ever blamed us directly. Press them further and they would mention the 29 April 2003 "massacre" in Fallujah, but more about the lack of an apology than the 70 plus unarmed citizens allegedly shot that day.

Another factor they would bring up was the shock and humiliation of having their army disbanded. The army was the one institution in Iraq everyone was proud of—Shi'a and Sunni alike—especially for what it had accomplished in protecting the nation against the Iranians in the 1980s. They perceived the disbanding as intentional contempt directed toward Iraq as a nation and as a people. They also saw it as the disarming of the nation. In the minds of many, this is when our status as liberators ended and that of occupier began.

Press the Anbaris one more time, and they would look you in the eye—but only if you are considered a friend—and they would state that after Baghdad fell and throughout the summer of 2003, the Americans overreacted to small acts of resistance or violence and fought in a way that was cowardly and without honor. Here they would talk about the senseless use of firepower and midnight raids on innocent men. They said that by our escalation, we proved true the rhetoric of the nationalist firebrands about why we had invaded, and our actions played directly into the hands of organizations like Zarqawi's al Qaeda in Iraq and Sadr's militia.

Ask the same Anbari citizens why sometime in 2006 they began to turn against the by then al Qaeda led insurgency, and the answer would be more direct. To them, their alliance with the radicals was a marriage of convenience to fight the U.S. occupation. Al Qaeda brought dedication, organization, funding, and a willingness to die. Over time, however, it overplayed its hand and wore out its welcome by forcing an extreme Islamic agenda on a generally secular and very tribal culture. Al Qaeda's campaign evolved from assistance, to persuasion, to intimidation, to murder in the most horrific ways, all designed to intimidate Anbari society—tribes and sheikhs alike—to adopt the most extreme form of Islam. At a certain point, al Qaeda's agenda became too much for the average Anbari to bear. It was increasingly directed at the sheikhs themselves, and just as importantly, it began to have an impact on the business interests of tribal leaders.

The 17 paramount dignified sheikhs of the major Anbari tribes and tribal federation turned away from al Qaeda for survival purposes and toward U.S. forces for the same reason. They will tell you that Iraqis were being hunted down and killed by both the terrorists and the Coalition forces in Anbar. They knew the unbending terrorists would never meet them halfway, but they were confident that the Americans would—and they were right. Many of these men were once as much a part of the insurgency as Zarqawi was, albeit for different reasons. Over time, it became glaringly obvious to them that it was in their personal interests, and the interests of their tribes, to put a stop to the war.

When I returned to Iraq in February 2008 as commander of I Marine Expeditionary Force and Multi National Force West (MNF W), I was amazed at what I found. Violent incidents, once over 400 a week in al Anbar Province, were down to 50 and had been in steady decline for months. Where Iraqis once avoided us, as any interaction jeopardized their lives and those of their families at the hands of al Qaeda terrorists or nationalist insurgents, they were now aggressive in wanting to engage with us. Things had turned. The obvious questions were why had the change occurred, and was it sustainable, or was it simply due to an operational pause in the insurgent's effort? For months, Major General Walt Gaskin and his superb II Marine Expeditionary Force team, our immediate predecessors as MNF W, had been wrestling with the answers. Their conclusions were ours to verify.

For MNF W's part, since March 2004 we had extended the hand of friendship and cooperation, even as we were forced into a brutal fight that knew no quarter on the part of the Iraqi insurgents and foreign fighters. It was the major theme of our campaign plan, and it never changed. The command philosophy, a philosophy programmed into every Marine and U.S. Army unit that served in al Anbar since we took the province, was that we had come to Iraq not to conquer, but to free, that we would always endeavor to "first, do not harm." This was often difficult, and sometimes you simply had to do a Fallujah II, even if Fallujah I had been ill advised and totally counterproductive to what you were trying to do in the first place.

No single personality was the key in Anbar, no shiny new field manual the reason why, and no "surge" or single unit made it happen. It was a combination of many factors, not the least of which—perhaps the most important—was the consistent command philosophy that drove operations in Anbar from March 2004 forward. Each MNF W commander and the troops under him continued to build upon the work of all those who came before. They took what their predecessors had done and ran with it, calling audibles as opportunities presented themselves. Consistency counts, and persistent presence on your feet puts you in more danger, no doubt, but also stacks the deck in your favor as you see more, hear more, know more, and engage more. It is these Americans—Marines, soldiers, sailors, and airmen, as well as civilians—who deserve the individual and collective credit for our part in the miracle that took place in al Anbar Province. They slogged it out for more than six years to help the Anbaris create a miracle that spread to other regions of the country in late 2007, throughout 2008, and now into 2009.

I urge a note of caution to those who might have an overly inflated opinion of the role they played in the Awakening, or to the "experts" who write today as if they, with complete clairvoyance, predicted the change in loyalties in al Anbar. The sheikhs, politicians, Iraqi security force officials, and even the former Ba'athist members of the military who reside in Anbar have a different opinion. They will tell you it was the sense of hopelessness the war had brought to the citizenry. The only hope for the future they could see was to be found in what members of MNF W had done and were doing on their behalf despite the heat, the criticism from home, and the killing and casualties. They began to see us as a force that was sharing in their agony. Once they tried reaching out to some soldier or Marine's outstretched hand in friendship, it was over.

The interviews collected in the two volumes of this anthology do what no previous work has done—they attempt to tell the story of the al Anbar Awakening from both sides, American and Iraqi. Not all the voices could be included, but there are many pertinent ones. The story they tell is a complex but important one, and it should be read with interest by all who want to truly understand what happened in Iraq between 2004 and 2009.

John F. Kelly
Lieutenant General, U.S. Marine Corps

Preface

This two volume anthology of interviews tells the story of the al Anbar Awakening and the emergence of al Anbar Province from the throes of insurgency. It presents the perspectives of both Iraqis (volume two) and Americans (volume one) who ultimately came to work together, in an unlikely alliance of former adversaries, for the stabilization and redevelopment of the province. The collection begins in the 2003 2004 time frame with the rise of the insurgency and concludes with observations from the vantage point of early to mid 2009.

The anthology demonstrates that there is not one history of the Awakening, but several histories intertwined. It is not a complete collection, but one that provides a broad spectrum of candid, unvarnished perspectives from some of the leading players.

The American volume focuses on the roles and views of U.S. Marines, who were the primary Coalition force in al Anbar from spring 2004 onward. At the time of their arrival, many military experts considered the province irredeemable. This collection chronicles the efforts of the Marines, and the soldiers, sailors, airmen, and civilians who worked with them, to consistently employ counterinsurgency tactics and to continue to reach out to the Iraqis during even the darkest days of the insurgency.

The Iraqi volume collects from many of the key Awakening players their views on how and why Anbaris came to turn against the insurgency that many had initially supported and seek the aid—both military and economic—of the Americans. Those interviewed include former Ba'ath Party military officers, senior officers in Iraq's new military, tribal sheikhs, Sunni imams, governmental representatives, and civilians.

This anthology is drawn from oral history interviews collected by field historians of the U.S. Marine Corps History Division, based at Marine Corps University in Quantico, Virginia. Field historians assigned to the History Division have collected hundreds of interviews since the beginning of Operation Iraqi Freedom I to serve as primary resources for future scholarship. In support of this anthology project,

Colonel Gary W. Montgomery and Chief Warrant Office 4 Timothy S. McWilliams deployed to Iraq in February and March of 2009 to interview Iraqis and additional American military and civilian personnel. Lieutenant Colonel Kurtis P. Wheeler had conducted more than 400 interviews in earlier deployments.

Like courtroom testimonies, oral histories are told from one person's perspective and may include discrepancies with, or even contradictions of, another witness's views. They are not a complete history, but they provide the outlines for one, to be fleshed out with documents and other sources not often collected or declassified this soon after events.

The interviews in this collection are edited excerpts drawn from longer interviews. They have been transcribed and edited according to scholarly standards to maintain the integrity of the interviews. Only interjections, false starts, and profanity have been silently omitted. Details added for clarity and accuracy are indicated by brackets. Omissions are noted by three dot ellipses for partial sentences and four dot ellipses for full sentences or more. With the Iraqi interviews, the interchange with interpreters has been omitted except in a few cases where the interpreter is attempting to clarify a point. Much of what has been left out of the American interviews is material that is duplicated in other interviews in the anthology. The full interviews and complete transcripts are part of the oral history collection of the Marine Corps History Division.

Ranks of officers, particularly American officers, reflect the rank at the time of the deployment under discussion. We have not tried to insert "then" in front of the ranks of all officers who have since been promoted.

We have attempted to verify the Iraqi person, place, and tribe names as best as possible, but undoubtedly there are several discrepancies, particularly in the Iraqi volume, where language barriers, dialects, the use of interpreters, and the mentions of many minor actors and areas made accurate transcription and identification challenging. There are also many variations in the transliteration of Iraqi names and terms.

*   *   *

The editors of this anthology acknowledge and thank a wide array of people for their support on this project. First and foremost, we thank the people whose stories are included for their time and candor. We particularly acknowledge Lieutenant General John F. Kelly, who wrote the foreword and who expedited the 2009 deployment of Colonel Montgomery and Chief Warrant Officer 4 McWilliams. In addition to the editors, those who conducted interviews included in the anthology are Colonel Jeffrey Acosta, Colonel Stephen E. Motsco, Colonel Michael D. Visconage, Lieutenant Colonel Craig H. Covert, Lieutenant Colonel John P. Piedmont, Lieutenant Colonel John R. Way, Staff Sergeant Bradford A. Wineman, Dr. David B. Crist, and Dr. Charles P. Neimeyer.

Dr. Neimeyer, director of the History Division; Mr. Charles D. Melson, chief historian; and Dr. Nathan S. Lowery, Field History branch head, provided guidance for the project. Mr. Kenneth H. Williams, senior editor for both the History Division and Marine Corps University Press, oversaw the editing and publication, assisted in the editing by Ms. Wanda J. Renfrow. Mr. Vincent J. Martinez provided layout and design for both volumes. Mr. Anthony R. Taglianetti, the History Division's oral historian, coordinated the timely transcription of the interviews. Lieutenant Colonel David A. Benhoff and Gunnery Sergeant Michael C. Coachman provided logistical support. Dr. Nicholas J. Schlosser, History Division historian, and Mr. Colin M. Colbourn, History Division intern, helped verify information.

Beyond the History Division, we are especially grateful to the interpreters. Those currently working in Iraq shall remain anonymous because of the inherent vulnerabilities peculiar to their vocation. Sometimes underappreciated and often overworked, their knowledge and perseverance was absolutely essential to our effort.

Many others labored to bring this project to fruition. Those who work outside of the normal publishing process are listed below. If we omitted anyone, it was inadvertent and not from lack of gratitude.

I Marine Expeditionary Force (Multi National Forces-West):
Lieutenant Colonel Bradley E. Weisz (G 3 Air Officer); Lieutenant Colonel Todd W. Lyons (G 9 Foreign Affairs Officer/Marine Corps Intelligence Activity); Major Adam T. Strickland (Engagement Officer); 1st Lieutenant Timothy J.

Malham (Economic and Political Intelligence Center); Sergeant Luke O. Vancleave (Economic and Political Intelligence Center); Corporal Travis L. Helm (Economic and Political Intelligence Center); Corporal Lamont J. Lum (Economic and Political Intelligence Center); Lance Corporal Cassidy C. Niblett (Economic and Political Intelligence Center); Lance Corporal Orell D. Fisher (Economic and Political Intelligence Center).

II Marine Expeditionary Force: Colonel Robert W. Lanham (G 9 Assistant Chief of Staff); Lieutenant Colonel Bowen Richwine (G 9 Engagements OIC); Major Steven K. Barriger (G 9 Governance); 2d Lieutenant Anthony M. Bramante (Economic and Political Intelligence Center); Staff Sergeant William J. Rickards (G 9 Support); Sergeant Robert A. Pittenridge (G 9 Governance); Lance Corporal Thomas P. Wiltshire (Combat Camera); "Jack" Mahmood S. Al Jumaily (Interpreter); Mythm Hassin (Interpreter).

Center for Advanced Operational Culture Learning, Quantico: Mr. Richard C. McPherson; Ms. Basema Maki (Interpreter); Mr. Hamid Lellou (Interpreter).

Marine Corps Intelligence Activity, Quantico: Colonel Philip D. Gentile (Commanding Officer); Mr. Dan J. Darling (Threat Analyst).

U.S. Marine Corps MARCENT LNO Cell, Kuwait: Gunnery Sergeant John M. Neatherton.

Marine Air-Ground Combat Training Center, Twentynine Palms, California: Staff Sergeant Michael A. Blaha (Combat Camera); Lance Corporal Ricky J. Holt (Combat Camera).

Marine Corps Base, Camp Pendleton, California: Captain Scott M. Clendaniel (Aide to General Kelly); Sergeant Eric L. Alabiso II (Combat Camera).

American Perspectives

Introduction

"If you help me get rid of those who mean me harm, then you're obviously my friend," a sheikh in al Anbar Province told U.S. Marine Major General Walter E. Gaskin Sr. in 2007. "If you fight along with me and shed your blood, you're my brother."[1] A year later, the Americans returned al Anbar to provincial Iraqi control and turned over Camp Fallujah to Iraqi forces.

Such a return of relative stability to al Anbar Province seemed unthinkable in the midst of the 2004 urban battles in Fallujah, the sustained insurgency of 2005, and the rising violence in 2006 and early 2007. This two volume oral history collection offers firsthand perspectives from many of the primary actors, both American and Iraqi, who worked together to accomplish this unlikely transformation.

The pivotal realignment that shaped the future of western Iraq for its residents and for Americans serving there was the Sahawa al Anbar, or al-Anbar Awakening. This indigenous movement to partner with U.S. forces to rid the region of al Qaeda in Iraq grew over time from multiple sources, coalesced in mid 2006, and blossomed in 2007. The Iraqi origins of the Awakening are captured in the second volume of this collection, while the efforts of Americans in al Anbar, primarily U.S. Marines, to establish conditions conducive to such a shift are chronicled here in the first.

Marines and their Coalition partners in al Anbar developed and persistently employed a strategy that that grew from the doctrinal seeds of the *Small Wars Manual* and from the Marines' 2003

---

[1] MajGen Walter E. Gaskin Sr. intvw, 11Jan08, Marine Corps Historical Center, Quantico, VA (hereafter MCHC).

experiences in Baghdad, Tikrit, and southern Iraq following the fall of Baghdad. That strategy, now preserved in Marine Corps Warfighting Publication 3 33.5 (Army Field Manual 3 24) *Counterinsurgency*, included proactive engagement of sheikhs and local leaders, respectful treatment of the populace, and sustained efforts to restore essential services and infrastructure. By working to reestablish local governance and by devoting extensive resources to build Iraqi security forces, the Marines sought to demonstrate that they did not seek to become a long term occupation force. At the same time, by pursuing opportunities to provide humanitarian aid, developing ties at the neighborhood level through active patrolling, and recognizing the role of traditional leaders, the Marines forged relationships that would pay dividends in 2006 2007.

The parallel challenge amid all of these "nonkinetic" approaches was to eradicate the foreign Islamist fighters and domestic insurgents who could not be convinced to lay down their arms—the "irreconcilables," as they came to be described. This task was essential to create the security and stability that would allow other elements of the plan to succeed. Underlying all of these actions was a foundation of information operations to communicate Coalition intentions.

The path to counterinsurgency success was not straight or smooth. The initial choice of many Sunni tribes and nationalist insurgents to partner with al Qaeda in Iraq enormously complicated efforts to separate insurgents from the population. The Coalition Provisional Authority's decision to disband the Iraqi military and conduct de Ba'athification in 2003 was especially disruptive to al Anbar Province given the concentration of Sunni military officers and former regime members there. Errors by some Coalition forces that included cultural insensitivity and heavy handed responses combined with widespread attention on stories such as the Abu Ghraib prisoner abuses to help fuel the insurgency and its information operations. The April 2004 orders from higher headquarters to conduct Operation Vigilant Resolve in Fallujah ran counter to the Marines' plan, while initiatives such as the summer 2004 overture to engage insurgent leaders went unsupported. Al Qaeda in Iraq's February 2006 bombing of the Golden Mosque in Samarra ignited Sunni Shi'a strife that undermined progress across Iraq. Although there was no sectarian infighting in al Anbar, developments such as these delayed Coalition efforts to build trust and partnerships with Iraqis both in al Anbar and across the country.

2003 Actions and Their Impact

I Marine Expeditionary Force began its efforts toward relationship building even in the midst of Operation Iraqi Freedom I. The decision to establish a civil military operations center immediately after the fall of Baghdad to coordinate restoring essential services demonstrated an underlying belief in the military value of winning the peoples' support. Marines employed the same approach in the unwelcoming environment of Tikrit, Saddam Hussein's hometown, as the Marines of Task Force Tripoli moved northward to conduct security and stability operations in April 2003. The task force placed an early emphasis on meeting humanitarian needs, such as providing fresh water, and on engaging local leaders.

That combination was replicated by all of I Marine Expeditionary Force as it moved into a dramatically different environment, taking over security operations in southern Iraq later that month. In this predominantly Shi'a region encompassing seven provinces (nearly half of the country), the security situation was largely positive in the aftermath of the collapse of Saddam Hussein's Sunni Ba'athist regime. Brigadier General John F. Kelly, assistant 1st Marine Division commander, recalled that "we took advantage of this lull without realizing we were doing it. And you know the division's motto, 'no better friend, no worse enemy,' worked out for us very, very well."[2]

A key theme dating back to 2003 was a determined effort by Marines to build capacity for local control and to develop relationships with Iraqis that defied the image of "occupier." The most kinetic portion of the Marine expeditionary force's new zone was in northern Babil Province, which included a significant insurgent presence. It was there that the Marines learned how to balance the iron fist of targeted operations with the velvet glove of civil affairs and engagement. Task

---

[2] BGen John F. Kelly intvw, 31Mar04 (MCHC).

Force Scorpion, built around the nucleus of the 4th Light Armored Reconnaissance Battalion (reinforced), proved equally adept at tracking down improvised explosive device makers and reaching out to local sheikhs and imams. This formula worked, as incident levels dropped to near zero by the end of July and stayed at that level until I Marine Expeditionary Force turned the sector over to the Army's 82d Airborne Division in September 2003.

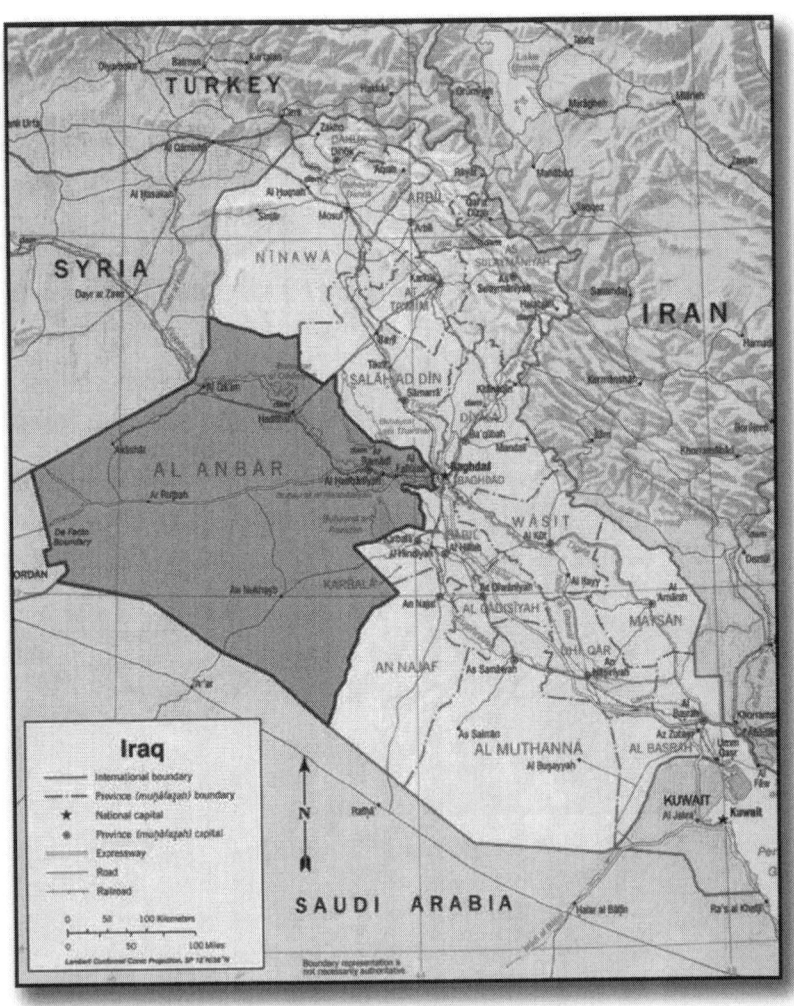

Returning to Iraq—The Plan for al-Anbar

As the Marines of I Marine Expeditionary Force prepared to return to Iraq in 2004, their leaders sought to apply the lessons of their 2003 experiences while also recognizing that they would be in a more hostile environment. "We thought that would be different in al Anbar," recalled Lieutenant General James T. Conway, who was commander of I Marine Expeditionary Force at the time. "It was a different sect of the population," and the people were "much more unsettled, unhappy with the scheme of things." According to Conway, "We went back to the *Small Wars Manual* for our initial doctrinal guidance. When we had conducted operations in the south, it seemed pretty valid to us, and we thought that we could do a continuation of the same type of thing in the al Anbar Province." They knew that the challenge "would be tough, we acknowledged that, but we really thought that, in time, those principles . . . would still be applicable."[3]

Prior to the return of 1st Marine Division to Iraq for Operation Iraqi Freedom II (2004 2005), Major General James N. Mattis, the division commander, sought to create an approach to guide his troops' actions. Recognizing that the key terrain in any insurgency is the population, Mattis and his staff began by assessing the demographics of al Anbar Province. Taking into account the cultural differences in western Iraq in contrast to the Marines' 2003 experiences in predominantly Shi'a southern Iraq, they identified three key groups: the tribes; former regime elements; and foreign fighters. Each of these groups required a different set of approaches.

The tribes, which made up the largest group, were guided by a network of sheikhs and elders. Success in undermining support for the insurgency within this core group would take not only enhanced security to allow economic development and restoration of services, but also engagement with traditional leaders. Former regime elements, a smaller but influential group, consisted of prior military and civil leaders with ties to the Ba'ath Party who sought a restoration of the old order. Some within this group could be converted to support the Coalition by appealing to their self interests. Others would have to be

---

[3] LtGen James T. Conway intvw, 21 June/7 July 2005 (MCHC).

5

defeated militarily. The final group consisted largely of foreign fighters with Islamist goals. The only effective approach for this most extreme and dangerous minority was eradication. The presence of purely criminal elements within all three cohorts further complicated planning and implementation of the counterinsurgency strategy.

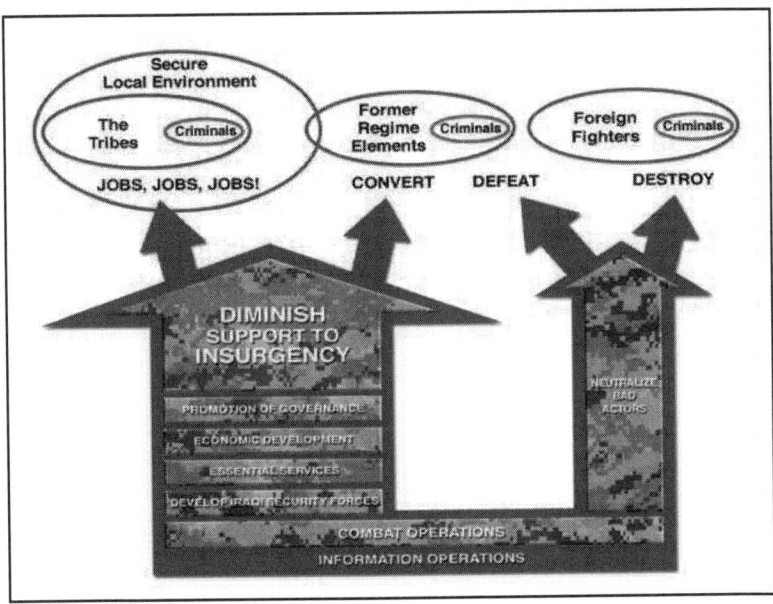

1st Marine Division's operational design for Operation Iraqi Freedom II

Interviews with Marine leaders at all levels from 2004 on reveals the integrated application of the principles described within this overarching plan. Posters summarizing the core philosophies of the approach hung in virtually every command post across Iraq. Mantras such as "first do no harm" and "no better friend, no worse enemy" were ingrained from the Marine expeditionary force staff to the fire team level. Given the diverse and decentralized nature of the western Iraq battlefield, the commitment to these core beliefs was noteworthy.

The Marines saw that the greatest challenge to their overarching strategy was the persistent level of violence and insecurity. Without stability, it was virtually impossible to create jobs and economic opportunities, which were key components for winning over the population.

2004–Fallujah I and Its Impact

The Blackwater USA murders on 31 March 2004 and their aftermath waylaid the Marines' operational plan. General Conway soon saw that "decision makers in Baghdad were being heavily influenced by public perception." His plea to higher headquarter to "not overreact to this" went unheeded, and the increasing pressure resulted in the Marines' plan being set aside in favor of Operation Vigilant Resolve, which Coalition forces mounted in April 2004 to clear insurgents from Fallujah.[4]

Although ordered in against the Marines commanders' better judgment, the "troops made great progress," according to Conway. "The snipers owned the streets, and . . . we were getting intercepts that they were about to run out of ammunition. We had killed a significant portion of the leadership, the rest were confused . . . arguing among themselves in terms of what they needed to do." What the insurgents did have going for them, however, was information operations, and soon Al Jazzera and others were erroneously reporting heavy civilian casualties in Fallujah, stories that many Western media outlets picked up. Despite Conway's message to higher headquarters that "we can give you the city in three more days," the Marines received orders to call off the attack.[5]

While the first battle of Fallujah hampered the Marines' efforts to directly implement their plans to engage the Anbaris, Colonel Michael M. Walker, commanding officer of 3d Civil Affairs Group, cites this period as yielding the first engagements that helped lay the groundwork for the Awakening. At a conference in Amman, Jordan, in July 2004 with many Iraqi business and tribal leaders, a Japanese investment banker told this group that "you can trust the Americans. When they say they'll work with you, they mean they'll work with you. They don't lie. They helped rebuild my country." Walker observed that among the Iraqis, "All of a sudden, the lights were going on that maybe the road out of this thing is with the Americans instead of with al Qaeda"[6] The concept did not find fertile ground with the diplomatic

---

[4] Conway intvw.
[5] Conway intvw.
[6] Col Michael M. Walker intvw, 24Mar09 (MCHC).

and political leadership in Iraq at time, however, and there would be many more months of fighting, but a seed had been planted with an influential audience.

Fallujah II—Operation al-Fajr

The abandoned assault in April led to the establishment of an insurgent stronghold in Fallujah, which could no longer be ignored by the fall of 2004. The operation to clear the city, initially named Phantom Fury, was changed to al Fajr by Iraqi Prime Minister Ayad Allawi shortly before the battle. Al Fajr translates as "the dawn," or "the new beginning."[7] Al Fajr tied directly into the Marines' counterinsurgency plan by destroying the most committed insurgent elements—those who could never be won over by other means—and by paving the way for improved security and economic opportunity for the majority of the population.

Even in the heat of the most intense combat of the Iraq War, the Marines were mindful of the implications of civil military operations for the long term success of the operation. Lieutenant General John F. Sattler, commanding general of I Marine Expeditionary Force during the battle, recounted that "we were phase four oriented before we went across the line of departure."[8] This focus on civil military operations at the highest levels went hand in hand with the tenacity and tactical success of the combat forces. While the civil affairs operations helped to deny the enemy the human terrain, the seizure of the city denied the insurgents a physical safe haven. Fallujah, explained Major General Richard F. Natonski, commander of 1st Marine Division during the operation, "offered the insurgents the ability to rest, rearm, refit, plan, and then go out and launch their attacks and then come back to a secure environment." It was essentially a forward operating base for them. "By taking down Fallujah," according to Natonski, the Marines denied "a sanctuary for the insurgents."[9] The operation also revealed more about the barbarism of some elements of the

---

[7] LtGen John F. Sattler intvw, 8Apr05 (MCHC).
[8] Ibid.
[9] MGen Richard F. Natonski intvw, 16Mar05 (MCHC).

insurgency, the types of things that would ultimately lead the population of al Anbar to turn away from the savagery of al Qaeda in Iraq.

The brutal tactics of the insurgents created an opening for Marine civil affairs operations. The contrast between the actions of al Qaeda's foreign fighters in Fallujah and the Marines' and the willingness to help the Fallujhans opened a fissure that would be exploited during the Awakening. As combat forces reached the southern side of the city, the Marines began the removal of rubble, bodies, and unexploded ordinance and took the first steps to restore water and other public works while other units were still conducting clearing operations. It would be weeks before the city could be systematically reopened for citizens to return. When they did, the Marines were ready to extend a hand with aid, including cash payments to help repair damages.[10]

2005—Elections, Named Operations, and Tribal Success in al-Qaim

While 2004 was dominated by events in Fallujah, efforts in 2005 centered on the October constitutional referendum and the December national elections. In contrast to the 3,700 votes cast in al Anbar during January 2005 for the Provincial Council, approximately 500,000 Anbaris voted in the December elections, an exponential turnaround in less than a year.[11]

While preparing for the elections, II Marine Expeditionary Force also conducted direct action against insurgent forces. In western al Anbar, the Marines undertook eleven named operations, including Matador, Iron Fist, and Steel Curtain, from May to December 2005. The purpose of these operations was to drive al Qaeda fighters from the western Euphrates River Valley and deny them that terrain as a place from which they could operate freely.[12]

Colonel Stephen W. Davis, commander of Regimental Combat Team 2 (RCT 2) during 2005, noted the challenge that his small force

---

[10] Ibid.
[11] BGen Charles S. Patton intvw , 25Jan06 (MCHC).
[12] MGen Stephen T. Johnson intvw, 26Jan06 (MCHC).

faced in an area of operations the size of South Carolina, observing that "we like to say [that] this is an RCT with a division mission in a MEF plus battlespace."[13] In al Qaim region, Davis and his Marines found that the foreign al Qaeda fighters had "come here to kill Americans, so they're not doing anything for Iraq." The nationalist insurgents were "fighting for Iraq, they're fighting for themselves, they're fighting for their families, for their tribes." They're not necessarily fighting for the Jihad, and that's where this big schism comes in."[14] Coalition forces would ultimately exploit that gap between the Iraqis and al Qaeda by appealing to the self interest of the indigenous Iraqis. Tactical successes cemented the status of the Marine Corps as the "most powerful tribe in al Anbar," a point that was not lost on the province's traditional leaders. Simultaneously, al Qaeda's interference with western Iraq's ages old and highly lucrative smuggling business contributed to the growing gap between al Qaeda in Iraq and the Anbaris.

In addition to the success of Marine driven combat operations, gradual progress continued with the development of Iraqi security forces. Iraqi and Coalition forces proved to be most effective in tandem. Coalition forces made the Iraqis more effective operationally, and the Iraqis provided cultural savvy to help separate insurgents from the population. By the end of 2005, the combination of military effectiveness, Iraqi security force development, and engagement of local leaders was emerging as the formula for long term success.

It was not always possible to see the significance of events as they occurred. Commanders during 2006 were able to look back on the actions of their predecessors in 2005 and see the foundations that had been built. Lieutenant Colonel Scott C. Shuster, commander of 3d Battalion, 4th Marines, was quick to give credit for the improved environment in the al Qaim region during late 2006 to the effective engagement of the Abu Mahal tribe by his predecessors. "Just prior to Steel Curtain," Shuster recounted, "the internal and external insurgents had a showdown, the external insurgents essentially won, and the internal insurgents decided that they would ally with Coalition forces

---

[13] Col Stephen W. Davis intvw, 20May05 (MCHC).
[14] Ibid.

to push the external insurgents out and then cooperate [with us] for a stable area."[15] The significance of these events, which paralleled later actions in Ramadi, may not have been apparent in 2005, but they stood out by 2006 when the strategy of "clear, hold, build" had clearly taken root in al Qaim.

State of Affairs in 2006

While tribal cooperation and the named operations during 2005 enhanced security in the western part of al Anbar, and the situation in Fallujah had improved following al Fajr, much of the province remained gripped by violence and insurgent activity. This state of affairs was captured in a briefing prepared by the I Marine Expeditionary Force Intelligence Officer, Colonel Peter H. Devlin, for Joint Chiefs Chairman General Peter Pace, who visited al Anbar in August 2006. As Devlin recounted, " I just wanted to tell him precisely what's going on here in Anbar Province regarding what the insurgency was and why our incident levels had increased." The briefing sought to explain the paradox of progress amidst some of the highest levels of violence of the entire war.[16]

Brigadier General Robert B. Neller, I Marine Expeditionary Force deputy commanding general for operations, observed, "We have killed a very substantial number of these guys, and yet the level of attacks has continued to go up. So we can attribute that to the fact that we've gone in areas where we weren't located before and we've dispersed the force and we've got more surfaces for them to contact against."[17] Anticipating follow up questions from General Pace or others, Colonel Devlin collaborated with Major Alfred B. "Ben" Connable at the Marine Corps Intelligence Activity to expand the briefing into a more detailed assessment of the situation as of August 2006. The classified report, portions of which were leaked to the media once it reached Washington, depicted al Qaeda in Iraq at the height of its power.[18] The irony was that, at the moment the situation looked most bleak, just as

---

[15] LtCol Scott C. Shuster intvw, 28Dec2006 (MCHC).
[16] Col Peter H. Devlin intvw, 31Jan07 (MCHC).
[17] BGen Robert B. Neller intvw, 23Jan07 (MCHC).
[18] Devlin intvw.

much of the media and political leaders in Washington were ready to abandon al Anbar and Iraq as lost causes, three years of investment by Marines and their Coalition partners were about to pay off.

Onset of the Awakening

In September 2006, Sheikh Abdul Sattar Abu Risha announced the formation of a tribal movement, the Sahawa al Anbar, or al Anbar Awakening. Frustrated with the extremism of al Qaeda in Iraq and its disregard for the traditions and leadership of the Anbar tribes, Sheikh Sattar and his allies began to target al Qaeda militants in their area and cooperate with Coalition forces. The tribes' most influential role was encouraging their military age males to volunteer for the Iraqi police. The movement grew steadily, first in the Ramadi area where it began, and then in other parts of the province. Unlike the largely localized 2005 effort of the Abu Mahal tribe in al Qaim, the Awakening became a province wide phenomenon.

Colonel Sean B. MacFarland, USA, commander of the 1st Brigade Combat Team, 1st Armored Division, in Ramadi, described the accelerating pace of change in a December 2006 interview. "One by one, the local tribes are beginning to flip from either hostile to neutral or neutral to friendly," he observed. "That's been probably one of the most decisive aspects of what we've done here, is bringing those tribes onto our side of the fence." MacFarland noted the impact of tribal cooperation on recruiting for the Iraqi police. With the blessing of local sheikhs, monthly volunteer totals went from 20 or 30 per month to several hundred.[19] With those additional forces, "inkblots" of stability, in the form of combat outposts or security stations, soon spread across Ramadi as the strategy of "clear, hold, build" was implemented.

At the heart of that effort in central Ramadi during the winter of 2006 2007 was 1st Battalion, 6th Marines. Commanding officer Lieutenant Colonel William M. Jurney described the battalion's focus in terms that paralleled the key themes of the Marines' campaign plan developed three years earlier. "We focused on . . . three lines of operations

---

[19] Col Sean B. MacFarland, USA, intvw, 13Dec06 (MCHC).

in our battalion. First and foremost is to neutralize those criminal and terrorist threats that would choose to do us harm." The second was on employing Iraqi security forces, and the third was civil affairs operations, to bring "life back to a sense of normalcy." One distinction that Jurney noted was the battalion's belief that "clear, hold, build" were not sequential, but concurrent efforts, with civil military operations to build in one area setting the conditions to clear the next, and combined U.S. Iraqi efforts to hold neighborhoods influencing both.[20]

While most attention during the Awakening period focused on the Ramadi area, the Marines and their Coalition partners were applying the same fundamentals across al Anbar. The Regimental Combat Team 5 commander, Colonel Lawrence D. Nicholson, observed of the collaboration in Fallujah that it was "quite a sight to see Iraqi police, Iraqi army, Marine planners hovering over a map, looking at intelligence, looking at names, comparing notes." Like many other commanders, Nicholson understood that the battle in al Anbar was one the Marines would not win directly. "Victory" would come when the Anbaris were willing and able to win the fight themselves. He emphasized the role of engagement, even with former adversaries, noting that "I've met with resistance leaders, I've met with guys who said, 'Hey, I was fighting you for two years. Now . . . we're fighting [al Qaeda].'" In addition to engagement, Nicholson emphasized the impact of civil military operations, reminding his troops to "treat everyone with dignity and respect, and we'll get a dividend from that."[21]

Engagement and Economic Development in 2006

While the focus of the Awakening was on the tribes, Marine leaders at all levels continued to balance engagement with the tribes and support for the elected governments. Major General Richard C. Zilmer, I Marine Expeditionary Force (Forward) commander during 2006, described efforts to support both traditional and newly elected leaders, noting that "to make those city councils, provincial councils .

---

[20] LtCol William M. Jurney intvw, 17Feb07 (MCHC).
[21] Col Lawrence D. Nicholson interview, 3Jan07 (MCHC).

.. successful, there's going to have to be a strong buy in from the tribal sheikhs, because that is the custom. . . . The most important social feature, I think, of the Anbar people, is that tribal sheikh relationship, and I think we had to learn that."[22]

A vital component of the tribes' engagement was the ability to promote enlistment in the Iraqi security forces. As Brigadier General Neller observed, "We've had really great success with the police out west and now with the police in Ramadi because of tribal engagement and civic support."[23] During I Marine Expeditionary Force's year in theater, the number of Iraqi police in al Anbar grew from 2,000 to 13,000, the maximum authorized at the time. Combined with two increasingly effective Iraqi army divisions, these police forces not only had a direct impact on stability and security, but they led to an improved flow of reporting from the populace to enable targeting of remaining insurgents. Al Anbar Province was rapidly becoming an inhospitable environment for the insurgents who had destabilized the region since 2003.

While General Neller focused on security operations for Multi National Force West, his counterpart, Brigadier General David G. Reist, pursued economic development opportunities. Whether meeting with Iraqi expatriots in Amman, Jordan, and beyond or helping Governor Mamoon San Rashid al Alwani obtain funding from the central government, he fought to resuscitate the Anbar economy. General Reist noted in early January 2007 that "the governor just . . . got his first allocation of reconstruction dollars from the federal government, and it equated to just under 40 million dollars. . . . Projects are starting as he distributes that money to his mayors." The synergistic impact of creating jobs, improving security, and undermining support for the insurgency envisioned in 2003 was becoming a reality by early 2007.[24]

Capitalizing on Success in 2007-2008

As anti Coalition incident rates dropped from 300 to 400 per week in early 2007 to near zero by spring, II Marine Expeditionary Force

[22] MajGen Richard C. Zilmer intvw, 3Jan07 (MCHC).
[23] Neller intvw.
[24] BGen David G. Reist intvw, 3Jan07 (MCHC).

had to move quickly to satisfy the emerging desire for self government and economic opportunities. Just as tribal leaders had helped to improve the security situation, their influence also played a role in enabling U.S. efforts to improve the economy. Sheikhs urged their followers to capitalize on American efforts to help rebuild during the window of time that remained and noted that attacking U.S. forces and contractors would undermine those efforts. Major General John R. Allen explained the key to understanding that dynamic: "Tribes and tribal leaders and sheikhs are all guided by self interest. Not selfish, necessarily, but self interest. . . . It is the nature of Arab tribes that sheikhs are concerned about the interests of their people."[25]

The 2007 "surge" improved the security situation across Iraq by giving the Iraqi government and security forces room to consolidate their gains. Major General Gaskin, commander of II Marine Expeditionary Force, described the shift in the al Anbar security situation early in his tour as surge forces arrived in theater. "What really grabbed us is that as we were able to take the population centers back," he said. "The incidents, whether it be IEDs [improvised explosive devices], small arms fire, indirect fire, dropped precipitously." The Coalition consolidated those gains by backfilling the secured areas with Iraqi police, who had familiarity with their communities and could leverage loyalty from local citizens that Coalition forces could not. Suddenly, al Qaeda's ability to stifle cooperation through intimidation and murder was eliminated. The police were instrumental in separating the insurgents from the population, a central principle of effective counterinsurgencies. The police grew not only in effectiveness, but also in numbers, increasing from about 11,000 to 24,000 during 2007 and serving in every population center in the province.[26]

By 2008, al Anbar was also able to leverage two greatly improved Iraqi army divisions. After years of investment in them by military transition teams, the 1st and 7th Iraqi Divisions demonstrated their readiness during a short notice deployment to Basrah to restore order there. The improved state of the Iraqi security forces and the

---

[25] MGen John R. Allen intvw, 27Jun07 (MCHC).
[26] Gaskin intvw.

dramatically better stability allowed reductions in Coalition forces no one would have thought possible two years earlier.[27]

John F. Kelly, who had been promoted to major general, commanded I Marine Expeditionary Force (Forward) during 2008. Looking back on his multiple tours, he noted the sustained commitment of Marine forces to the phrases emphasized by General Mattis, "no better friend, no worse enemy," and "first, do no harm." Kelly recalled that "the sheikhs would tell me that 'in spite of the fact that we were killing you guys . . . you were still trying to force us to work with you.'"[28] That commitment to engagement paid dividends throughout the war.

Major Adam T. Strickland, who served as General Kelly's engagement officer from December 2007 to December 2008, related that "our motto was, 'There are no good and bad people. There are just self interested people.' So individuals chose courses of action in the past because they thought it was in their best interest. Now, we hope to show them that regardless of what they've done in the past, [through reconciliation there is] a path to a better future with the government." It was that spirit that led to cooperation with many of the Coalition's former adversaries.[29] By 2007 and 2008, the misguided policies that disbanded the Iraqi military and made enemies of those most able to reconstruct Iraqi society were finally being reversed. The "conversion" of former regime elements recommended in the Operation Iraqi Freedom II operational design has led to a reconciliation that benefited both Coalition forces and Iraqi society. The late 2003 vision of local governance, economic development, restored services, and employment of Iraqi security forces to create a stable environment for the people of al Anbar is an increasingly secure reality in the western Iraq of 2009.

Kurtis P. Wheeler
Lieutenant Colonel, U.S. Marine Corps Reserve

---

[27] BGen Martin Post intvw, 18Mar09 (MCHC).
[28] BGen John F. Kelly intvw, 26Mar09 (MCHC).
[29] Maj Adam T. Strickland intvw, 26Mar09 (MCHC).

2004

Marine Deployment to al-Anbar
and the Rise of the Insurgency

Interview 1
Preparing for Counterinsurgency

Major General James N. Mattis

Commanding General
1st Marine Division
Multi National Force • West

August 2002 to August 2004

Major General James N. Mattis is a career infantry officer who commanded 1st Marine Division from August 2002 to August 2004. While serving in that capacity he completed two tours in Iraq, leading the division's attack toward Baghdad during Operation Iraqi Freedom I and then during subsequent stability and support operations as part of Operation Iraqi Freedom II. Following that assignment, he commanded I Marine Expeditionary Force, where he served concurrently as the commander of U.S. Marine Forces, Central Command. In November 2007, he assumed command of U.S. Joint Forces Command, where he serves concurrently as Supreme Allied Commander for Transformation for the North Atlantic Treaty Organization.

In this interview, Major General Mattis discusses preparations undertaken in anticipation of the 1st Marine Division's redeployment to Iraq in March 2004, the development of a counterinsurgency strategy designed to engage the Iraqi people, and security operations conducted throughout Anbar Province, including the first battle for Fallujah. He notes that a key element in the division's counterinsurgency effort was to "try and turn down the cycle of violence." This was pursued through a two pronged, intelligence driven approach, designed to neutralize their adversaries' influence over the population while simultaneously promoting governance, economic development, and essential services within the community.

Major General Mattis was interviewed by Dr. Charles P. Neimeyer, director of the Marine Corps History Division, on 17 June 2009 at the Pentagon.

Charles P. Neimeyer: What was the plan for the return of I MEF [I Marine Expeditionary Force] assets back into Iraq in the 2004 time frame?

Major General James N. Mattis: Well, some of the ships were still at sea with our equipment and would not arrive in southern California ports until November [2003] and even December, early December, with our gear. So initially there was a two pronged approach. One was on planning, and one was on logistic preparations of gear that we knew we had to get turned around. In many cases, the mechanics and all from the FSSG [force service support group] and even our own were sent down to the ports, where they would work on the gear there and basically reload the ships. This is during the holiday period, Thanksgiving, Christmas of 2003.

As soon as I received the warning order, and I believe it was on November 7th, . . . I immediately directed my deputy, [the] assistant division commander, Brigadier General John [F.] Kelly, to get over there right away and determine what needed to be [done], get the lay down of where the 82d Airborne was at, size up the mission, and do all the initial planning things that you need to do to starting filling in assumptions with information, rather than having information gaps. The plan for the deployment was basically that we would get an advance team in. They would start integrating with the 82d Airborne Division. We would ensure a good turnover of the battlefield situation, understand what they were doing, and try to exploit and move along the lines that 82d Airborne Division had underway.

[Kelly] got there and returned. We decided that I would go out next—this is in early December—and take with us engineering officers, intel[ligence] officers, who would actually start working on the camps that we would need, making certain that the camps were ready for us to move into them, handle the turnover from 82d Airborne to I MEF. All this is going on under the auspices of I MEF's efforts. The intel aspect was twofold. We had to get the enemy's situation, so we understood what was going on, which was a little unclear, since we had not operated in western Iraq before. But we also needed to organize the intel effort correctly, and this was really done by the MEF intel officer, Colonel [James R.] Jim Howcroft, who determined that the nature of this fight would require a fusion center of all intel assets at the division level, SigInt [signals intelligence], HumInt [human intelligence], analysis, this sort of thing, so that it was closely connected to and integrated with the operational effort. So you'd have a logistics preparation going on, you have a planning preparation going on, and inside the planning there's a specific focus on intel.

Additionally, we immediately set up a rudimentary orientation that our units had to go through at an abandoned housing site up in the March Air Force Base housing area that had been shut down. We had Marines play acting like what we expected to have going on over there. This was the start of what eventually grew, by the way, into ... Mojave Viper, eventually gaining great support out of the Marine Corps Warfighting Lab at Quantico. They were the ones who really helped us. Eventually, TECom [Training and Education Command] came in and helped further, but the efforts that they had conducted on urban warfare back in the '90s, some of that expertise was still there. The thinking was fresh to them, and they were a great help. So we also have a training effort underway, which also included in each battalion trying to craft one platoon that would be organized to work as a CAP [combined action program] platoon and [on] how could we get language and cultural appreciation improved.*

We contacted the best Arabist we could find, Barak [A.] Salmoni, ... at the Naval Postgraduate School. ... He had a unique ability to talk to Marines about the culture they were going into and try to start the cultural and linguistic preparation of units going in with the idea [that] some of the units would actually live in amongst the Iraqis. ...

We identified three groups of enemy, or potential players on the battlefield. The tribes, there were criminals amongst them, and what we thought we needed for them was jobs and securing them, the locals. Then we had the former regime elements. These were the recalcitrant ones, the ones who chose to be irreconcilable. There were criminals amongst them, too. And then we had the foreign

---

* The combined action program emerged during the Vietnam War where a platoon of Marines integrated with local Vietnamese force to protect a designated village. In Iraq, these CAP platoons would be embedded with Iraqi security forces [ISF] and evolve into police and military transition teams [PTTs and MTTs], partnering with ISF as mentors and trainers.

fighters, not many, when you ran into them, because you generally didn't take prisoners. They fought to the death.

Neimeyer: You wanted to destroy these guys?

Mattis: These we would destroy. We would defeat or convert, try to move the former regime elements into the reconcilable ranks. The ones we could not, we would defeat, destroy them. But the main effort was to diminish support to the insurgency [by] promoting governance, economic development, essential services, and the supporting effort was to neutralize the bad actors. In other words, take them out, either imprison them, kill them, whatever it took, the irreconcilables.

These were how we constructed what we called combat operations. You can see the main effort was diminishing support to the insurgency, and the whole thing . . . was done inside a bodyguard of information ops [operations]. And this would be the scheme that would eventually have us addressing situations like Fallujah, that we knew was going to be a tough nut. And we had an idea of how we'd diminish support for the insurgents there by doing things around the periphery, for example, that sort of thing, as we continued to maintain this effort, to include strong interaction with the tribes.

Immediately, how could we get a hold of the tribes? Down south [in the southern provinces where the Marines had been], the imams and some of the tribal leaders were the main people we had dealt with. Out in the west [al Anbar Province], we were aware— this was based on our reconnaissance and 82d Airborne's superb briefings to us—we were aware that the tribes would be the center of our efforts out there from the very beginning. And this is reflected a few months later. Even on the worst days of fighting in Fallujah, I would oftentimes return to Ramadi and meet with the tribal leaders there, who were very upset. But I just kept working with them, kept listening to them, and all of my officers were doing that as we were working with the tribes. The tribes, the tribes, from the very beginning—that [was] the plan going in.

The Army Special Forces, Major Adam A. Such, came in, linked up with us. I believe it was in December, before we deployed. . . . Adam would be the one who, with his guys out in the Hit/Haditha area, made initial contact with the Abu Nimer tribe and actually began what eventually morphed into the Anbar Awakening. This is, by the way, in April May June of 2004. Also, Colonel [Arthur W.] "Buck" Connor [Jr., USA], who commanded the 1st Brigade, 1st Infantry, that held Ramadi, served under us for our first several months there. He also had a vigorous tribal engagement going on there in the Ramadi capital. So you see, Army and Marine efforts to engage with these folks, and that's kind of how the planning was coming together as we went in.

Neimeyer: Let me ask you about the SASO [stability and support operations] training that you organized prior to going back in. I noticed LAPD [Los Angeles Police Department] was assisting you in some of this street gang stuff and things of that nature, understanding criminal elements.

Mattis: The LAPD was superb.... They flew us over the city [Los Angeles] in their own helos [helicopters], showing us how they police, what kind of issues there are. We sat in classrooms with them. We spent the day with them. It was very, very helpful, and their counter IED [improvised explosive device] guy basically helped train our people and then deployed with us. [Notes that he helped train 55 infantry battalions.] But the LAPD, based on a good working relationship, was most beneficial, from the chief down to the detective level.

Neimeyer: This SASO [security and stabilization operations] thing ... is a rather unique approach. Did it just come to you, or did you basically understand that you were going in the second time in a completely different than you did on the march up?

Mattis: We knew it was a very different environment. We had pulled off the preceding five and a half months and sustained I believe one killed and 55 wounded. Out of the division, I think it was two killed. [Referring to Phase IV Security and Stabilization Operations in 2003 during Operation Iraqi Freedom I where Marines governed seven Shia provinces in southern Iraq at the end of decisive operations].... But going back in, it was clear that we would be facing a much more entrenched enemy in al Anbar.

However, we were still very optimistic after General Kelly's initial visit that we would earn the population. We didn't know how long it would take, and, frankly, it probably took longer than we imagined, but that's why you see the immediate main effort being to diminish the reasons for the insurgency, why we were training our troops, not just to be "no better friend, no worse enemy," but [what] we'd applied by this point during the preceding deployment and reemphasized now was first do no harm and protect the people.

I'd studied the [French] 10th Parachute Division in Algeria in 1960, and trying to turn down the cycle of violence is one of the lessons I drew from that. We kept doing that, even, like I said, during the worst fighting in Fallujah. We were still working with the sheikhs, even though we knew many of them were actively operating against us, to try and turn that down. So this was based on a study of history, understanding of COIN [counterinsurgency] doctrine, and a recognition that this was going to be an ethically and morally bruising environment that we had to prepare the troops for. The lessons were pretty obvious. But we had to prioritize working with the tribes and providing a secure local environment, which was going to be very difficult, with the number of troops we had.

Neimeyer: Did you find it hard to hold the Marines back and switch from a mostly kinetic sort of attitude, when they did the march up, to a nonkinetic sort of avenue?

Mattis: No, I did not, and part of the reason was we were able to go back in—do you have a copy of my letter to the troops?

Neimeyer: I do. I do have that.

Mattis: You'll see where we actually say . . . that the enemy wants you to hate all of the Iraqis. Don't allow the enemy that victory. We put it in terms that Marines understood [about] how the enemy was going to try to manipulate them. It was not difficult, although the excitement of that combat for young Marines, you always want to bring everything to bear. We just had to keep stressing to them, "Be careful. Don't allow a single innocent person to be injured. We're the good guys." The Marines, it took a lot of talk, but it's a balancing act.

Neimeyer: Could you describe the situation on the ground when you arrived back in country for the second time? I mean, was it the way you expected it, or did you find any surprises that hit you when you got back there?

Mattis: It was pretty much as we expected it, although the infantry rich formations that Marines bring, where we have in some cases hundreds more infantrymen than the Army units we were replacing, allowed us to do foot patrols and to go into areas they had not been in. In Ramadi as we did that, we uncovered a significant enemy presence that was probably not as well defined during the turnover as I thought it had been. I thought I had a pretty good idea what was in Ramadi, and then Lieutenant Colonel Paul [J.] Kennedy's 2/4 [2d Battalion, 4th Marines] kicked over a real hornet's nest, even while we were fighting down in Fallujah.

Fallujah we knew would be a tough nut, and our approach was going to be to get the lights turned on in one nearby community, get jobs in another one, working around it in that manner, so that we did not go charging into Fallujah. The theater commander, General [John P.] Abizaid, [USA], and General [Charles H.] Swannack [Jr., USA], the 82d Airborne commander, had been attacked on their latest visit there, so we knew it was going to be a tough one there. But our idea was to use agents inside the city to identify enemies, support special forces operations to go in and kill those people, but continue to do good works outside the city, where it was a more benign environment, and draw people's attention to those things.

We were not naive about it. We didn't intend to convert the hard core, but we knew that there were a lot of people that we could convert, that were not committed to being adversaries. However, we knew too we were taking an American, largely Christian force into a part of the world where that combination did not play well, so we would have a very skeptical audience. We were going to have to be very stoic, and it was going to be hard. But we were very confident we would eventually turn them. So the Fallujah situation was understood by us from the beginning. We had Colonel John [A.] Toolan [Jr.], the regimental commander responsible for the area, he had a very good plan to deal with it. We were all on the same sheet of music, and of course the Blackwater [USA] thing had an impact on that plan.

But I think there [in Fallujah], and even further west, we were unaware of just how deeply, not entrenched, but how well the enemy had organized and the numbers of troops he had. We had some serious challenges as that threat manifested itself from Husaybah, near al Qaim, on the Syrian border, to Haditha area, on down to Ramadi, that 2/4 stumbled into, and then of course Fallujah.

Furthermore, at this very time, as we're turning over, this MSR [main supply route] between Kuwait and Baghdad is cut, and significant numbers of our troops under General John Kelly had to be committed to restoring the bridges and reopening those lines, even as we were fighting in Fallujah. Obviously, 2/4 had one squad overrun and decimated, and meanwhile, we have the situation in Husaybah, where we have a company lose its company commander and five staff NCOs [noncommissioned officers] killed in the first hour, then has to fight its way back through this. It's all going at about the same time, immediately following the turnover with 82d Airborne.

Neimeyer: We talked a little bit about Fallujah, and we're going to get back to that, but were there any areas in Anbar when you got there that you considered what you'd call no go areas, where you weren't going to go there yet, and you were going to wait until you'd figured out the situation or built up more forces on the ground?

Mattis: No. No, there weren't. We had the forces we had. We did make requests for additional forces. For part of the fight, there were forces shifted around. First Armored Division was actually turned around. General [Martin E.] Dempsey's [USA] division was turned around and sent back up to relieve some of our southernmost units, Army and Marine, that were then brought up closer into the fight for Fallujah.

But I mean, obviously, when you're in the middle of fights, there are no go areas. There was no area that we said we're going to surrender. There were just areas we could not address because we didn't have enough troops. The area north of the Euphrates River

Valley, the area up towards Lake Tharthar, areas like that. For Fallujah itself, a city of 350,000 people, all I could bring to bear initially were two infantry battalions. We eventually got four, and that would have been sufficient because the enemy hadn't prepared for this. Of course, then we were stopped.

Neimeyer: One of your hallmarks, I think, in the march up [to Baghdad] was your demand for speed. Did you have that same attitude in the midst of the fighting the second time around, or were you more deliberate?

Mattis: Well, we are now going into what we consider to be a counterinsurgent effort, and that required what I called the three P's: patient, persistent, presence. Patience you understood. That word sends a message. Persistent, you can't go in and come out, you can't be episodic. And presence, you've got to be there or you're not influential. And this included building Iraqi security forces, which unfortunately had been basically put together with uniforms and a modicum of training, rather than taking the time to build them correctly. And they basically collapsed pretty much—not everywhere—but basically pretty much collapsed or joined the enemy's side during the uprising there in March April.

Neimeyer: Did you find the historical example of combined action platoons useful to you in the second time you went in?

Mattis: We did. We had attempted to organize in each battalion one platoon, for example, that would be given extra language training, extra cultural training. Remember, we have very little time. These troops have just returned home. We've dropped people who under stop loss or whatever had to go home or extended for the deployment to fight with their buddies. We're getting recruits in. We're repairing gear, and getting it back on the ships, and sending it back over, [and] meanwhile trying to train these units. So the CAP units in each battalion, and that approach of being out among the people, was our basic approach.

Neimeyer: Did you make adjustments once you got on the ground? Is there anything that popped up that you had to adjust to that you didn't really think about?

Mattis: No, no, not really. Obviously, the fighting, frankly, the fighting piece became heavier than I desired, but I mean, to me that's the normal give and take of war. But we maintained. Even, like I said, on the worst days of fighting, I would come back from Husaybah and visiting there, or from out in town in Ramadi, or most often down in Fallujah area. We'd come back, and routinely there'd be anywhere from two to 40 sheikhs wanting to see me. And I would continue to talk with them. I would talk with them down in Fallujah, outside of Fallujah. It was just constant discussions, keeping the dialogue going, but the whole emphasis was on the tribes out there. . . .

Neimeyer: How would you describe the enemy at the beginning of the deployment? How did the enemy react to the presence of Marines in Anbar, once you started becoming more effective?

Mattis: Well, the enemy didn't like us. But at the same time, we did not have a lot of interagency support, so all we had to offer them—the people there—were some projects that were being planned, or CERP [Commander's Emergency Relief Program] funds, where they could pay people to work, and this sort of thing. Or we could provide a generator for the Abu Nimer tribe, because they were helping us.

The enemy obviously didn't like us, but we kept believing that most of this enemy was actually reconcilable. We didn't use those words then, but we kept thinking. We used the word "convert," but "reconcilable" was probably the better word, which General [Graeme C.M.] Lamb, the British three star, eventually breaks the enemy's logic train. At this point, we've not broken it, and we can't define the enemy. We hear "former regime elements," "dead enders," "former Ba'athists," all this sort of thing. Eventually, a couple of years later, General [David H.] Petraeus [USA] comes in, and General Lamb, and he'd come up with this reconcilable/irreconcilable, [which] is really the definition here, and keep moving as far as you can to bring reconcilable people [to your side]. Those you cannot, you take them out—out of the fight.

Neimeyer: The enemy, in reacting to you, stepped up their murder and intimidation campaign against folks who were on the fence. How did you deal with that? I mean, how do you deal with especially the foreign fighters who were assassinating some of the guys who were potentially reconcilable?

Mattis: Well, that's where ambushes and working intel, HumInt and all, as we had efforts underway to create HumInt. Some of the intel support we got, nonmilitary, was not that good. But you try to identify who's doing it, and you try to secure—consistent with our going in proposition—secure the local environment. That's very difficult when you have an area that big, as big as probably North Carolina, and you have the paucity of troops we had, and the untrained and questionable loyalty troops of the Iraqi security force at this point, who have been thrown together, cobbled together, as best both 82d Airborne and we could, but without the time to vet them, with the enemy message gaining credibility, our message getting muted. It's just a very, very difficult time.

Neimeyer: Did you observe any indications that Multi National Force Iraq, government of Iraq, U.S. government, regarded Anbar Province as a hopeless situation? I recall the intelligence assessment of one colonel that said Anbar was most likely lost.

Mattis: First of all, that colonel did not speak for the Marine view. I thought it was an unfortunate assessment, and inaccurate. From the very beginning, General Kelly and I, Colonel [Joseph F.] Dunford [Jr.], who became the chief of staff, eventually the deputy commander, assistant division commander, we were of one mind—as we were right down through battalion and company and platoon commanders—that in these areas, we could turn these people. Some were more convinced than others based on where they were at. Inside Fallujah, it was going to be tough. But in many other areas, we were seeing progress already.

Neimeyer: So you believe that, in fact, the assessment was inaccurate?

Mattis: That assessment comes years later, right at a most unfortunate time. But the bottom line is, there was a sense that Anbar would be the last area, I think the word used was "pacified," or "stabilized," that we would just hold on. It was an economy of force theater throughout. It was never the main effort.

We believed that if we could turn Anbar, we could set a new tone for the whole war, and we were convinced that we could do that from the very good briefings that 82d Airborne Division gave us. That was our assessment. I'm not saying it's theirs, but they gave us good briefs, we considered what they were saying, and we thought we could do it if we had the right approach, which I lay out here.

Numerous times, . . . the priority for bringing in more forces seemed to go elsewhere. During the surge itself, we received two more Marine infantry battalions—several years later—but it was difficult across the country. The command in Baghdad had prioritized other areas, and we did sense that the Sunnis were seen as the most recalcitrant and least likely to come over to our side. We disagreed, seeing with the same data reasons why they might be the first to flip.

For the first time in this war since 9/11, and probably if you go back to when this war really started, which was in the '80s, . . . this is really the first time that you see an entire Arab Middle Eastern population turn against al Qaeda and the extremists. We never doubted we could do it. How long it would take, we knew you can't calculate these things, [that] you can't predict the future of these things. The tipping point would come probably due as much to our own restraint as it would have to do with the enemy's mistakes.

And the enemy, they were so stupid. They made mistake after mistake. And eventually we, by maintaining our ethical stance, our moral stance, the people there—watching the reality of us versus the enemy—shift. It starts with Adam [A.] Such, Army Special Forces major, in Hit, Haditha, out west of Ramadi, with the Abu Nimer tribe. It then leapfrogged somewhat, although many people are staying with the program, Marines keep rotating back time after time to al Anbar. But Dale Alford's battalion, Lieutenant Colonel [Julian D.] Alford, out in the al Qaim area, then guts the enemy's program in terms of its information message and all, and he makes great progress out there, clearly a man extremely attuned to the counterinsurgent mindset.

But you see this throughout the battalion commanders who simply, stoically take the casualties, hold their troops in check, do not allow the enemy to drive us too far, although some battalions fighting in downtown Ramadi during the difficult days are literally fighting every day. It's not counterinsurgency in the sense of winning hearts and minds. It's firefights. . . . But the fact is the Marines are able to adapt and quickly shift to nonlethal activities, and it is the forbearance of the troops, the self discipline of the NCOs and junior officers, that almost always keeps us on the side of the angels here, and the people are watching this. And as the enemy cuts off the heads of young boys, as they kill a sheikh and leave his body to sit out there in the August sun for four days, as they continue this sort of behavior, these forced marriages, what you and I would call rape, where they marry someone for three or four days, these are all telling. . . . And so eventually these mistakes, and our forbearance, pay off, and in a very short period of time, all of a sudden the tribes realize whose side they're really on, and it all shifts. . . .

Neimeyer: Give me your assessment and role of, or intentions of the Anbari sheikhs in 2004. How did they strike you?

Mattis: They were angry. Their Sunni domination of the political life of Iraq obviously was jeopardized by us coming in and dumping Saddam [Hussein]'s regime out. We, by going with the de Ba'athification campaign, we had basically disenfranchised all of those who had been in authority, which is obviously many of the Sunni sheikhs. By disbanding the army, many of the Sunni boys out there, they're very tribal, had joined the army. They were now out of work. They had been trained, trained quite well, and so it was a difficult time for them.

At the same time, we had time to get into very strident discussions. I was asked on one occasion, during a negotiation outside Fallujah, by several, "When are you going to leave?" I said, "I'm never going to leave. I found a little piece of property down on the Euphrates. I'm going to retire there." But my point was that I wanted to suffocate any hope that the enemy had that we were temporarily there. [I wanted them to believe] that we were going to stay as long as necessary. That was difficult, because at times they'd be reading things off the front pages of U.S. newspapers about pulling out and all, but I told them that we would not leave them adrift and that they had bought in with the wrong people.

I knew they couldn't admit that publicly right then, but the fact is that they had bought in with people who said no cigarette smoking, who would marry their daughters if they wished, whether or not the parents wanted that. These were people who had no interest in the good of the people. In fact, they would try to get innocent people killed by firing from their homes and all on Marines. But the bottom line was that eventually they were going to see that we were their only best friends.

Neimeyer: I'd like to talk a little bit about the Blackwater [USA] incident.... On two sides of the question, the first is, how important is this? How did you handle this incident, the bridge incident? And then the second thing is, did you feel pressure coming from the American high command to do something about it?

Mattis: Our first warning of it, I was out on the road, and . . . someone called saying on CNN [Cable News Network] there was this incident being broadcast around the world. I said, "Okay, just continue with what we're doing and do what you can to recover the bodies. Let's find out who did it and then we'll kill them." I talked with General [James T.] Conway. I said, "I don't want to go into the city." He agreed. He said, "That's exactly what the enemy wants us to do right now. We will continue the operations around the periphery of the city."

We had people actually in the city at the time, but only for short periods—in and out—and we would do our best to recover the bodies and to identify who had done it, and then continue the special forces raids. . . . I said, "Steady as she goes." We were working with the police chief and the then mayor to do this sort of thing. There were a lot of tribal factions that didn't necessarily get along in the city, so we were able to work that. We had fairly good information come out of inside the city. For several days, we continued along these lines, recovered some of the bodies, starting to get names and this sort of thing.

Then, eventually, I was ordered to have a sustained U.S. Marine presence inside the city within 72 hours. And I don't know all of the background as far as who did what. . . . And so we basically were ordered to go into the city, with two infantry battalions available at that point.

Neimeyer: And obviously you probably would have preferred to have more. But the incident itself, how did it affect the overall lay down of forces? Did this affect your ability to do other things in other areas, because now you've tied up two infantry battalions?

Mattis: Oh yeah. See, at the same time that we tied two infantry battalions here, and that's insufficient to even put a ring around, we can't even isolate the city at this point, don't have enough forces. At this point, the supply lines are being cut. Bridges are being dropped between Baghdad and Kuwait, including going through our southern sector.

Meanwhile, 2/4 is in a hell of a fight in Ramadi and Husaybah, out near the Syrian border. I eventually tell RCT 7 [Regimental Combat Team 7] to get one of its battalions—it turned out to be 3/4 [3d Battalion, 4th Marines] on its way back—chopped to Colonel Toolan. The Army 1st Armored Division, under General [Martin E.] Marty Dempsey, comes in—thank God for them—and frees up 2/2 [2d Battalion, 2d Marines], that moves against the southern sector of the city, and the 1st of the 32d and 10th Mountain Division that moves up on the peninsula. Those soldiers were helping to isolate there. But already, 1/5 [1st Battalion, 5th Marines] and 2/1 [2d Battalion, 1st Marines]—1/5 from the south and east and 2/1 from the north—are moving into the city. Many people have been evacuated, this sort of thing, and I then tell RCT 7 to leave detachments—left them out across its zone—and move swiftly down south of the lakes because we're losing control around the city outside of that.

As I pull these units in, 3/4 actually initially has to go into the Karmah area, north of Camp Fallujah, before I can even bring them in, in order to at least throw the enemy off balance there. So Colonel [Craig A.] Tucker [of RCT 7] leaves elements at all locations and comes south of Ramadi, south of the lakes, up into the peninsula area, to the west of Fallujah, drops down and pushes through an area . . . and then turns towards Baghdad, goes through the western fringes of Baghdad, and comes into the Karmah area. And what he's doing this whole time is he's trying to put enough of a threat to the enemy that they cannot get braves in areas I've had to denude of troops. And, eventually, I move him back to the west, where we are again having trouble. So we're trying to stick our fingers in all of the holes of the dike, and we don't have enough troops to go around.

Neimeyer: Yes sir. Can you give me an overview of Operation Vigilant Resolve, . . . the two battalions going into Fallujah?

Mattis: Basically, my intention was to squeeze in at the enemy. I knew we would eventually find where they have hard points, where they tried to hold, and then we would take them out. I had been, as you know, I thought this was not the best way to handle it, but I was ordered to do it. No problem. I did ask to receive the order in writing, which we eventually got, and I asked that we not be stopped once started.

We went into the city, [and] 1/5 and 2/1 made good progress. We were not fast, because I didn't want to push so fast that we couldn't secure behind them, or we just pushed the enemy elsewhere in the city where I didn't have troops. I wanted to do it methodically at this point. We used no artillery, no matter what Al Jazeera put on TV. That was manufactured, or bought tapes from some other fight somewhere else, but we were not firing artillery into the city. As we were pressing in, we were bringing up the 32d [Infantry Regiment] to block the peninsula area, where the enemy was running a good propaganda campaign out of a hospital. We brought 2/2 up from the south. That sealed that area, which had been wide open, and eventually 3/4 came in for the east side.

At that point, we were poised to really crush them. I would say that we were probably 24 hours away from the time when I'd say "go" and all of it would now move against the enemy. They had not had time to pre stage ammunition. I don't think they had expected us. They had not built bunkers in most of the homes. And at that point, we were stopped. . . .

This is some of the most primitive kind of fighting, I guess you'd call it. It's house to house, it's street to street. Probably the best thing was the snipers. . . .

When I was stopped and told to start negotiating, I had no terms of reference that were given to me. So I would go in, and basically, I'd get guidance from General Conway, who tried to filter and refine to me what I was supposed to do there. They would oftentimes say, "Gosh, you have to pull your snipers back," and I wouldn't do it because without a doubt the most effective force in there were the Marine riflemen and snipers. . . .

Neimeyer: How did you measure progress [in the overall effort]?

Mattis: Well, it is very difficult, because what matters most in war is oftentimes the least easy to measure. We were looking for a tipping point, and we knew we had to simply maintain our self discipline and our fire discipline, maintain our faith that it would work, observe what was going on, and look at the numbers of attacks, the number of IEDs found, the number of IEDs exploded, the casualty rate on our side. We tried to color code areas for what was getting more stable, what was getting more normalized. But really, during my period there as a division commander, it was very, very difficult to do, because just getting ground truth from the ground was difficult, and you had only episodic involvement with the people because the troops are spread too thin. I've got to move 7th Marines out of its area just to regain control of the countryside around Fallujah.

It was very, very difficult to measure. Much of the measuring came from my discussions with the sheikhs, and that is very hard to quantify, again, but I could sense if they thought we were surging—our side was surging, [if] it was gaining or not. And when we started having good effect on the enemy in Fallujah, they [the sheikhs] were quite upset, because they'd kind of pitched in with the enemy, and this would not look good for them. So they're trying to bring pressure on us to say you've got to quit this, you have to leave, you have to stop killing all the innocent people. We weren't killing innocent people. That sort of thing. So I could gauge a lot from the kind of the tone of my talks with them.

Come back two and a half years as [commander of] MarCent [U.S. Marine Forces Central Command] and I'm meeting with people, two of whom came up in suits and said, "You threw both of us in

Abu Ghraib prison, but you were right, and we're with you to the end now." This was at a meeting at Sheikh [Abdul] Sattar [Abu Risha]'s house, where there were over 70 sheikhs and sub sheikhs out there.

Really, in this kind of a war, you do the best you can, quantifying various measures, and you apply your military judgment. At this point, you're as well off if you've read *Angela's Ashes*, and Desmond Tutu's writings, and if you've studied Northern Ireland and the efforts for rapprochement there, [and] in South Africa following their civil war, as you are if you've read [William T.] Sherman and obviously [Carl P.G.] von Clausewitz and all.

It's a very humanistic war, this war amongst the people. So it's hard to measure, but the indicators that I would consider most significant were when I walked down the street, did people look me in the eye and shake my hand? That was more significant than whatever.

There was almost an over quantification. We had a checklist of 77 questions to ask police stations, in each police station. We went out and asked those questions, and one of them that had the most yeses, when the fighting broke out badly against us, they joined the enemy. One decrepit little station with a half dozen officers who shared two weapons and had zero yeses on training, uniforms, radio equipment, anything, stuck with us out on the highway. So it just shows that when you go with this idea of effects based operations, you're very likely to be measuring the wrong thing.

Interview 2
U.S. Marine Security & Stabilization Operations

Lieutenant General James T. Conway

Commanding General
I Marine Expeditionary Force

November 2002 to September 2004

Lieutenant General James T. Conway is a career infantry officer who commanded I Marine Expeditionary Force [I MEF] during Operation Iraqi Freedom I in 2003 and the first half of Operation Iraqi Freedom II in 2004. Following this assignment, he went to the Pentagon as the J 3, Director of Operations for the Joint Chiefs of Staff before being promoted to general and becoming the 34th Commandant of the Marine Corps.

In this interview, General Conway describes the role I MEF played in operations in post Saddam Hussein Iraq and circumstances that led to I MEF returning to Iraq in 2004, including the decisions to move the headquarters to Iraq. He recounts the situation in Fallujah, the relief in place, transfer of authority with the 82d Airborne Division, and the state of Iraqi security forces in 2004. He also describes I MEF's reaction to the Blackwater USA murders and the circumstances leading to the first battle of Fallujah and the premature unilateral cease fire. General Conway provides a commander's level overview of the battle and describes the role of the western and Arab media.

Lieutenant General Conway was interviewed by Major John P. Piedmont and Dr. David B. Crist on 21 June and 7 July 2005 at the Pentagon.

Major John P. Piedmont: When did I MEF [I Marine Expeditionary Force] receive word that it would be returning to Iraq for OIF II [Operation Iraqi Freedom II]?

Lieutenant General James T. Conway: I can tell you exactly when it was. I was sitting on the BG [brigadier general promotion] board in probably the first week of October [2003] when I received a call from the Commandant [General Michael W. Hagee]. His initial question was would I MEF want to send three battalions back to Iraq. The thought process was that the commitment would be fairly small. At that point, I said absolutely. We had had two battalions who had not had the opportunity to go out of 1st Marine Division, and I knew we could come away with another one. So I said, yes, we would take that, as opposed to II MEF [II Marine Expeditionary Force], which was the option at that point.

Well, three grew to six pretty quickly. Six became nine, thanks to what we call the Wolfowitz Regiment. [Deputy Secretary of Defense Paul Wolfowitz] wanted to see an addition to the force, felt that more Marines was probably better. I think we actually deployed eleven battalions. With that you wind up with an aviation component, a CSS [combat service support] component, necessarily, and a headquarters component. And within probably two months, we realized that 63 percent of the MEF was going to be there, so there was no question in my mind as to where the MEF CG [commanding general] needed to be at that point. So we took the whole group back to Iraq.

Piedmont: Once you had received the word and you began planning, what were your greatest operational concerns in preparing the MEF for this second mission?

Conway: Well, when we went over for OIF [I], clearly we were going to be in the attack. It was a very different construct for what we call reconstruction, or nation building, or Phase IV operations. So we needed to look at those things, those lessons learned if you would, that came out of our five and a half months in the Shi'a provinces after OIF and try to determine which of those would be applicable to what was likely to be a different environment in the al Anbar Province. So that was our essence.

Certainly, the division went about immersing themselves in language training, civil affairs types of efforts, all those manner of things, I would say enhancements over what we had done in the southern provinces. We looked again at lessons learned, how we would reorganize, and those manner of things. We consciously made an effort to push all of the intelligence down from MEF level to division level. We really felt that large intelligence gathering meant for large scale units, and a large scale conflict would not necessarily be the best approach in this environment. In fact, we wanted to get it as low as we could, and the lowest level where that eventually made sense was in the division.

We looked at how we would do the lay down—it's a very large province—what would be the best lay down of those available forces to accomplish all those types of things that we thought had to be done, maintain security for logistics lines, MSRs [main supply routes], those types of things. There was a whole assortment of things, as you can imagine, that we needed to look at . . . [in] a fairly brief period of time, [particularly after] we finally realized that that percentage of troops was going to go.

Piedmont: Why was the MEF sent to al Anbar Province, and what was your commander's estimate of the situation there?

Conway: Well, we had spent five and a half months initially with the provinces in the south. We initially took over nine. Eventually, the British came out from under MEF command and control. So they took two, [and] that left us with seven. And then there was a further adjustment that gave us five, so we were continually downsizing our presence. Although we sustained a significant number of attacks there, we were fortunate. There were some Marines that were grievously injured, but nobody [was] killed.

We thought that would be different in al Anbar. It was a different sect of the population, people much more unsettled, unhappy with the scheme of things. We thought that it would probably be a more competent enemy than some of the folks we had faced in the south because Saddam [Hussein] drew his leadership for his own military out of the west and out of the Sunni populations. So our assessment was that it would be a nastier place.

That said, we went back to the *Small Wars Manual* for our initial doctrinal guidance. When we had conducted operations in the south, it seemed pretty valid to us, and we thought that we could do a continuation of the same type of thing in the al Anbar Province. It would be tough, we acknowledged that, but we really thought that in time, those principles, out of that 1920s doctrine, would still be applicable.

Piedmont: Sir, if you would, give us a sketch of the MEF's plan of operations for the campaign for OIF II.

Conway: Well, we knew that there were certain population centers in the province that were going to be critical to our scheme of operation. Ramadi is the provincial capital, and that's where we decided to lay down the division. There was much discussion as to whether or not division and the MEF needed to be at the same location. We had done that after the division moved from ad Diwaniyah over to al Hillah in OIF II, and it seemed to work well for day to day coordination, communication, those types of things. In this instance, because partly of the lay down of the 82d [Airborne Division] and partly because of the projection at the theater level of continuing bases, continuing facilities that would be used for some time, we didn't do that.

The MEF took shape at Camp Fallujah, and the division moved into Ramadi. And that was principally because, again, of the lay down the 82d had, but as importantly, and probably more so, is we realized that there would need to be close coordination with the governor and his folks, and they operated out of Ramadi. But Fallujah was also critical to us. Fallujah is on the road between Ramadi and Baghdad. Fallujah was clearly causing the 82d a good deal of difficulty. So we knew Fallujah was going to have to be high in our sight picture as well.

The other area was out on the border at Husaybah and al Qaim. And we realized, of course, that the foreign fighters, the cross border activity that we saw between Iraq and Syria, had to be curtailed, and we thought that we would have to position a sufficiently powerful force out there to be able to do that. So that was our initial look. We needed to control the population centers. We needed to take on the insurgents where we could find them. We needed to provide a level of stability and security to the people [and] at the same time improve their quality of life through CA [civil affairs] efforts. . . .

Piedmont: What were your relations with higher headquarters?

Conway: That's an interesting question. When we were in the south, CFLCC [Coalition Forces Land Component Command] had transitioned to CJTF 7 [Combined Joint Task Force 7]. General [David D.] McKiernan became General [Ricardo S.] Sanchez. On a personal level, our relationship was good. There were some things that happened that gave me cause for concern. I went back to the States three times. Two out of the three times, [General Sanchez] visited and poked my number two in the chest, Major General [Keith J.] Stalder, and said essentially I want you to do this, do that, do some things that are very different to the approach that we were using at the time.

We were paying particular concern to the northern Babil Province. It was probably the most hostile of all the areas that we owned south of Baghdad. And on one occasion, [General Sanchez] wanted to completely change our method of operations and have us sweep through the province. On another occasion, he wanted to sign over the province, or that portion of the province, for a period of time and let the 1st Armored Division roll tanks and tracks through there for a period of two weeks and then give it back to us. And we said no, those things are absolutely not going to happen. But I didn't like the idea that they tried to bludgeon the MEF into doing certain things while I was gone.

So that led to my belief going into OIF II that we needed to have a Marine three star on deck. We had our ways that were probably more akin to the British method of operation than the U.S. Army methods, and we probably needed a three star to provide top cover to our ground combat element and others to be able to do those things. The relationship continued to be cordial, but we stood on principle any number of times. I was convinced after a period of time that it was a wise move on the part of the Commandant to put a three star in there, again, not the least of which is because we had a very tough province to deal with, and that 63 percent of the MEF was there. I mean, it's hard to justify sending your people forward and sit back in California or elsewhere not being a part of that.

I and others have attempted to convince the Commandant we probably need to retain a three star presence there so long as there are 25,000 Marines, but I think he was chastised once by the Secretary of Defense [Donald H. Rumsfeld] over it. The Secretary asked why I was there. The Commandant gave him an answer, maybe not an answer he was comfortable with. But I think that has altered the thinking some in terms of the senior Marine in theater. Maybe the conditions are better than what they were as we went back. I don't know that, but I tend to think that where you've got that number of Marines operating as a MAGTF [Marine air ground task force], you probably ought to have the MEF commander there. That's a personal perspective.

Piedmont: Do you think that the higher headquarters, especially when it's headed up by one of our sister services, fully understands the capabilities of a MAGTF, or was that something you had to continually educate them on?

Conway: I think they understand it. It was very interesting, and I never got the full story, but at the end of OIF [I] when General McKiernan had his first commander's conference in Baghdad, and we used an old palace there for the appropriate setting, he had probably 20 Army generals of all sorts of background sitting around the table. All of his commanders and me, a couple of Air Force guys, I don't remember there being any Navy being there. But he kicked off the conference saying, "I don't want to hear any more about this g**d*** MAGTF." He said, "We don't have it, we are not going to get it. I want that to end the conversation." And I thought that was very unusual, and I had no idea what he was talking about. And I looked at him, and I didn't know where that came from at all.

From what I could find, our sister services were fairly impressed with the blitzkrieg effort of the MEF. They were particularly impressed with the direct air support that we were able to get on a continuing basis; our ability to use the other air [elements] that came our way. And I think they liked the idea of combined arms supported with your own air, your own logistics, the self containment that we have as a MEF. That's all I can draw from that. So I think at least during the war, if they didn't appreciate it initially, they certainly came to.

In an insurgency environment, the MEF as a MAGTF is still effective, but it's less obvious to most folks because you are going to get air support from the Navy and the Air Force and all that type of thing. You are not gaining ground. You are doing the day to day things that have to be done to overcome an insurgency. So it may be less apparent, but I think people still understood it better than ever before, perhaps after OIF II.

Piedmont: Was the Marine Corps' rotation plan of six to seven months, vastly different from the Army's, ever a contentious issue?

Conway: Well, it was contentious when the Commandant fought and won the issue. He initially was of the thinking that our folks needed to be there a year. I didn't believe that way at all. I thought six months—what we initially proposed—would be sufficient, especially when you looked at the percentage of the people that were going back. So we argued for six months. I got great support from [Lieutenant General Wallace C.] "Chip" Gregson, who was MarForPac [Marine Forces Pacific] at that point. He did the rigor, if you will, in showing what it would mean, the preservation of the force over time, and we eventually convinced the Commandant, and then the Commandant had to convince SecDef [Secretary of Defense]. But he did so against all odds, against all expectations of the people in this building [the Pentagon] at that point. It has since been heralded as the way to do business. I am satisfied the Army would change in a heartbeat given the opportunity. I've talked to any number of soldiers, . . . and I don't think I've talked to a single one of them who didn't say you guys have got it right.

We're going to break the Army, and this whole thing of reenlistment and retention is going to get real ugly over time with these one year assignments. And what you lose in terms of the continuity, the spatial orientation of the troops, those types of things, I think are well out balanced by the morale aspect of it. The fact that Marines traditionally do six , I'll argue now seven month deployments, you can recock, refresh, all those kinds of things. It has caused some gear issues, what you leave behind, what you bring out with you, and those types of things. Headquarters is working through that right now. I still think we made a good decision there, too, in terms of stay behind equipment. Not having to transit without armor protection in or out of the country, those types of things, make it advantageous.

No, it never really caused contentiousness on the part of our higher headquarters, although I got a couple of odd comments. I think in the end, those people would have traded what we were doing in a heartbeat, so they couldn't say much about it.

Piedmont: Move on if you would to the RIPTOA [relief in place/transfer of authority]. The MEF begins to flow in February [2004], the division subordinate units begin the very detailed RIPTOA with the 82d. What did the 82d Airborne brief you on the situation?

Conway: Well, I had read before we went over there, and I think it was probably generals trying to paint the best picture they could in terms of the effort that their troops had accomplished, but the 82d highlighted to the media that they had broken the back of the insurgency in the al Anbar Province. We took that with a grain of salt, and we realized that Fallujah was still the "Wild, Wild West." And we said before we ever went over that can't be because there's no place in our AO [area of operation] that we're going to say we can't go. And yet the word that was getting to us on the West Coast that you really can't go into Fallujah, and you can't go there and stay long because you are going to get shot at. And in fact that very much was the case. General [John P.] Abizaid [USA] was nearly assassinated there. Our regimental commander who had responsibility for Fallujah got shot at on the way into town, got shot at a meeting, got shot at on the way out.

Piedmont: And that was very early on?

Conway: That was his orientation to Fallujah. That was his first meeting downtown with the membership. And when we started peeling back the onion, and realizing that you sort of dash through Fallujah if you were part of the 82d and call it a patrol—that let us know that we had a problem. Anyway, it was a good turnover. Good guys in the 82d.

The second night that I was in Camp Fallujah, unfortunately, we lost five soldiers and a corpsman to an indirect fire attack. In fact, there was a lot of indirect fire coming into Fallujah. It made us realize again that it was going to be a very different place. I highlighted to you earlier that we didn't lose a single Marine in [the southern provinces] in five and half months. By the time we had turnover with the 82d Airborne, we lost five Marines in the al Anbar Province. The awareness that they [the insurgents] had contested the turnover, if you will, and that it was going to be very different for us in the al Anbar Province was quite real even by the time of the turnover. . . .

Piedmont: General, I would like to talk about Fallujah right now. You just set the tactical stage. Here we are roughly at the end of March [2004], the final RIPTOA went on the 26th of March, I believe, and four days later, the four contractors were murdered in Fallujah, thereby presenting us with something of a conundrum, a quandary. What were the courses of action that the MEF staff presented to you in response to this?

Conway: Let me highlight for you that on the same day that we lost four contractors in Fallujah, we lost five soldiers in Ramadi, and they were literally blown away. They hit what up to that point was probably the biggest explosive device that we had seen. They were riding in a [M]113 [armored personnel carrier], and all we found was the tailgate and a boot. The size of the explosion was monstrous, 15 to 18 feet across, 10 to 12 feet deep. We don't know for sure what they hit, but it was certainly something very large, probably stacked.

I need to characterize for you our first reaction to the contractors because that will, I hope, make what else I say make more sense. We started seeing the reports initially on TV. And that fit, because we had no idea these guys were going into Fallujah. And the first of the effort was that we had to get those bodies back, and we did that. We had three bodies back by the end of the day, a fourth body that the police chief helped us with that we recovered the next morning. So we got the bodies back very quickly.

Our next questions, then, as military people responsible for the area, is who were these guys? Where did they come from? Who sent them into Fallujah, and why didn't they tell us, because quite frankly, four white guys in a soft skinned vehicle could die in a lot of cities in Iraq at that point, and Fallujah was no exception. Now, how they died was absolutely terrible, but we felt like there had been a serious mistake made in causing that to happen in the first place, and one that was very avoidable through some very simple coordination.

So that was our first reaction. And at the same time we are dealing with what's happened to the 1st of the 1st [1st Engineer Battalion, 1st Brigade, 1st Infantry Division, USA] with the five soldiers out in Ramadi. It didn't take long at all for us to sense that the public reaction to this thing was significant and that in some regards, decision makers in Baghdad were being heavily influenced by public perception. So we cautioned people, started saying at the outset, "hey, let's not overreact to this, okay? We've got a plan for Fallujah." We [had] already . . . launched a battalion sized operation up on the northwest side of the city to ensure freedom of movement. We were in close coordination with the Special Forces in the area. We felt like that we were going to solve Fallujah. There was no place in our AO that we wouldn't go. . . . [We believed that] our courses of action of developing the intelligence, developing a credibility with the people, gaining additional tactical intelligence from them, would eventually lead us to the leadership of what we thought was an enclave of foreign fighters there . . . and we would take the head off of the insurgency in and around Fallujah.

And so we cautioned people, "let's not overreact to the death of the contractors." That was a mistake, frankly, and one that should not drive our policies, or our strategies in and around the city.

In the midst of trying to push back against that, we got word to attack Fallujah—a division level attack, whatever amount of force that we thought we needed. . . . Once again, we pushed back, and I went to certain levels in the chain of command to try to determine where this was coming from. Again, harkening back to an earlier question, I felt the Army could be fairly heavy handed, and I wanted to make sure this just wasn't CJTF 7 telling us we had to attack. In fact, it came from higher than that, and once we discovered that, we said, "Okay, if this is well understood by everyone up and down the chain of command, we're Marines, and we will execute our orders."

We looked at various ways to conduct the attack. Essentially, we looked at a feint to the south, the main attack coming in from the north, and in the end three battalions in an attack on the city. We were about three days in the attack; we had taken about a third of the city. People talk about Marine casualties associated with Fallujah. In fact, the casualties were light. We had six Marines killed in three days of attacking the city and I want to say 18 wounded. . . . But if you look at what our guys had done, they had done very well. There were some other deaths outside the city. They continued to attack our convoys. We had a very unfortunate incident where we lost four Marines to a large IED [improvised explosive device] south of Abu Ghraib. So total MEF casualties were mounting. But strictly looking at those forces attacking Fallujah, [the casualties] were not bad over a three day period, and we killed a lot of bad guys. They were doing some really stupid things in the city, [like] 40 to 50 guys skylarking at a roadblock inside the city that our AC 130 picked up. Groups walking down the streets trying to move into attack positions that our people could see that were flying with the close air. Snipers were introduced to the Iraqis. We brought in a lot of snipers, realizing that they would be a very viable weapon in a built up area. [It was the] first time we had to fight in a heavily built up area really since Baghdad.

So these troops made great progress. The snipers owned the streets, and we felt like, in fact, we were getting intercepts that they were about to run out of ammunition. We had killed a significant portion of the leadership, the rest were confused . . . arguing among themselves in terms of what they needed to do. They were starting to look at how to slip out of the city. We could never, just based on the numbers of forces, put a complete cordon around the city, so there was some filtering out down by the river. We had not had time to evacuate the civilians, so we had young military aged males coming out with some of the civilians at the checkpoints. We couldn't confirm or deny. Probably if we had had some Iraqis there, they could have helped us, but they really, once again, as I said, the Iraqi forces had essentially dissolved, although the 36th Commando, they were tigers, they did their part.

But in any event, after about . . . three or four days, we got word to stop attacking the city, and that at that point was the entirely the wrong thing to do. What had happened in the process was that Al Jazeera and some other Arab media had worked their way into the city, and they were reporting that we were killing hundreds of women and children and old people, when in fact just the opposite was true. I think probably some women and children did die. We were dropping bombs and shooting artillery, counterbattery, into Fallujah, no question about it. But we were being very careful. We were checking all of those missions to try to make sure that collateral damage was absolutely minimized, and I am satisfied that we did that.

There were a couple of doctors over at the hospital who were bigger insurgents than the insurgents were. So they were only too happy to make comments about how we were filling the hospital with women and children, and so the whole myth was precipitated, and just the hysterical, I would say irresponsible, reporting of the Arab press I think inflamed the whole region. In fact, it started giving me some cause for concern that not only did you have the Sunnis who were being agitated by it all, but the Shi'a down south were reading these reports [and] believing them. And about the same time, [Muqtada al] Sadr and his people came to life in Najaf. We never wanted to see a general uprising of both Shi'a and Sunni because we did not have enough forces in the country to handle both of those writ large.

So anyway, there was cause for concern that the whole thing was potentially going to get out of hand. I think we owe that all collectively to the Arab media and their lack of journalistic integrity in terms of reporting of what they were actually seeing.

Once again, we thought we had gotten some bum steer out of Baghdad, so we pushed back, saying hey, you know, "you couldn't anticipate that you were going to have Sunni objection to this in the governing body?" It was pretty shortsighted. Okay, you've got this attack into motion now. You don't just call off three battalions of Marines just like that, especially when they have lost some of their fellow Marines and they want to see this thing done. It would be a huge mistake at this point to cease the attack. We can give you the city in three more days.

And yet our orders were our orders, so we were told to hold what we had and go into a series of negotiations. We did that with the city fathers, but they never swung any weight. They were very heavily influenced by the insurgents that were still there. They had no real authority over the people. They were just trying to cut the best deal they could, and delay, and do some other things to try to draw the thing out, which I think they successfully did. So after a time it was pretty much just stalemate. We thought at one point that the national will was going to be there again to go back into the city, and we tried everything imaginable. We tried to get them to turn in their heavy weapons, to turn over the insurgent leadership, those kinds of things. Again, they could not have possibly pulled that off, I am convinced of it, because they had no real authority or couldn't indicate any ability to make those things happen. Anyway, we negotiated with them. They sent some people out of Baghdad. Between them and me, and a number of others, we talked to them, but the talks never came to anything substantial.

We in the process . . . evolved to the Fallujah Brigade in an effort to try to take advantage of what we called a charismatic old Iraqi general that could muster forces in the area, and bring security to the city, and turn over the insurgent leadership, and that type of thing. That was essentially a concept that was, General Abizaid and I, had talked about it before, and we always thought that was a key to putting this Iraqi lead in place out there with a competent and capable force. On the heels of that, we had a suggestion. I met one night with General [Mohammed Abdullah Mohammed] al Shehwani, who was the head of Iraqi National Intelligence Service, and he said that he and his people knew of some Iraqi generals like that in that area, and that he thought it was worth the effort. It matched the thing General Abizaid and I had talked about. It gave us a way to break the standoff, if you will. We were dealing with no aces in the deck after it was determined that we would not reattack. We were always bluffing to say that if these things don't happen, American forces will resume the offensive, but they didn't know that, and so they were inspired to try to do some other things.

Once again, the Fallujah Brigade indicated sort of the ineffectiveness of locals attempting to do a security thing. We appealed to the honor and nature of the Iraqi army, any number of things, to try to get these guys to, to get the old spirit back, but they just would not—could not—do it, and after a time, once again, when we saw we were killing some of these guys in uniform right alongside the insurgency, we took back the weapons and equipment that we had given them, and that was sort of the quiet demise of the Fallujah Brigade. . . .

[Further discussion of the stalemate before General Conway had to end the conversation. The interview resumed three weeks later.]

Piedmont: We left off last time toward the end of the battle of Fallujah. The very last thing we were discussing was your concern that the stalemate you were involved in was locking down three battalions that could have been used elsewhere. Please pick up on that thread and take us through.

Conway: What we had found was we had about the right amount of troops for service in the al Anbar. But that said, we didn't have enough to bring in for a focused attack on Fallujah and take care of the rest of the area of responsibility. So the division commander massed his troops to the extent he could from areas that were not as affected as others. But in the process, we saw that the bad guys started to come in behind us and exact some retribution on people who had been contributing and cooperating with us. We were concerned that . . . we were going to start having large numbers of troops sitting in positions and baking, in the sun, achieving no measurable purpose. So we wanted to get past the impasse that we saw starting to develop.

A couple of interesting things I would add to it. One is that there was reporting, much later after the fact, that Marines were driven out of Fallujah based on casualties and some other factors. In fact, if you go back to check your record of those three battalions in the fighting in Fallujah, they lost some other Marines and sailors outside of the city through IEDs and that type of thing, but actually fighting inside the city, we had six Marines killed and six wounded as a result of their attacks. And we were pretty satisfied with that. We hated to lose anybody, but at the time we stopped, [we] own[ed] about a third of the city, and [for] the casualties to be that relatively insignificant I thought was a testament to the good tactics and operations use of combined arms and so forth by the small unit commanders. The other thing of course was the nature of the press reporting. . . .

Piedmont: What role did the media play in shaping the battle? If I have it right, there was a scarcity of "embeds" versus OIF I. Is that correct?

Conway: I don't think we ever saw the number of embeds in OIF II that we saw in OIF I. And by embeds by the pure definition of the term, we had some people that came and lived with us for a couple of days, and did what the troops would probably classify as a "drive by shooting," and then left. That caused us to say, "hey, either you are an embed or you are not." If you're just here to do a story, there's a difference between calling yourself an embed. An embed lives with, sleeps with, gets to know the troops over an extended period of time. I don't think you can reach that status in a three or four day period, which was some of what we were seeing.

Our concern wasn't so much with the U.S. press as it was with the Arab press. That was where we came to understand that some of these folks—not all—but some of these folks have absolutely no journalistic integrity, and they were not the least bit hesitant to virtually be the enemy combat camera. I mean, there were reports— and this is what [reached] part of the people in Baghdad, and especially the Sunnis as a part of the transition government—that we had killed 750 women and children. And these guys are only too happy to go interview the doctor at the hospital, who by the way was probably one of the biggest insurgents in the town. But the credibility associated with the doctor at the hospital "who says" was obvious.

In fact, we were pretty pleased with the efforts [to avoid civilian casualties] in the attack. There probably were some women and children who were killed, frankly, because we dropped bombs on hard targets in the city. But we were also quite precise. We had AC 130s up at night, and this was the first time that they had learned to deal with that weapon system. In one instance, we had a radio call back, "We've got 50 guys loitering around a roadblock in the middle of town. Do we take them out?" We said yeah, take them out. Another instance we had 40 or 50 come out of a mosque headed toward positions. Again, an F 16 saw them. Again, we put a precision weapon in the middle of them and hit large numbers.

Anyway, this hysterical and irresponsible reporting got to the Sunnis in the country, the rest of the Arab region. . . . It was just, it taught us that these bastards cannot be trusted, and we tried different things over time, embedding them, making sure that they had proper reporting, and so forth. I confronted, and that's the only word to use, one of our battalion commanders with a statement that he had made in Al Jazeera, and he said, sir, those people were with me all day, and you can ask anybody, I didn't say anything like that. All they got right is his name and his hometown. So they used that to fabricate whatever they wanted to say that would continue to inflame, and just print it.

Things like that were just incredible to us, and again, it brought us to realize that this whole IO [information operations] aspect of the fight was indeed important, and very well understood by our adversary. . . .

Piedmont: The final question on the actual battle of Fallujah and the immediate aftermath as the whole thing was going on—what was your greatest concern?

Conway: Well, we had a concern for civilian casualties, of course, and we had a concern for what was happening in the outlying areas. I never had any doubt as to how it was going to turn out. But I think on a larger scale, I had a concern that we were going off plan, in that we had gone in there with the idea of trying to employ the same techniques that we had seen work in the south. And we felt that given our head that we could have done things differently in Fallujah, not overreacted to the idea of contractors, which I consider as sort of the root of all evil here, but by being on deck five days after turnover and then assaulting the town of Fallujah.

Okay, that's not exactly in accordance with our doctrine out of the *Small Wars Manual.* Once we had Fallujah, what were we going to do with it? There was no police force. There was no army. So we were going to have to garrison Fallujah and tie down large numbers of troops in a city that would probably be seething and hostile to our presence. So we were concerned about what was going to be the aftermath of that. And again, the fact that the Marines come to the al Anbar, and the first thing we do is start killing people. We had said before we ever got there that we knew the Army didn't go into Fallujah, and thought that was a bit of travesty to be saying the insurgency was broken—you know, we've got complete control of our AO, and yet nobody goes into Fallujah. There's a reason for that. So, a little bit transparent. And we had said we'll go anyplace in our AO, whatever that takes. And we certainly will have freedom of movement for our convoys, and that type of thing. That's what started piquing our interest almost right away. But we knew that we were getting away from this whole idea of developing the trust and confidence of the people, and trying to win him over through what was both reducing the insurgency and creating a better quality of life.

The thing that probably should be posted for the record before we leave Fallujah is that as late as the 25th [April 2004], we thought we were going to reattack the city. You know, we sat for about two, two and half weeks, with these useless conversations that were taking place with the city representatives and leadership. They were under the gun of the terrorists and the insurgents. We knew that. And it was a cat and mouse game that was being played, but okay, that's all right because when this fails, unfortunately, we are going to get orders to attack anyway. We thought that those were coming on about the 25th, only to find out that apparently in Baghdad, and maybe even in the capitals, the Brits and later the Italians had said, and I think it was again subject somewhat to what they were reading out of the Arab media, that you are being too heavy handed there, and if you do that, you risk us leaving the Coalition. And that was a bucket of cold water in the face of a lot of people. Immediately, the whole thought process changed about us going back into Fallujah because whatever else we were doing there was not going to be worth the breakup of the Coalition to include our best ally.

So you know, it gets back to this whole idea of overreaction, and the fact that we should have taken the deaths of the four contractors much more in stride, realizing that . . . our reaction was exactly what they wanted it to be. We should have been smarter than that, and it's unfortunate that it simply served to inflame the nation, and probably the region, and now we've got what we've got. . . .

Piedmont: As we wind down your tenure, your personal tour of command of the MEF in Iraq, how would you characterize the situation when you left? Had you seen the point at which the initiative had passed back to us?

Conway: Yeah, listen, we were always optimists, guardedly optimistic at times, but they could only hurt us in certain ways, and I think that we always had the initiative. They were reacting in great part to what we were doing, and we sensed that, and it made the troops feel pretty good about things, feel pretty good about Iraq.

You can't just talk about the kinetic aspect of things; there's an economic line, a governmental line. There were five lines of operation that really we were operating on. We were having intermittent talks with some of the bad guys who said, thought that they represented a Sunni insurgency. We were creating business conferences with Iraqi businessmen, some of them right out of Fallujah, both in Bahrain and in Jordan. We looked for a way to try to secure the contractors who would come to our area to build the projects.

We had a method. It needed some tweaking, I think, before it was all over, and security is still the principal issue there. But we were looking for ways to try to generate business growth, and employment associated with that.

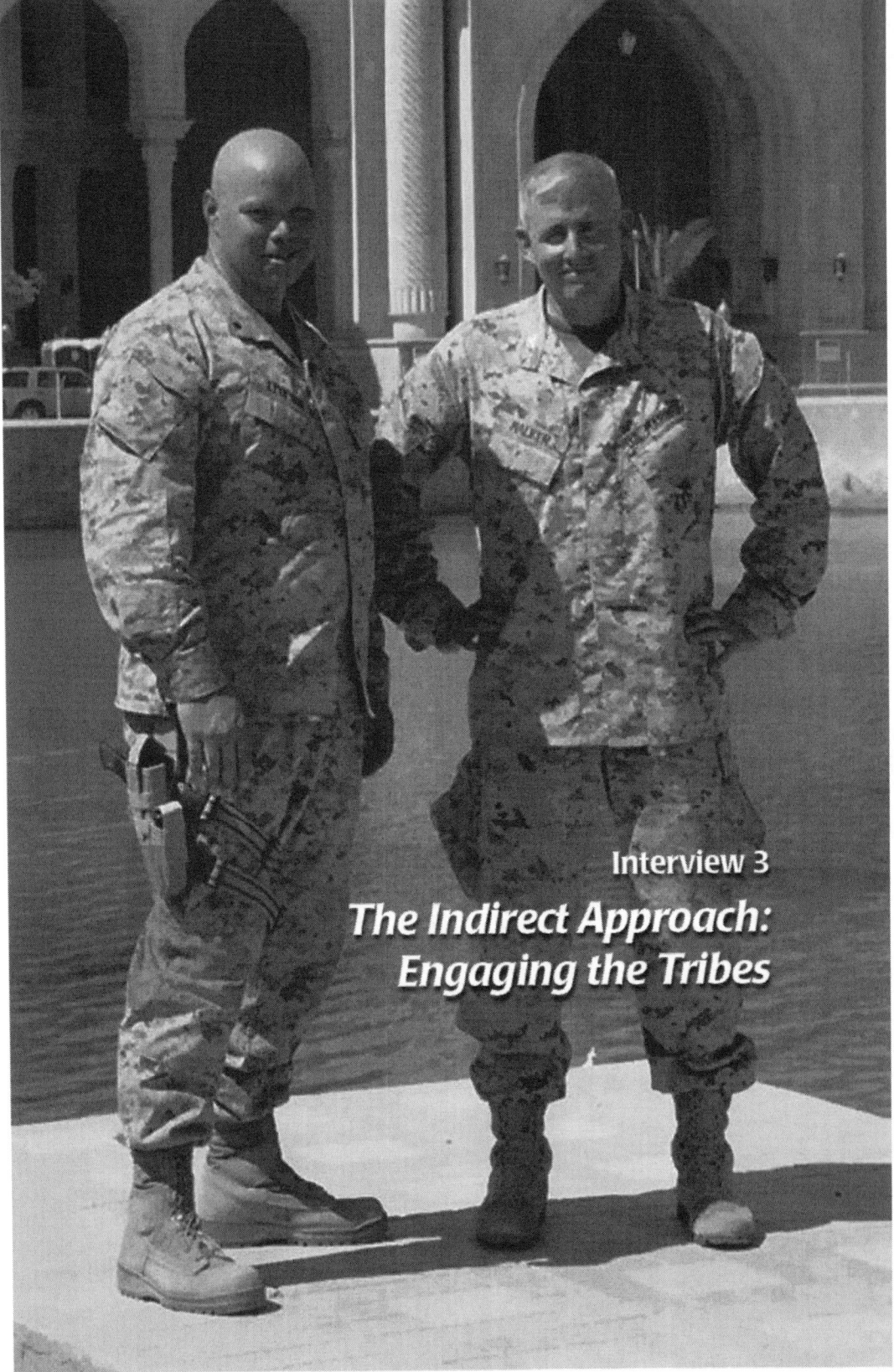

Interview 3
The Indirect Approach:
Engaging the Tribes

Colonel Michael M. Walker

Commanding Officer
3d Civil Affairs Group
I Marine Expeditionary Force

October 2003 to September 2005

Colonel Michael M. Walker commanded 3d Civil Affairs Group during the first deployment of Marine forces into al Anbar Province from February until September 2004. Previously, he served with the Defense Intelligence Agency, Defense Intelligence Service, and in 2003 he was in charge of captured document exploitation for the whole of Iraq. In this interview, he describes the first battle of Fallujah and initial efforts to engage Anbari leaders and split the insurgency.

Colonel Walker was interviewed by Colonel Gary W. Montgomery on 24 March 2009 at Twentynine Palms, California.

Colonel Gary W. Montgomery: What was your impression when you first got there? What was Anbar Province like, and what was your impression of the insurgency?

Colonel Michael M. Walker: Well, actually, I had an opinion that the insurgency was far more sophisticated and developed. . . . The previous tour, I saw how sophisticated the Iraqi intelligence service was, . . . and all these guys were out there. And we saw them connecting themselves back together again in the summer of 2003. . . .

That whole first Fallujah fight fiasco—that was probably the single most frustrating experience of my entire career, bar none, nothing even close to being second. So here you go. You have probably the best prepared Marine combat organization in the history of the Marine Corps going back with a great campaign plan, approved all the way up through the whole friggin' chain of command. Set to go, set to execute. . . . We did the transfer of authority between I MEF [I Marine Expeditionary Force] and the 82d [Airborne Division, USA], . . . I'd say the last few days of March. And either the next day or the day following, those Blackwater guys drive into Fallujah. . . .

So the Marines were saying, look, we've got a campaign plan that's going to win here. Why in the hell would you deviate from your campaign plan four or five days into its execution? It's a 190 day plan. Realistically, probably it was longer than that, because it was obviously built for continuing operations. And you're going to throw that thing out of the book and go make a major fight in Fallujah? And . . . we did. . . . But now we're tied up in this terrible fight in Fallujah, and the same guys who ordered us to attack now order us to quit, so they stopped the fighting. . . .

Reacting to those four guys getting killed in Fallujah immediately handed the tactical and operational initiative to the enemy because now we were reacting to what they were doing. Now we were on their agenda. Like I said, I'm endlessly frustrated, and it's not like the Marine Corps didn't see it, that we didn't know that, and we weren't fighting tooth and nail not to execute that operation, OVR, Operation Vigilant Resolve.

So we did that, so now what do you do? Well, now you really better start thinking out of the box, because we've got a mess on our hands. We threw our campaign plan away. Now we're going to go try to start it up again. . . . What are we going to do since we're not going to go in militarily? So we started opening up lines of communication, went through a whole series of negotiations. They were going to hand over the prisoners, and they were going to turn over their weapons, and all this other stuff, and we all knew that it was hokum.

I've been to negotiations in my civilian work, and I studied negotiations at Harvard. . . . You've got to have something to be able to negotiate with somebody, and they knew we had no cards. Our card was, "Well, if you do this, we're going to go resume military operations," and they knew we couldn't. So we did that kabuki dance for a number of weeks, but the good thing that came out of that is we finally started talking to these guys. And the thing that General [James T.] Conway did that I thought was so keen was that he would not only have you talk to the guys while you're working, but during the breaks, and everything else. . . . He had us start to talk to these guys, and a number of things came out of that.

We found out that a bunch of military officers were interested in going back into an Iraqi army in the future, and these guys, right now, their alternatives were: starve; try to make ends meet in a desperate way for my family; have no future; or try to get back in the army.

At this point, there were a lot of guys I spoke to up in Baghdad at CPA [Coalition Provisional Authority] who I think were looking at life through rose colored glasses and going, "The Iraqi army was a bad thing, and we don't need it, and the worst thing we can do is bring back the Iraqi army." From the Iraqis I spoke to, even up in the Kurds, the Iraqi army had always been considered one of the most respected professions in Iraq. It certainly wasn't [like] being in the intelligence services. It certainly wasn't [like] being a Ba'athist Party guy for the Kurds. The Iraqi army was a respected organization. It was respected by the Sunnis, it was respected by the Shia. Bringing back the Iraqi army was an important thing, so we started seeing this as a possible way to crack the insurgency.

Some of those conversations led to the famous Fallujah Brigade. That was out of the box. That was highly controversial. A lot of people just went nuts when the Marines did that. I think that was a great solution. I'll defend that to my dying day. First of all, it created a crack—again, which was one of General Conway's goals—in the insurgency, because now at least you had some of these guys saying that, "Hey, I'm going to work on a day to day basis with the Marines," and you had some of their guys saying, "No we won't." Well, prior to that, it was all "No we won't," so we started to create that dialogue. . . .

One of the things General Conway did was to have us integrate economically back into the region, so we had an LNO [liaison officer] office in Kuwait, we had an LNO in Jordan, and we were using those guys to try to get the economy going by having the regional Arabs integrate with the Iraqi local economy here in al Anbar and see what we could get going through that end. . . . So then we started these [discussions], "Try to get the economy going again. The fighting's over. Let's try to carry out the campaign plan as best we can." We put together the idea of trying to identify leaders in al Anbar, and we'll take them out of al Anbar. We'll get them out of that place, because it's like a kid who was growing up in a gang environment. You live your whole life in a gang environment, you think that's the only world there is. . . . So maybe if we could get these guys out, we could broaden them to a different way of seeing it, a different future for Iraq, and embrace that, and take it back with them.

So we arranged to have a trip to Bahrain, and we brought a bunch of these business guys and leaders and so forth to Bahrain, and one of our rules was that anybody could go as long as they all agreed to it. The insurgency wanted to figure out what the hell we were doing, so we knew we were bringing some bad guys along.

So we got there, but now we're in a setting where there's no flak jackets, no incoming, no nothing. You're in another Arab country. . . . Saddam [Hussein] wouldn't let people leave Iraq. A couple of these guys in the delegation had been to Bahrain, but the last time they'd been in Bahrain was in the mid 1970s, so we're talking 30 years earlier. When they left Iraq in the mid '70s to go to Bahrain, Iraq was the country with the higher per capita earnings. Iraq was the country with the nice buildings. Iraq was the country of wealth and stability, and Bahrain was a kind of backwater. And now Bahrain's got skyscrapers, and everyone's driving fancy cars, and there's landscaped highways and fancy hotels. And all of a sudden they see, for the first time, some of these guys saw what the hell happened to them. They went from being the top of the pile in the mid '70s to being way behind by the 2000s, mid 2000s.

And I remember we were up in this one holding company, a major corporation in Bahrain. Their first business deal in the '50s had been exporting rice from Iraq into the Middle East and into India. And they said, "Hey, my family started doing business with Iraqi guys half a century ago. We'd love to start business again up with Iraq." And these guys were all anxious—"yeah, let's do it"—and all this stuff. And then we would sit there saying, "Wait a minute. I don't think the security situation in al Anbar is appropriate for you to bring your business in right now. No, we've got to get the fighting under control. We've got to make this place a safer place to be before we start closing these business deals." So we still closed some business deals, but we wanted to keep sending that message that if you want this for your future, you've got to change the reality that's back in al Anbar. At that time, also we would have dinners and stuff so we could talk informally, and that's when we first got the first kind of overtures of some quid pro quos: "If we come work with you, can you do this for me?" And they didn't go too far, but it was just some feelers.

So then we decided, okay, that was launched out of Kuwait, so . . . the Kuwait guys started integrating. What's going on in Jordan? We've got an LNO sitting there in Jordan. What's going on there? So I took a trip to Jordan to meet with our officer there, by the name of [Lieutenant Colonel Roy D.] "Dave" Harlan. Dave takes me all these places, and we start meeting those people, and he's got a list of connections of people in al Anbar that I'm just like going, "I can't believe this." But nothing's happening. It's all talk, and it's all contacts, but we're not getting anywhere.

And that's when I realized that tens of thousands of Iraqis from the al Anbar had gone to Jordan. And not only just tens of thousands, tens of thousands with talent: engineers, doctors, scientists, former high ranking government officials, guys with PhDs in economics, guys with—you name an American university, they've got a degree there. And they're all sitting there, and they want to do something. So I'm like, "He's sitting on a pile of golden eggs here." So we came back, and I got my econ guys and said, "Look, Dave is a great salesman. He is great at finding contacts. He's got contacts out the yin yang. We need to start closing some of this." So I sent the econ team over there to go start putting something together, and that led to our first economic development meeting, which was okay. And I say okay in the sense that it accomplished all of our goals of economics, but it was still, it wasn't a major step forward. But they liked what they saw, evidently, so then they said let's schedule another one in late July—18, 19, 20, somewhere around there.

So then all of a sudden I'm getting these e mails from the former ambassador to France who is a senior vice president for Citicorp, . . . and I'm getting an e mail from a guy who led one of the USAID

[United States Agency for International Development] projects for reintegrating Eastern Europe after the fall of communism. And they're saying, "Hey, we're getting some Iraqis [who] are contacting us and saying they want to come to this business meeting, and it's supposed to be with the Marines." And I'm going like, "Oh, the more the merrier," but I'm letting the chain of command know there's an unusual list of characters coming to this thing. . . .

So, I arrive the first day, and an Office of Secretary of Defense White House liaison was there, Jerry [H.] Jones, and Ambassador [Peter W.] Galbraith, and a number of other guys were there. There was representative, what's the name of the U.S. bank? It's like the U.S. bank for international development. . . . And then there was the Japanese bank for international cooperation, or whatever. They were there. . . . And Jerry Jones calls me over and says, "Hey, look, one of the Iraqis here says that there's going to be a representative from the insurgency in al Anbar that wants to talk to you guys, open up an informal line of communication." So it was, "Okay, fine." So then I sent that e mail off to J.C. [Colonel] John [C.] Coleman, [I MEF] chief of staff. . . .

So then, the next day we go in—and this gets back to your earlier question about how organized did you think the insurgency was— I thought they were fairly organized militarily. I was a clueless wonder on how well organized they were until this meeting the next day. So we go in there, and these guys have got five or six committees organized. They've got a political committee, an economics committee, a governance committee, a military committee. . . .

Montgomery: They've got their own lines of operation.

Walker: They're ready to take over the country. I mean, so these guys are totally organized. They're not just organized militarily. They're totally organized economically. They're organized politically. They're organized from a governance standpoint. They've got all three of our lines of operation matched. They've got a security line of operation. They've got an economic line of operation. They've got a governance line of operation. It's up and running and set, and some . . . PhDs in economics are on their economics team, and their military committee's got former

Republican Guard corps commanders and other generals, and things like that. These guys are ready to go. . . .

So we sent that message back to MEF, and they're going like, "Well, that's pretty interesting," and now J. C. Coleman is like chomping on the bit. He wants to get on a plane and fly out. But during lunch that day, Jerry Jones gets pulled aside, said, "Hey, the representative from the insurgency's arrived. They want to meet you guys up in his hotel room this afternoon." So he tells me that as we're going out to lunch. So we eat lunch, go back, head count, more of this stuff. . . . We were no longer running that conference. They were running the conference. They were having their committees come up and discuss what their vision of Iraq was going to be, their vision of al Anbar, and what role they wanted us to do. And it was pretty enlightening. . . .

The other thing that amazed me was the gentleman from Japan gave an impassioned talk about becoming the friends of America. . . . He's saying, "You can trust the Americans. When they say they'll work with you, they mean they'll work with you. They don't lie. They helped rebuild my country. They said they were going to rebuild the country after the war. No one believed them. They did. We expected them to occupy our country and take everything we own, and leave us destroyed, and they didn't, and now they're one of our best friends." I'm paraphrasing, but no American could have made that speech to another audience.

Again, that showed a vision of maybe being with the Americans instead of being with al Qaeda—and I'm talking Sunnis now, because screw the al Qaeda guys. These are Sunnis—and these are the diehard Ba'athists for the most part—all of a sudden, the lights were going on that maybe the road out of this thing is with the Americans, instead of with al Qaeda, and al Qaeda was Frankenstein's monster. They brought them in, thinking they were going to be able to control them, and they were not. They lost control of the beast, and al Qaeda started taking over them. So that all started helping us.

Montgomery: The campaign plan that was diverted because of the Blackwater incident, as a consequence of that and the first fight in

Fallujah, you said it caused them to start opening lines of communication.

Walker: That's correct.

Montgomery: But was that consistent with the campaign plan you already had?

Walker: Absolutely. . . .

Montgomery: Let's see, this meeting, you said there was a meeting in August, and this one is after that, right?

Walker: No, this was in July. This one set up the August [meeting]. . . . Let me back up just a second. What we did was we wanted to establish the bona fides of the insurgent guy we met with, the representative of the resistance, which I never pause calling terrorists, because they hated it, which I think did us a lot of good. And I said, "Well, if you do this, you're a terrorist." So, anyway, he was going to go back to his guys, and I got all of the stuff, the list of demands that they had and so on and so forth, and we were going to go in, and we were going to see if he was really, truly representative, so they were going to do a cease fire. And if they could do a cease fire in Anbar, then we believed that they had control, and that therefore you're a legitimate player, and we'll take it from here.

For a number of reasons, it just didn't work. We tried to do it towards the end of the following week in July, which is a very tight timeline. We really didn't connect on their demands and our demands, on what we thought was supposed to happen, what they thought was supposed to happen. I don't think the trust was there. You don't build trust and rapport with somebody in one two hour meeting, not for something of this magnitude, not for a cease fire in the entire province.

So we waited for the cease fire. We didn't see it. We were doing statistical—how many IEDs [improvised explosive devices] went off, how many firefights, how many contacts were reported? Was there a statistical drop during the cease fire period? And then it didn't happen. We didn't buy it. We had notified up the chain of command because they also claimed to control part of the area around Samarra, north of Baghdad. The Army commander said he didn't see anything happening there. I think we both set conditions that were impossible to meet. . . .

We said okay, let's try it again in August, so we'll meet again in August. So we set up another meeting. . . .

So I go back, report to the deputy chief of mission [James F. Jeffrey, at the U.S. embassy in Baghdad]. I'm thinking he's going to want to talk about, "Do you know what we just saw—about how organized the Sunnis are? Do you know that they're having one of the armed resistance wants to come talk to us about a potential cease fire?" No. He didn't want to talk about that at all. He was interested in "what in the Sam Hill was some guy from the Office of Secretary Defense doing there in Amman?" That this should all be Department of State, not Department of Defense. And "what do those guys think they're doing?" And "what was he doing here?" And "when is he leaving?" And "what's his name?"

And I'm sitting there going like, "Am I or am I not sitting here in the U.S. embassy in Baghdad, and aren't we in a kind of nasty little shoot 'em up right now?" I didn't say any of this, of course, because I'm just sitting there. But I'm going, like, "You're talking some turf war back between Foggy Bottom and the Pentagon. And here we have an opportunity to possibly exploit a big crack or seam in the enemy in the war here that might start moving us forward toward resolving this thing." I tried my best to pitch all that stuff, and he would just brush that stuff aside, yeah, yeah, and go back to the OSD DoD DoS turf battles. So I said my piece and I left.

Now, I said that to compare the reception that I got at the U.S. embassy in Baghdad in the last days of July in 2004, and how I MEF was looking at this, and 1 MarDiv [1st Marine Division]. And they were looking at this thing very seriously, and looking at this as a real avenue to try to pursue. But you can see the disconnect. It's going to be really hard for the MEF to go off on a policy if it's not in sync with the mission [of the U.S. embassy]. And even more so, now I'm wondering how are we going to sell this to the Iraqi interim government and PM [Prime Minister Ayad] Allawi, because if the U.S. mission isn't on board, Allawi is certainly not going to be on board with this thing, and we're liable to kill this thing. It's going to be a stillborn opportunity here.

So we went back in August. Now by August, we know that the second Fallujah fight is coming. I don't know what date it is, but everybody's gearing up for it. That train's left the station, and it's going to happen. And we kind of viewed the August meeting as the last chance to maybe avoid this fight. But again, the first Fallujah fight had warped their perception of how strong they were. At that August meeting, there was a special Fallujah delegation that came, and our position was we weren't going to talk to them. . . . They were even a separate delegation from the rest of the Sunni resistance because they had gone off on their own world. They were being run by [Abu Musab al] Zarqawi . . .

Montgomery: [Abdallah al] Janabi, maybe?

Walker: Yeah, yeah. . . . Those guys were just a bunch of bad actors, and we didn't want to talk to them, but we did. . . .

So these guys [Fallujah delegation], they were totally convinced they were going to beat us again, which they don't realize they lost the first time. They won because of politics. They won because the Iraqi governing council at that time, which was the advisers under the CPA [Coalition Provisional Authority], said that they were going to resign, four of the council were going to resign if we didn't stop operations. So [Ambassador L. Paul] Bremer had said, "Look, stop it." They viewed that as they thought they beat us cold. They thought they had fought us to a standstill, . . . and they weren't interested in negotiating. They were basically just giving us ultimatums. . . . I knew there was no way that there wasn't going to be a second Fallujah battle. . . .

This Fallujah delegation gave us a real interesting description of how Fallujah was being governed at that time. And I can tell you that the closest comparison I can give to you, if you're a student of history, is the Reign of Terror in Paris after the [French] Revolution. It was a bone chilling description of how to run a population. . . . Things that were just horrific, and it was all star chamber, informants and counter informants, executions and summary executions, and torturing. It was just terrible what was going on inside that city. The term we used was a cancer growing on the face of Iraq. Fallujah was a cancer that had to be eradicated. . . .

We came back the second time from the meeting. This was the first time they gave us a detailed proposal arming the Sunnis to fight with us, and it's sad that that [idea] got sidetracked for about a year, year and a half. And their proposal, in my personal opinion, was unrealistic, even unrealistic for the future. But not only was it unrealistic for that time frame, it was an unrealistic solution. But it had the key components to create an armed Sunni force in the Sunni provinces; northern Babil; al Anbar; I think Samarra Province, I mean, the Sunni province that has Samarra in it; and parts of western Baghdad, that they would do that and join with us and do that, follow that out, which in essence became the Sunni Awakening.

By that time, my tour was coming to a close. Fourth CAG [civil affairs group] was coming on board, and the State Department was not interested in this line of communication, and I felt that it would probably get picked up again after the second Fallujah fight. I know subsequent Marine rotations attempted to rebuild those lines and re create that dynamic again, and eventually we succeeded. . . .

Before Brigadier General [David G.] Reist deployed, he was keenly interested in reviving this, and he kept it going. I don't know if he was able to move the pot from the back burner to the front burner, but he certainly kept the flame on it. And a number of people just kept working it and working it. I would still get e mails from these guys two years later, three years later. . . .

This just goes to show you how much trust the Marines built up with the Sunnis at this time, and how much they really, truly trusted the Marines to do the right thing by them. Al Qaeda was really taking over the western end of al Anbar, and they were absolutely savage to the Iraqis. . . . These guys were [really bad], and they'd always have a torture chamber set up, and they always had their informants and executions going, and it was rule by terror. And then absolute rigid, extreme Islamic proselytization. And so that's what I'm saying. The Marines were offering security, governance, economy, and al Qaeda's offering a trip back to the Dark Ages. . . .

So what finally happened, and I believe this was in 2006, one of the local tribes [near al Qaim] said, "We've had enough with al Qaeda," and without the Marines or anything, they started going after al Qaeda, and they were losing the fight. And they called back to the guys in Jordan, the Sunnis that we had been talking to, who knew how to get a hold of the Americans, who got a hold of John Coleman, who was now the base guy [at Camp Pendleton]. . . . And they're literally calling him from Iraq to tell him, "Help us. Send air support so we can beat al Qaeda." And J. C. [Coleman] knows all the numbers. He calls the command center at I MEF (Rear), who knows they can immediately contact I MEF (Forward), and they work the comm[unication]s through, and the Marines were able to bring in air support.

My personal opinion was that was the tipping point. That was where it hit the tipping point for the Sunni Awakening, because that's when they reached out to the Marines and said, "Come help me." Now, there were a lot of fits and starts after that, and steps forward and steps back, and progress gained and progress lost. I'm just saying it was an amazing continuum that started through that. . . .

We weren't able to get, initially, the U.S. [State Department] mission behind it, which is the number one reason why we couldn't build, because at the end of the day, you follow orders. If the mission's saying this, then that's what you're going to do. But where you have your own latitude within your own AO [area of operations], you continue to keep that pot on the oven.

Well anyway, that's my view of how the whole Sunni Awakening continued on. So then, of course, then General Reist kept it going, and then it started hitting real success. I remember Colonel [Michael F.] Morris, before he deployed. I gave him a data dump as best I could. I always gave the data dump to any CAG guy, CAG commander, who says, "Hey, what's going on?" [I'd say,] "Here's names, here's people, here's lessons learned, here's whatever we've got." And I'm saying that as a representative of a whole host of people who were doing that. So I'm saying everyone who got connected with that stuff all tried to keep building the network, and building the network, and keeping that thing alive, and working it, and keeping it going.

I'd like to back up and tell one short story. We've talked about when we tried to do a cease fire to see whether or not the people we were talking about were legitimate, and that didn't particularly work out. But there was a second unintentional sequence of events that seriously proved that the people we were talking to were who they said they were. During the afternoon of one of the dates in July, the Iraqi gentleman, [Talal] al Gaood, who was a sheikh, and who also had, I believe, a PhD in engineering, brought out the mayor of Ramadi into a room where I was. . . . The mayor of Ramadi had had a falling out with the insurgents. Now I'm talking the Sunni insurgents, not al Qaeda. Al Qaeda was gunning for them, too. But they did not trust him, and they were looking at him as not someone that they wanted as part of their organization. And so they had a reconciliation meeting there, where they made up, and the mayor of Ramadi then became acceptable to the resistance.

At that exact same meeting, the discussion of the governor of al Anbar came up, Governor [Abdul Karim] Burghis [al Rawi]. . . . The insurgency was livid with Governor Burghis, and they said he had to go . . . because they felt he'd taken too much money, and he was corrupt. . . . [After returning to Iraq,] all of a sudden I get this report [from the provincial support liaison team in Ramadi] on learning about the relationship between the governor of the province, the mayor of Ramadi, and what that authority is. And it was as if someone was starting to delineate who was who in the pecking order. And I'm going like, "why is this coming up right now?" I mean, a week and a half ago I was in Amman, and they were talking about they wanted the mayor of Ramadi, [and] they wanted the governor out. . . . So now all of a sudden I'm getting this thing out of Ramadi saying that they're having all of these discussions about the role of the governor and the role of the mayor of Ramadi, and yadda, yadda, yadda. It had nothing to do with the day to day operations; it was a completely out of the ordinary report. So I'm wondering what's going on in Ramadi. . . .

Well, several days later, they broke into the governor's home, kidnapped his kids. Then they made him go down to Fallujah, resign his office, and make an anti American video. These guys would have knives and clubs and things. So he did that, and he was out.

Now, for those of us that knew about the July meetings, that was all the bona fides we needed. Skip the failed cease fire. These guys said, "This guy's gone. This guy needs to go," and within two weeks it's a done deal. So then we knew that these guys were what they said, and the amount of influence they had in al Anbar was every bit as significant as they proposed it to be. . . .

I would just close by repeating what I said earlier, was that in my opinion the Awakening began in the summer of 2004, and through some very difficult up times and down times, and good times and bad times, a whole host of Marines always picked it up. And if they didn't advance the torch forward, they at least kept that thing lit and held onto it until someone else could move it forward. I think the Sunni Awakening that eventually happened is an unbroken chain from what happened in 2004, and who knows how many unknown Marines, whose role is important in that, who we never get a chance to talk about, played a role.

Interview 4
Fallujah–
The Epicenter of the Insurgency

Lieutenant General John F. Sattler

Commanding General
I Marine Expeditionary Force
Multi National Force • West

September 2004 to February 2005

Lieutenant General John F. Sattler assumed command of I Marine Expeditionary Force in September 2004, midway through Operation Iraqi Freedom II. At the time, Marines were beginning to shape the battlefield for the decisive fight against the insurgents. Prior to this, Sattler commanded the 2d Marine Division and was the J 3 operation officer for U.S. Marine Forces, Central Command.

In this interview, Lieutenant General Sattler describes assuming command following the conclusion of operations in an Najaf the previous month and applying the lessons learned from Najaf and the first battle for Fallujah in planning the second battle for Fallujah. He notes the role of information operations, Iraqi security forces, and joint forces in the second battle for Fallujah.*

Lieutenant General Sattler was interviewed by Lieutenant Colonel John R. Way on 8 April 2005 at Camp Pendleton, California.

Lieutenant Colonel John R. Way: One of the things that I was struck with when I first got to Fallujah was the importance of information operations and what was being done. Please talk a little bit about your guidance in terms of conducting information operations.

Lieutenant General John F. Sattler: Well, we found out that if you're going to wait for guidance to come down, a strategic communications plan, which was going to push information operations down to us with themes, that in some cases, the themes were too late in coming or weren't applicable to al Anbar. So when

---

* For more detail, see the article that LtGen Sattler coauthored with LtCol Daniel H. Wilson, "Operation Al Fajr: The Battle of Fallujah—Part II," *Marine Corps Gazette*, July 2005.

we took our IO [information operations] team, Colonel [Robert M.] Mike Olivier was designated and came in to run the IO campaign. [He] came in about the same time I did.

When we bombed targets during the shaping phase, whatever target we hit, even though we did positive identification, we did the collateral damage assessment to make sure there wouldn't be collateral damage to noncombatants, and we deconflicted friendly forces. . . . We watched the hit and we knew who we killed, and we knew what collateral damage was done.

The next day there was going to be a press release coming out from the insurgents that would show [that] we killed women, children, and elderly men. And there would always be pictures of hospitals with children, women, and old men in it as they talked about who we had bombed, and that [our bombs] never killed any insurgents, they never killed any of [Abu Musab al] Zarqawi's [al Qaeda] network. It was always a standard thing.

And then we would try to rebut that. Well, we figured out that . . . even if you have the moral, legal high ground, you're not going to win, because you're trying to put a genie back in the bottle, [which is] much harder than letting the genie out of the bottle. So a couple of weeks after taking over, [we brought] all the smart folks together. There has to be public affairs, and I know public affairs and IO are separate; they have two different missions in life. The way you attack the theme is different when you're IO or public affairs, but the themes can be relatively the same. And they need to know each other's themes so they can play off 'em inside their own arena. So we had public affairs, civil affairs, and IO all sitting down at the same table, working through the themes, to make sure we were getting the effect that we wanted.

What we basically did, before we dropped a bomb, after about the two week mark, [a] press release went out from us, telling what we did, why we did it, [that] the individual was a thug, a two bit criminal who has killed over "X" number of Iraqi civilians, has destroyed this much of Iraqi infrastructure, and has kept this much off the table in the form of contracts that would return essential services to your town. So every time we struck, we told 'em who went after, who we thought we killed—i.e., a member of the Zarqawi network—and then we were able to also remind everybody that this is not Robin Hood. . . . We twisted that over time; we turned it around to play the way it should be played. And believe it or not, after about a week of us getting the first shot out, their IO campaign fell apart. . . . We started to drive a wedge between the terrorists and the local residents, and then we drove a wedge between [Omar] Hadeed, one thug lord; Zarqawi, another thug lord; and [Abdullah al] Janabi, another thug lord. Each one of our themes was set to open the gap. . . .

Way: You invited some of the media deep into the inner sanctum of the MEF [Marine expeditionary force] at one point. Can you talk about that?

Sattler: Well, they [the reporters] were [using] words like "indiscriminate bombing," and that would be words that the insurgents, or thugs, or murders would use, because it "played ball." And I was going to press conferences, and they would say, "well, you bombed." You know, you "indiscriminately bombed." And I'd say, "Stop. We have never indiscriminately bombed. Every bomb that we have dropped has been a precision munition." Not one armed bombed was dropped during the whole fight, the workup, or the campaign. Well, then we figured out that we need to get "truth in lending." Transparency works well. Embedded media, tell the story. They're going to tell the good, the bad, and the ugly. And you can't censor the ugly, or then you're no longer perceived transparent. . . .

It paid off during the Fallujah fight. We had them in the town to show [that it] was not a humanitarian crisis in the town. The people had left. They had gone out, based on the IO campaign and the shaping campaign. They voluntarily left the town of Fallujah because they saw the signs, and we made it clear, that if they don't cooperate, we're coming. They did not want to be there in the middle of the fight like they got caught up [in] last April [2004]. So they left on their own. But that was all driven by the IO campaign and alerting them to the fact that we're going to come, and you probably do not want to be here. . . .

Way: At one point there was an ABC reporter . . .

Sattler: It was Martha Raddatz. What we decided to do, I looked over at General [Thomas F.] Metz [USA], my boss, and said look, let's bring in somebody who has tremendous credibility, who is not pro or con, who has been very balanced, and let's bring them in and show 'em the whole targeting procedure, show them how we build targeting orders, show them how we update the folders, and when we hit the culmination point, when the positive identification and the criteria that we've established for that particular target's met, how we clear it, how we discuss it quickly, and how we strike it. So we brought her into the COC [combat operations center], and she actually showed it on *Nightline*, where she's sitting there with myself and General Metz . . . and all the fires guys right there, and we're watching the last phases of the target unfold to where we strike it, where we're watching on the gun camera of the aircraft that actually struck the target.

So she saw the pains we went through to ensure we limit the collateral damage, to include the lay of the fuse, the size of the warhead on the bomb, the angle of approach that the aircraft's gonna use, and that we knew by a mathematical model, how many noncombatants may be injured, and that balanced as to what target we were going after. Some targets might be worth a risk of noncombatants being injured, other targets aren't. So she got a chance to see that. She also had a chance to see how accurate the system was when it hit. And she also got a chance to see that you can take out a building with buildings on four sides of it, . . . and when the dust clears, only the building you wanted to strike is rubbled. It imploded on itself, and the other one might have a cracked window, or a crack in the wall. She was just amazed that our systems could be that accurate and our targeting was that painstaking. So, again, it's transparency. . . .

Way: Sir, talk a little bit about the issues and, perhaps, some of the frustrations in terms of the process of defining when [Operation Phantom Fury/Operation al Fajr] was going to happen and the involvement of higher headquarters and the Iraqi government.

Sattler: Well, we were working very closely with both Multi National Corps, General Metz, and Multi National Force, General [George

W.] Casey [Jr., USA], on the timing issue—gonna go, not gonna go? And, if you remember, it was during Ramadan. And it was: "Are we to go before Ramadan? Do we prepare ourselves to do it during Ramadan? Do we start, and if we don't finish, we stop? Do we have a pause during Ramadan?" All those things were being discussed.

But the bottom line was, it was an Iraqi call. Prime Minister [Ayad] Allawi had to be the one that set the conditions, with not only the Iraqi people, both the Shi'a and the Sunni. He had to exhaust all opportunity for a peaceful conclusion, and then he had to let the international community know he had done so; mainly the GCC [Gulf Cooperation Council] countries, which surround Iraq. He had let Muslims worldwide know that he was only going to fight other Muslims because it had to be done. We had to paint the picture of what was going on inside Fallujah, and was being exported out of Fallujah. We were going have to go [into the city] because it wasn't working.

The prime minister knew it wasn't going to work, either, but he had built a timeline, and he even came out two days before we attacked and met all the Iraqi warriors, and then sat down and looked me in the eye. And that was the night when he said, "What is this operation called?" And we said, "Phantom Fury." And he said, "That's not an Iraqi name. That doesn't tell Iraqi people why we're fighting this epic fight." And that's when he changed it; he's the one who changed it to al Fajr, which means the new dawn, the new beginning, because he saw the crushing of the insurgency inside of Fallujah as the breaking of their dream, as the elimination of their battle cry, "Remember Fallujah" . . .

And the prime minister, when we talked to him, the night right before he made the decision, we told him. I looked him right in the eye and said, "You know, Mr. Prime Minister, don't tell us to go and expect us to stop. When you have exhausted all the political, all the opportunities to solve this problem, and that we can no longer let them export their terrorist ideas, their VBIEDs [vehicle borne improvised explosive devices], their IEDs [improvised explosive devices], their raids." They were exporting terrorism out of Fallujah and bringing people in, hostages, etc., that they were terrorizing inside Fallujah. "When you reach that point," I actually said, "Just tear your phone out of the wall. Don't think about calling us and telling us to stop because once we get going, we're going to have to go all the way. We're not gonna stop 'til we hit the southern end of the town.". . . And, he said, "I understand. When I tell you go, we will accomplish the mission, we will complete the mission." That was right from the prime minister.

[During the first battle of Fallujah in April 2004], the international community got involved because of the insurgency IO campaign that painted all the death, all the destruction, and all the humanitarian crisis in the town. During the shaping operation [for the second battle], we were aware of that, and [as] we continued to shape, we brought all the press in. We had over 70 to 100 embeds with our forces so that the world could see it live, not through me, standing up at a press conference at the Pentagon, but through daily, hourly press releases coming back from cameras held by noncombatants and people who were sworn to an oath to tell the true story. And it worked.

Way: As Phantom Fury, or al Fajr, kicked off on 7 November, what were your lingering concerns? What were your thoughts on that day?

Sattler: My lingering concern was casualties. Obviously, casualties was number one, casualties was number two, and casualties was number three. I'm sure if you cascade down to the platoon commander, everyone was concerned about casualties. Not fear of not doing your job, but fear of having your warriors injured or killed because could have done something better. Because you only get one chance in this. . . .

Way: At this point, stepping into the battle of Fallujah, if you could recall your recollections of how those first couple of days went and how you tracked it.

Sattler: Well, the first the attack up the peninsula was executed flawlessly, to include the takedown of the hospital. . . . [The initial attack] was based on the shaping and the feints, the turnaways we had done before. We were convinced that the Iraqis still weren't real sure what was going on. Not the Iraqis, but the thugs in the town. When the sun set that second day, when the sun rose the next morning, we had moved all the forces into position. The town was completely encircled. And then we shaped about 17 targets during that day, took 'em out daylight, which we had never done before. We always struck at night. We took out targets in daylight, and we had been working these targets for a long period of time, and that sent 'em another message. And then when we actually worked to shut down some of the communications, the electric power, etc. And then we crossed that LD [line of departure] that night; that would have been the night of the 8th, after sunset.

Then, it was, we just came leading with the two [U.S.] Army battalions, the Army mech[anized] battalion in the front, with two Marine battalions on each side of them. So it was a six battalion Coalition attack coming from north to south, with two regimental combat teams. Then we also pushed five Iraqi battalions in behind them, and then eventually out to the side. During the early phases, we reached MSR [main supply route] Michigan, where the phase line [Fran was] which bisects the town, running from east to west. We figured it might take 48 hours or a little more to get there. We actually eclipsed that within the first 24, especially on the eastern side, with the Army mech forces. There was still a lot of heavy fighting, house to house, with Marines and soldiers involved, mainly Marines. We continued the attack [until] the sun came up on the 10th . . .

We had to stop and hook back to clean up some isolated pockets that had either gone into rat holes and popped up behind us or had worked their way through [our] lines. So we were fighting a 360 degree fight, to be totally candid, north of Michigan. So we turned around, and we had to attack back towards the north while forces were still coming north to south. And we were also sweeping east to west, along the Jolan District, because we did do a hook there to clear out the Jolan and the old city there* . . .

---

    * Originally, the Marines were going to execute a turning maneuver when they reached MSR Michigan (Phase Line Fran), driving the insurgents into the Euphrates River. However, LtGen Sattler met with BGen Richard F. Natonski and decided to execute a branch plan to have both regimental combat teams continue south, driving the insurgents into the anvil of the Army's Black Jack and Stryker brigades.

They [the insurgents] went back, and we just kept a force oriented [toward] the south. We paused, went back, cleaned up the insurgents who snuck in behind us, and then continued with the six battalions pressing north to south. Actually, we left one battalion in each sector north of [MSR] Michigan to go ahead and continue to clean up along with the Iraqi battalions. Then we pushed on south to go ahead and culminate the fight at the southern end, and we blocked the southern end with the Black Jack Brigade out of the [U.S. Army] 1st Cav[alry], which was already in a position on the southern side. They also had [U.S. Marine] 2d Recon[naissance] Battalion, which was cross attached to them, fighting with them in that southern sector. The [1st Marine] division executed it flawlessly. They did a great job.

Way: Was the planning to return the city of Fallujah to its [original state]?

Sattler: Phase IV [security and stability operations] was totally planned before we crossed the line into Phase III [decisive combat operations], to include getting guarantees from the prime minister and our higher headquarters, these resources and assets would be available. . . . During the ROC [required operation capacity] drill and during the planning phase, we planned a civil military operations phase: the rebuilding, the reestablishment of the central services, to include the reestablishing of the Iraqi security forces to run the town. Not us, but them. And we thought we had 10 days. We thought after we secured the town to the southern end, we would have 10 days before we would become targets of the people, and we would no longer be liberators, we'd be occupiers. That was our assumption, [but] we were wrong there because the people had all left the town. So until we opened the gates to bring the people back, we really had more time to occupy with Iraqi army and Coalition forces.

We sent two Army battalions back out, so we had four [Marine] battalions up through the reoccupation phase, which we wanted to start as late as possible. The prime minister wanted to start as soon as possible, building the town back up. He wanted to do it ubiquitously, just open the gates and let everybody come back. We wanted to do it very orderly. They already had 18 districts defined. . . . We came forward with a plan to populate by subdivision so we could clear rubble and establish water and minimal essential services in a sequential way. In other words, instead of having to have the whole town ready, we could start with one district, and keep the rubble clearing and the water and everything coming in, plus the removal of standing water. We could populate the town as we cleared. We got it ready to go, and that's what we were able to do.

The only place we disagreed is we were not going to permit any cars to come in. We had built park and rides. We had hired buses, where you stop, park your car, go through your bedding, go through the protection system, whether it was BAT [biometric assessment tool] scanner radar or some other system. And then once you proved where you were from, you got on the bus, and they took you down to that district. But two days before [the Marines were to allow citizens to return to Fallujah], the prime minister cancelled the park and ride, so we had to redo the berms, redo the barriers, build a serpentine, and be prepared to let private owned vehicles into the town. That obviously opened it up for easier smuggling and vehicle borne improvised explosive devices; somebody making a vehicle bomb, getting it through a check system, or building it in the town. . . .

Way: The planning for Phase III, combat operations, and Phase IV, the rebuilding, were done in a parallel manner?

Sattler: Correct. Simultaneous.

Way: At what point did your focus switch from combat operations to civil military operations and rebuilding?

Sattler: Before we crossed Route Michigan to continue the attack towards the south. Once we took the governor's complex, the civil military operations Marines, the CAG [civil affairs group] moved in right with the SeaBees [construction battalions] and started relaying wire . . . while we were still taking fire from across the street. So we were Phase IV oriented before we went across the line of departure.

Once we got into the fight, General Natonski didn't need my help to fight the fight. Where he needed my help was to get the conditions set, the right forces, the right resources to fight the fight. And my help was required in Phase IV to start pounding on the ministries for the money and the resources, and to get the ministries to come in and build the little team, which we built at Camp Fallujah. We were actually holding town meetings at Camp Fallujah with ministers out of Baghdad before we opened the town back up. One of the big arguments was when do we open the town up. And if you remember, we opened it on the 23d of December. They wanted to open it on 1 December, and we—my job was to show the prime minister, General Casey, and General Metz why that was not a smart move, and to buy as much time as we could, because each day, the town got better. The stagnant water was being pumped out, the rubble was being cleared, and you could watch it, and it was a very systematic approach to cleaning the town up. . . .

We had the complete town opened up before the 30th [December 2004]. We had to ensure we had polling centers inside Fallujah that were safe and secure so the Fallujahan citizens felt comfortable coming to vote. And about 7,000 of them did vote inside Fallujah. . . . That was very rewarding to every Marine that was involved, every sailor, every soldier that was involved in the election process. We felt good. And they continued to feel that way.

Because they voted, [the Iraqis] felt that they were reenfranchised, they felt better about what they'd done. And the attitude of the security forces, and the attitude towards those security forces, from the Iraqi people, changed from the old days of, "if you've got a uniform, you're either gonna arrest me, arrest my family, or take something I had under Saddam." They now started to understand that security forces were there for them and not for their own self interests.

Interview 5

Operation al-Fajr and the Return to Security and Stabilization Operations

Major General Richard F. Natonski

Commanding General
1st Marine Division
Multi National Force • West

August 2004 to March 2005

Major General Richard F. Natonski took over command of the 1st Marine Division from Major General James N. Mattis in August 2004. In this interview, Natonski describes the shaping and preparation efforts leading to the second battle for Fallujah. He notes the effects of insurgent propaganda, the transition into security and stabilization operations, and the security efforts pertaining to the January 2005 provincial elections.

Major General Natonski was interviewed by Lieutenant Colonel John R. Way on 16 March 2005 at Camp Pendleton, California.

Lieutenant Colonel John R. Way: I'd like to ask you about pre Operation Phantom Fury [second battle of Fallujah], the shaping phases and some of the challenges that went along with that.

Major General Richard F. Natonski: I think part of our success in al Fajr [Iraqi name for second battle of Fallujah] was the shaping campaign. We ultimately attacked from the north side of the city. However, we executed a number of feints on the east side of the city to give them the impression that would be the direction of attack that we would execute on. Whenever we did any of our kinetic shaping or tried anything new in Fallujah, it was always important to make sure that 2d Radio Battalion was collecting. If we did a feint and we received fire, we had troops in contact, then we would attack kinetically and hit the target. And that would light off additional command and control networks to be collected on by radio battalion, who would do things like fly an F 18 low level to see what response we would get and what signals intelligence we could gather. Firing illumination solicited a different response. At the same time, we had 626 [Iraqi National Guard Battalion] that was hitting targets in the city, high value targets affiliated with the

[Abu Musab al] Zarqawi network. So we were hitting some of the higher level leadership. We were trying to hit the insurgents.

Now, not only did we have the kinetic shaping piece, but we also had nonkinetic. We were dropping leaflets, leaflets that tried to drive a wedge between the insurgents and the people that were the residents.* We knew that the residents of Fallujah were just innocent victims of the insurgents. And when I say insurgents, I mean the whole gamut. We had former regime elements, criminals, but also a lot of foreign fighters from all over the Islamic world. We would drop leaflets that would tell the people of Fallujah that you would have a water treatment plant this month except that your city is full of insurgents. And we tried to explain what they were missing [out on] because of the presence of the insurgents.

Just prior to the attack, we made sure [through] leaflet drops and radio broadcasts that the people that were in the city— fortunately for us, most of the people left the city—they knew the fight was coming. And I think that made it easier when we did go into the city. We told them that any vehicle would be considered as hostile, because we knew there was going to be a great threat of suicide vehicle borne improvised explosive devices, or SVBIEDs. We told them that anyone outside with a weapon would be considered hostile. We told the people to stay in their homes for their own safety. So we also looked at it from that nonkinetic side.

We also executed a lot of the electronic warfare pieces. Since this is an unclassified briefing, I can't go into detail, but there were a lot of nonkinetic pieces that went into the shaping. Probably my biggest disappointment was, because of collateral damage and positive ID [identification] limitations, we could not hit as many targets as we wanted. I believe for the enhanced shaping day, which was actually D day on the 7th of November, we had over 60 preplanned targets. But we were not able to hit, I think, somewhere in the neighborhood of a dozen, almost on par with the previous days. There was no enhanced shaping with kinetic fires because of the positive ID. You had to definitely ascertain that they were enemy and that the collateral damage would not hurt or kill a specific number, as given to us by higher headquarters. That number is classified as well.

So that really limited what we could hit. Even though we knew there were insurgents in there, I think that it was validated that a lot of the targets we had identified before but were limited from attacking in the days and weeks and the months going into Fallujah turned out to be insurgent strongholds, which we ended up destroying as troops became in contact. So sometimes the ROE [rules of engagement], in an effort to protect the people, worked against us. And maybe it was good, but come to find out the only people in Fallujah when we went in were insurgents; very, very few civilians.

Way: As you went around to talk to the Marines as they prepared to go in, what did you tell them, what did you talk to them about?

Natonski: Well—and I did go around to all the units—I just told them how proud I was, and that here was an opportunity now to take the fight to the enemy. Prior to Fallujah, we had Marines on OPs [observation posts], on patrol, and they hadn't really been able to take the fight to the enemy like we were going to in Fallujah. And I drew a parallel to the *Patton* movie. They said, you know, someday that grandchild is going to be sitting on your knee, and they are going to look at you in the eye and say, "Grandpa, what did you do in the war?" And you can say, "well, we weren't shoveling s*** in Camp Lejeune or in Camp Pendleton or in Hawaii," you were fighting in Fallujah. And I will tell you that the troops looked forward. Let's face it, that's why we come into the Marines, for that. They were ready for the fight. And it was more my way just to thank [them] for what they did and what they were going to do.

I told you about the deliberate planning process. Well, we also did a rehearsal on D 2. Wow, when I think of what we did in terms of just like the book, we executed a movement of all our attack forces from their assembly areas to their attack positions. We tested our command, control, and communications. We tested our timing to get to the attack positions. And we made a feint so that we moved up from the north this time, where we were actually going to attack from, and then we pulled back. The enemy thought, well, we'd just [feinted] from the north.

I really think that having that rehearsal paid dividends in terms of getting everything right in terms of timing, because D day was actually the enhanced shaping day. The assault into the city actually took place on D+1. That was driven by MNC I [Multi National Corps Iraq], and to this day, I don't know why the assault into the city started on D+1. But on D day, we conducted our enhanced shaping, which included the movement up the peninsula to take the hospital and block the two bridges. We wanted to block the two bridges leaving, on the western side across the Euphrates, to prevent the enemy from escaping.

On that day, we also moved 2d BCT [brigade combat team] into their blocking positions on the south and east side of the city to prevent enemy from escaping in that area. At the same time, we moved our assault units into the north side of the city so they were in position to attack the following day on the 8th of November. But the actual attack, as they moved into their assault positions, I went out and I went through all of their units. I spent the whole day of the 7th traveling from unit to unit just to see them. I told a number of reporters that day, at that moment, the most potent fighting force on the face of the earth was assembled around Fallujah, and that once they started the assault, there was nothing on the face of the earth that would stop those Marines and soldiers.

As part of the plan, we knew, unlike [in] April, that when we commenced our assault, we had the blessing of the president of the United States to attack through the entire city. So I knew that nothing was going to stop us, unlike the situation the previous April. So when they started the attack, we went all the way. There was tremendous support from [Multi National Forces Iraq and Multi National Corps Iraq], because they literally had to bring all the units from Baghdad and elsewhere to help support what became the main effort of the fight in Fallujah.

By taking down Fallujah, which was a sanctuary for the insurgents, it's just like any FOB [forward operating base] that we have, for example Blue Diamond, Fallujah offered the insurgents the ability to rest, rearm, refit, plan, and then go out and launch their attacks and then come back to a secure environment. [Taking out Fallujah denied insurgents of that.] Plus it was an IO [information operations] victory for them. How could you have control in Iraq when you have this cancer called Fallujah? So it had to be eradicated before you could even conceive of having a successful election in January [2005]. And I think that's what turned the tide in terms of going in and assaulting Fallujah.

Earlier, I recall, the plan was essentially to keep a lid on al Anbar and Fallujah while we exploit the success we're having in the rest of Iraq. I think it came to people's realization by the end of September [that] Fallujah could not continue to exist in the state it was. And by taking out Fallujah, I think we then had the momentum in the rest of the country, that the Iraqi people understood that we meant business, that we could now hold an election at the end of January. And even then you can recall the news and the lead up to the election, that people thought, many countries thought, there would never be a viable election. I think the Iraqi people proved them wrong, the fact that they came to the polls. Today we're reaping the benefits of that election.

I'm a firm believer that you've got to be aggressive and take the fight to the enemy. Otherwise, if you sit back, they will take advantage. As long as you keep them moving, hoping that one day Zarqawi's going to run into a checkpoint he didn't know where it was, and we're going to grab him, just like we grabbed a lot of other foreign fighters and insurgents. You keep them moving, you keep them guessing, you roll them up. They never know when you're coming. They can't do all of the planning that's going to be required to attack. I think that's what we've been able to do....

Way: On the eve of the battle, back on 7 November, what were the lingering concerns in your mind?

Natonski: Civilians were certainly a concern because we really didn't know what we were going to find in the city. I mean, there were no doubts in my mind about the capabilities of our Marines. I knew we would be victorious. I wanted it to go fast. I felt that the quicker we got in, that penetration was key. We found in an Najaf that if you could outrun the enemy into the city, . . . if you could get in behind them, they wouldn't stay. They would retreat back, and then they couldn't detonate the explosives that they had laid out.

By that rapid penetration, we were able to achieve with both the 2d of the 2d [Task Force 2 2, 2d Infantry Regiment, 2d Infantry Division] and the 2d of the 7th [2d Battalion, 7th Regiment, 1st Cavalry Division], followed by the Marines clearing, we made that rapid progress that we had hoped for. We did find some chemical labs. We found a lot of what we coined "torture chambers," "slaughterhouses." I never imagined the amount of ordnance and weapons that we would find in the city.... I didn't realize how entrenched the insurgents were in the city....

So they continued to fall back, but as we advanced, we had to clear every single building. And they were fighting.... We talked about Abu Ghraib, and what a stain it was on the reputation of the United States, and the effect it had in the Muslim world from an IO perspective. One of the second or third order effects of the Abu Gharib prison scandal was the fact that many of the insurgents who had fought in the city had been brainwashed by films and photographs of the Iraqi prisoners being maltreated by American soldiers, and they were told that if you are captured, this is what's going to happen to you. So they did not want to get captured. They wanted to fight to the death. And they did that. Some were on drugs ... speed, amphetamines. Others had tourniquets around their arms and legs so that if they got shot, they could continue to fight. But they literally fought to the death. So the fact that we had that scandal in Abu Gharib made the resistance that much tougher when we had to fight in Fallujah....

Way: You mentioned rubble cleanup and getting the power and water turned back on. Surely in mid December, just after I think Prime Minister [Ayad] Allawi declared the city secure, the 4th CAG [civil affairs group] moved in ...

Natonski: 4th CAG ... I can remember going in with Colonel [John R.] Ballard probably around the 11th of November. We were still getting shot at, and I said, "John, you are going to set up your CMOC [Civil Military Operations Center] over there in the government center?" And we walked over there, and I said, "I want you in there tomorrow." They were moving in as the fighting was going on. We wanted to get started on that, on the rubble cleaning.

Prime Minister Allawi did declare that we had secured the city by the—I don't remember. The assault commenced on the 8th. I don't know what day that was. I think it was on Monday. I think by Saturday or Sunday, we had basically cleared through; we had pushed all the way to the south end of the city, and it was just clearing operations after that. In terms of the restoration of services, we kept the residents south while we continued to clear buildings, clear remains of the dead insurgents, and also clear out tons and tons of unexploded ordnance and caches.

At the same time, we wanted to clear out the rubble, start the restoration of services, water. . . . There was some flooding, because the water table is so high and some of the water mains were broken, and water continued to be pumped in. So from a sanitary perspective, we needed to get the pump stations that removed the water from the city working. And the SeaBees [construction battalions] played a big role in that, as well as getting the city engineers back in.

It wasn't until around the 16th of December that we started to open the city up, a district at a time. . . . And as we opened up each district, and they had to prove that they lived in that district, then we would let them in. They could survey and take personal possessions out. Not too many people stayed initially because there were no stores. We were passing out humanitarian rations, water, blankets, because it was cold at that time. But people started to come in, check the damage to their homes.

I think it was in January [that] we gave a $200 solatia [condolence] payment to all the heads of households in the city to buy the good will. We wanted them to know that we appreciated them, the fact that they were back, and that we were sorry for the damage. More and more people as we opened the districts from the west side of the city to the east. We got more and more people, and today, a few months later, people are living in the city. I'd say we have somewhere between 40 and 60,000 people that live in there. Businesses are open. Food is plentiful. You'll see a barbershop, maybe a window is broken, bakeries are open, and we're going around giving cash payments to start up businesses again. I mean, the city is really flourishing. It's still rubble, and the next piece is claims payments by the Iraqi government. That will let the people of Fallujah know that the central government of Iraq wants them to be taken care of. And that's really a key, because they are Sunni, and in an Najaf after the battle, the central government of Iraq came in very quickly and paid claims and started the restoration and rebuilding of an Najaf. . . .

Way: Are there any other comments, any other things you'd like to address, sir?

Natonski: I would just say in closing that this was an exciting period of time to be in Iraq. As I mentioned previously, and as I told the Marines going home, they can hold their heads proud for what they've accomplished. When we look back on the operations that led up to Fallujah, through Operation al Fajr, then the subsequent operations that we've conducted around the Fallujah area, in preparation for the election, and now River Blitz and River Bridge in preparation for the RIP [relief in place, with II MEF], I could not have asked for a better performance from our troops. My only regret are those that we've lost in action. I hope that our country will never forget the sacrifice that those Marines, soldiers, sailors, and airmen have made not only for our country, but for the people of Iraq.

2005

Stabilization and Elections

Interview 6
Targeting al-Qaeda in Iraq

Major General Stephen T. Johnson

Commanding General
II Marine Expeditionary Force (Forward)
Multi National Force • West

February 2005 to February 2006

Major General Stephen T. Johnson commanded II Marine Expeditionary Force during the unit's first combat deployment when it took over Multi National Force West from I Marine Expeditionary Force in February 2005. In this interview, he discusses rebuilding the Iraqi security forces in al Anbar Province and 11 named operations conducted under the umbrella of Operation Sayeed. These operations were aimed at driving al Qaeda from the western Euphrates River Valley, ensuring that people were allowed to vote in the October 2005 referendum elections, and restoring the control of the border to the Iraqi government. He also describes the progress resulting from Operation Sayeed, which include disrupting al Qaeda's leadership, operating with Iraqi forces, and the Marine air ground task force fight. Johnson discusses the planning factors leading to the successful October 2005 referendum elections and the achievements resulting from the embedding of a U.S. State Department representative in Fallujah.

Major General Johnson was interviewed by Lieutenant Colonel Craig H. Covert on 26 January 2006 at Camp Fallujah, Iraq.

Lieutenant Colonel Craig H. Covert: Could you comment on the Iraqi security forces, particularly the Iraqi police, the Iraqi army, and the growth in effectiveness that you've seen?

Major General Stephen T. Johnson: First of all, the Iraqi security forces encompass a number of things—not only the Iraqi army and the police, but also the special police commandos; public order battalions; the Department of Border Enforcement forces, who guard the borders; the highway patrol; and the traffic police. So there's a number of different things that are all generally lumped under the term ISF, Iraqi security forces.

When we arrived here in al Anbar Province in February of 2005, there really weren't very many Iraqi security forces. There were a couple of small Iraqi brigades. They had been together for a considerable period of time at that point. They'd fought in the [battle of Fallujah (Operation al Fajr)]. They were fairly capable, but that was all it was. Throughout the rest of the province, there were a number of what they called Iraqi national guard battalions and companies. They were left over from a previous failed experiment in terms of putting together security forces. They were fairly corrupt, ineffective, and in many cases worked against the Coalition forces, so one of our first duties was to disband them. Many of them chose to go in the army. Others just went back to the civilian world.

There were no police in al Anbar when we arrived. There were some local police left, but again, they were corrupt and created more problems than they were worth. So we assisted the Iraqis in disbanding those organizations as well.

Since that time, the Iraqi army has made remarkable progress. Where we had approximately 2,500 soldiers in the Iraqi army when we arrived, now there's close to 20,000. [Their units have] all been formed at different periods of time over the past year, so they're not all at the same experience level. Four of the brigades are at a level two training readiness status [nearly fully trained], and nine of the battalions are at a level two training readiness status. The rest are at different stages of preparedness, and over the next year, the rest of them will come online. There are two divisions in al Anbar now. The last brigade of the second division to be formed is still finishing up its recruit training in Habbaniyah. In February [2006], they will join the rest of the division in western al Anbar Province. So over the next year, these forces will continue to improve, continue to get stronger. And by this time next year, I think they will be a significant force.

The police is a second entity that we need to look at. As I said, there were no police in May [2005]. We started off with a program to train police for Fallujah. Over the months of May through about October, the Iraqis screened, embedded, and hired a number of

Iraqi citizens to be policemen. We assisted them by sending them to school and training them to be policemen, equipping them, and helping to provide facilities. Over that period of time, 1,200 policemen were formed in Fallujah. There's an outstanding police chief there, a man of integrity and energy. He's made a big difference. We have another 500 policemen for Fallujah being trained now, and equipped. So here in the next month or so, there will be roughly 1,700 policemen in Fallujah. They are just learning the ropes, but they're improving, and they're providing services to their people. Right now, we've started to see an improvement in security based on the police. So that's a big step forward. In the rest of al Anbar Province, there are no other police, and we're working with the Iraqis to correct that over the next several months. Upwards of another 10,000 Iraqis will enter the police force, be trained, be equipped, and provide police services in the other cities in al Anbar Province, the primary city being Ramadi.

The Department of Border Enforcement forces has also grown over the last several months. The Iraqis, in coordination with the Coalition forces, have built a number of border installations in the area that we're responsible for. I'm talking about the border with Syria, Jordan, and Saudi Arabia. Those border [installations] are manned, and the border police continue to go through training. There are now two [Iraqi] brigades out there, making progress, turning control of the border to the Iraqi government and to the Iraqi people. It's not a unilateral effort. They are partnered with Iraqi army forces, and they also get support from Coalition forces. So it's a three way effort out there, but the Department of Border Enforcement forces are showing their improvement. . . .

Covert: Would you say that the addition of all these forces has effectively increased security for the Iraqi people, or are we still facing a point where, yes, they're growing, but they're still somewhat ineffective?

Johnson: Well, like I pointed out earlier, they're at different levels of readiness. Some of them are standing on their own. Several of the brigades have been given areas of operation which they operate. They do the majority of the operations and receive basic support from the

Coalition forces. Others are very reliant, still, on the relationship they have with the Coalition. And that will continue over the next few months until they get in the saddle. [The] takeaway from the situation now is that all of the Iraqi army forces, and soon the police forces as well, are partnered up with Coalition forces.

In al Anbar, two thirds of the units there are partnered up with Marines, and the other third are [partnered with U.S.] Army forces. The partnering allows the Iraqi unit to operate with, to train with, [and] to get mentoring from [Marines and soldiers]. That is one of the ways in which we improve the readiness of the Iraqi battalions, by linking them up with a U.S. Coalition battalion.

The second point is that each of the Iraqi forces, the Iraqi army battalions, has a military transition team with it. These transition teams are either Army or Marines, and they're embedded with the Iraqi force. They work with them on a daily basis, they teach them the battlefield functions, and they help them learn, and help them grow, plan, operate, and so forth. The military transition teams also provide a link back to the partnered battalion. So in these ways, we are improving the effectiveness of these forces and enabling them to get better faster. They still have a ways to go, and like I said, it'll be over the next year until we see all of those forces reach a common level two standing.

Another key element of what we're doing here is providing presence in the communities. These Iraqi forces are not just centralized at one location, like Ramadi or Fallujah. They're spread out now across the entire battlespace, all the way up through the Euphrates River Valley, in the big towns there—Hit, Haditha, the al Qaim region, Husaybah. In all of those places, there's a combination of Coalition forces and Iraqi forces. They're partnered up, and they work together in those areas. That partnering, that relationship, is not only good for them, but it's also supportive of the people in those communities. It provides more security, an environment of security in those towns that hasn't been noted before. It makes it far more difficult for the insurgents to come back in and begin disruptive behavior again in those towns. It also shows the people that we're committed to seeing the job through and getting the security forces on their feet. So the combination of partnering together and being present in the communities in al Anbar Province, those two things are making better security for the Iraqi people.

Covert: Could you comment on the accomplishments and successes of Operations Iron Fist, Steel Curtain, and Sayeed, and what it meant for the MEF (Marine Expeditionary Force) to succeed in those operations?

Johnson: First of all, Operation Sayeed was the umbrella operation. Operation Steel Curtain and Operation Iron Fist were named operations under the umbrella of Sayeed. There were 11 named operations under the Sayeed umbrella. Those operations stretched from July of 2005 until just after the December '05 elections. The purpose of those operations was to drive al Qaeda from the western Euphrates River Valley and to eliminate that as a place where they could operate freely. We accomplished that mission.

The operation was also designed to ensure that we had the climate and the environment to conduct the referendum in October and the national elections in December. The operations under Operation Sayeed were designed to ensure that we had the conditions so that people could vote. I think that the results of the election showed, the election and the referendum both showed that that was successful. A third goal of Operation Sayeed was to restore the control of the Iraqi border to the Iraqi people. As I pointed out earlier, we assisted them by helping to get the border forces out there, and to assist them in providing security along the border. So those were three key elements of Operation Sayeed.

There were a number of accomplishments and successes that occurred during Sayeed. First of all, we put the insurgent back on his heels. We disrupted his activities there, we killed a lot of his foot soldiers, we took away some of the places where he felt secure, and we disrupted the leadership of al Qaeda and caused them to not be able to operate freely in that part of the country. Another success you can note there, about Operation Sayeed, was that it was the first time that we'd operated on a large scale with the Iraqi security force, the army security forces. It wasn't until about

September that we had a full brigade of Iraqi army forces out there west of the Euphrates. They came, actually, after the operations under Sayeed had begun. They joined their

Coalition partners during the operation and made a significant contribution to the operations in the western Euphrates River Valley during that period of time. The third thing, a key point to take away from Sayeed, from a Marine perspective, is the outstanding way that the MAGTFs [Marine Air Ground Task Force] fought that fight. The 2d Marine Division, and RCT 2 [regional combat team] in particular, did a magnificent job of fighting a counterinsurgency fight, taking the fight to the enemy. . . .

So it was an incredible effort across the board in the MAGTF, not only the GCE [ground combat element], but supported very well by the ACE [air combat element] and the MLG [Marine logistics unit]. So those things were the successes of Operation Sayeed, and its 11 named operations underneath.

Surely you can't forget that concurrent with Operation Sayeed is Operation Liberty Express, which was the named operation for the referendum in October and the national election in December. That operation ran concurrent with Sayeed, but it was very important, too, and also very well done. It required all the elements of the MAGTF to function together to make that happen as well.

Covert: How did the operations, particularly Sayeed, affect the national elections, as well as the referendum?

Johnson: Well, I think that you can probably look at that in three parts. One is the amount of planning that went into that election, [both] the referendum and the election. We started the planning for both of them last June [2005]—it might even have been May. . . . The planning process went on that whole summer and continued to change. It didn't really go dormant, because this was a new experience for the Iraqi people. The Independent Election Committee of Iraq, IECI, was the governing body that set all the rules and did most of the planning. But the Coalition forces were involved in the planning all the way along.

The fact that this was a new experience for the Iraqis sometimes made it very difficult. There were some planning decisions made by the Iraqis that weren't particularly easy to live with, but our folks worked closely with them. There was a lot of patience involved. There was a lot of compromise on the part of the Coalition forces. In the end, had it not been for that detailed planning all the way along, we wouldn't have been able to help them conduct the successful elections that they had. Some idea of some of the things that had to be planned: to move poll workers into this province, because they could not hire enough people out here, because of the security situation. People didn't feel secure enough to sign up to be poll workers, so they had to be brought in from the outside. They had to be housed, fed, and protected during the time they were here. All that planning and preparation had to be done. There had to be transportation to move them to the polling sites. On the election day, we returned them to where they were staying at night. There was a tremendous amount of transportation involved. All of these things required extensive planning.

In the preparation phase, right before the election, there were an incredible amount of things that had to be done. The Marines and soldiers, who were engaged in an operation right up until a few days before the referendum, finished that operation, turned right around, and went to work on the election. They were doing such things as putting in barriers, transporting poll materials, arranging for security. Those types of things had to be done on a short fuse in order to be prepared for the 15th of October and the 15th of December. So again, it's a good example of how planning and preparation, and being able to be flexible, made a big difference.

The third piece of this is the Iraqi people themselves. I think many of them came out to vote because they knew that it gives them an opportunity for something better than the violence that they'd been subjected to for so many years. Many of them came out and voted, even though it wasn't particularly safe in many places, even though they were subject to threats. They still made it to the polls, and the results of the election are self evident. A vast number of people voted—I think well over 50 percent voted—in al Anbar Province alone. If you remember, about 2 to 4 percent had voted in January of '05 for the interim transitional government. Then a full year later, over 50 percent of the people turned out to vote, which is pretty remarkable in my view. So those are the three pieces I would point out to you for the success of the election.

I would point out one thing that we learned here. All through the planning process, we and the Coalition planned to provide security around the outside of the polling sites. That was a key element of our plan. Right before the referendum, the IECI announced that they would not want the Coalition to be used for security, that they would take care of the public themselves. This of course caused us a lot of angst. We thought that that meant that there would surely be a lot of security problems and so forth. But it was their desire, and it was their election. They were in charge, so we did what they asked. We stayed very much in the background.

What happened was, though, that there weren't a lot of incidents, either in the referendum or the election itself. They did do a good job of running their election, providing security, and using the local police, at least in Fallujah, to help augment the security. So in that sense, I bring that up because it surprised us. We thought that they couldn't do it without us, but yet they did. They did a very good job without us, and there's a lesson there for the future. They probably can do more, and quicker, than we give them credit for.

Covert: You mentioned that in Fallujah, but I believe also in Ramadi, sir, there was quite a big success, despite the fact that right now, it's a little more kinetic and more dangerous.

Johnson: Well, for the referendum, there was not a big turnout in Ramadi. There was a very small turnout because we believe that the senior leaders had not emphasized it enough to the people, or had told them not to go vote in the referendum. For the election, however, the circumstances changed, and they had a good turnout for the election. You're correct—in the election in December, they also took care of their own security for that as well. They expanded the areas which they took care of. It was a good operation in the sense that we learned a lot about our Iraqi partners and their capabilities.

Covert: Could you comment on the employment and effectiveness of the CAG [civil affairs group] within your AO [area of operation]?

Johnson: We had two groups. We had the 5th Civil Affairs Group that deployed with us, and then they were replaced in August and September by the 6th Civil Affairs Group. I think they've done a superb job of getting out into the communities and looking for ways that we can be useful to the Iraqi people. There are a number of examples of the things that they've done. They have been very proactive in looking for ways to ensure that reconstruction money was invested in projects that were productive to the communities. When we got here, there was a tremendous amount of reconstruction funds available. The trick was not so much getting the funds, but applying them in the right place, where something could be accomplished for the good of the community, and in accordance with the desires of the community.

The civil affairs group was plugged into the communities, particularly Fallujah, and to a certain degree later on in Ramadi, but primarily in Fallujah. They were able to help the Iraqis in a way that the Iraqis wanted to be helped. There was a tremendous amount of bravery on the part of the Civil Affairs Group. They spent a lot of time on the roads, in the towns. By their nature, they have to interact with the people, and you can't interact with the people on the FOBs [forward operating bases]. So they'd been out there, and I'm very pleased with the performance that both CAGs have shown us. Neither one of them was a pure civil affairs groups. They had, certainly, a [collection] of people who had that skill, who had the requisite MOSs [military occupational specialties]. But most of them were folks from other MOSs, other units, where there were not civil affairs specifically. They got trained, they applied their training, and they did a superb job.

Covert: You've got a pretty incredible State Department rep here [John Kael Weston]. Could you talk about the positive effect of having him embedded here in Fallujah and how it has helped you out with the MEF?

Johnson: Well, having Kael here is like having a political advisor that the combatant commanders have. Kael is a very dynamic young man, personally courageous, and interested in seeing a positive outcome here. He's been with the Marines here, I MEF and now us, and soon to be I MEF again, for almost three years. He spent a lot of time in town, particularly Fallujah. He has been integral in acquainting us in the personalities here and the atmospherics that are there. He also has been very good at conveying our intentions to the Iraqi leadership in the town. He was instrumental in helping them have their first elections for a city council, for a mayor. He has been instrumental in helping them learn how to be a democratic body. And frankly, I think he's a good friend to many of them. He was very hurt by the savage death of Sheikh Hamza [Abbas al Issawi] several weeks ago. He knew the sheikh, and he respected him, and recognized that he was a leader in the community. Kael was very taken aback by that tragic event.

So he's done a great job, and he's taught us a lot about how to deal with the Iraqis, how to deal with issues on the political side of the house. He's very much attuned to the balance between military and political events. He's not jealous of the role that the Marines play, but he is quick to let us know when it's time to use the political piece, which is part of his tool kit. So we've got a great relationship with him. He has a lot of friends here, and we will hate to say goodbye to him.

Interview 7
Setting the Conditions for a Turn

Brigadier General James L. Williams

Assistant Commanding General
2d Marine Division

July 2005 to January 2006*

Reserve Brigadier General James L. Williams served as the deputy commanding general of I Marine Expeditionary Force (Forward) from January to March 2005. He focused on security and force management while in that position. He returned to Iraq in July 2005 as the assistant commanding general of the 2d Marine Division.

In this interview, Brigadier General Williams describes the transition in focus of effort after the second battle for Fallujah and discusses a series of important meetings leading to the creation of the Anbar Security Council. He also describes the changes and successes in al Anbar Province during his two tours.

Brigadier General Williams was interviewed by Colonel Jeffrey Acosta, 6th Civil Affairs Group, on 20 February 2006 at Camp Fallujah, Iraq.

Colonel Jeffrey Acosta: Can you describe the situation in al Anbar Province?

Brigadier General James L. Williams: Well, if you look at the '04 to '05 time period, al Anbar Province was a province that was in essence being inundated by the influx of insurgent and foreign fighter activity, which led up to a couple of things. Obviously, if you take a historical perspective on this, you have to consider what occurred during 2004. April of 2004 was very significant, when the Blackwater [USA] team was killed and hung up in Fallujah. That kind of created a false expectation, I think, of what was to come, in

---

* BGen Williams was deputy command general, I Marine Expeditionary Force (Forward)/Multi National Force-West, from 31 January 2005 to 31 March 2005; assistant commanding general, 2d Marine Division, from 1 July 2005 to 12 January 2006; deputy commanding general, II Marine Expeditionary Force (Forward)/Multi National Force-West, from 12 January 2006 to 13 January 2006; and deputy commanding general, special projects-al-Anbar security plan, I Marine Expeditionary Force (Forward)/Multi National Force-West, from 13 January 2006 to 15 March 2006.

the sense that I think when we came back, we thought things were going to be much better, that there was going to be more of an open arms approach by the Iraqi people, and there was probably a miscalculation of the expectation of insurgent activity.

So all through the summer of 2004 was essentially the preparation to do Operation al Fajr, which occurred in the October November time frame of 2004. That very kinetic operation really set the tone for 2004.

As I came into the theater, the activities of getting Fallujah back on its feet really became the focus of effort in 2004, early 2005, and of course that carried through much of 2005 in construction, getting the compensation for the damages that were done during the kinetic war, and then also providing, if you will, a model for what cities in al Anbar could be like.

And then, of course, during this time we had operationally probably nine battalions within the Fallujah city limits. When 2d Marine Division came in, it essentially moved those battalions out of Fallujah and started looking at the surrounding areas, which essentially became a model of activity, operationally, that led to the kinetic operations that went from March of '05 until the most recent operation.

Acosta: Let's talk now, sir, if we could about the 28 November 2005 meeting. What was the importance of that meeting? How was the meeting set up?

Williams: This is why history is important. The original engagement was with MML, Mohammed Mahmoud Latif, who was the number two or three insurgent on our list. . . . General [Richard A.] Huck, back in the May June time frame, had a meeting with MML, which included several go to guys, and Sheikh Thamer [Ibrahim Tahir al Assafi] was one of those, which was being imam, and Latif was imam as well. But Latif decided that he probably wasn't going to participate like the governor [Mamoun Sami Rashid al Alwani] has, because it's a government entity now. And then he started a little group on the side, not at this point directly competitive to the al Anbar Security Council, but was meeting nevertheless, which he called the People's Committee. What we said was, "Hey, well, that's good. They're meeting. Maybe they're cooking up something, maybe they're not."

The [November] 28th meeting essentially got started from the Sheikh [Abdullah] Jallal [Mukhif al Faraji] piece, which was, okay, how do we do this? How do we stop guys from blowing our guys up? Which didn't mean we were going to stop any operations. What it meant was, "What do you guys have for a solution?" And so part of that discussion was withdrawal of the Coalition forces from the city, and I just simply said, "Oh, we can do that." That wasn't anything different than what General [George W.] Casey [Jr., USA] [said] back in April of '04—and he reminds everybody about that, too—he says, "Hey, I've already said that the goal is to reduce forces out of the cities, not to put permanent American presence out there."

So with that as a backdrop, the 28th meeting, which was pulled together very quickly, because I think it was November 15th when we had our next meeting, and the governor said, "Well, let me talk with these guys and see who we get." And then it outdid our greatest expectations. The room was filled. . . .

But the 28th meeting also sprang the follow on meeting, which was the meeting of the al Anbar Security Council, so 12 people, thereabouts, 14 people maybe, were selected by the original crowd of 200 to actually go and have this interface. And as a result of that, this group of 12 now has become essentially like the advisory group of the governor. The downside is that we've had one assassination attempt, and that one successful, Sheikh [Nasser Kareem al Fahdawi], a big guy in his [Albu Fahad] tribe. And that essentially has unnerved many people in Fallujah; not so much in Ramadi, because I think they're just used to all of the incoming stuff flying around. . . .

Acosta: Could you discuss the December 12th milestone meeting?

Williams: Well, they didn't stop talking. The issue was that Minister [of Defense Sa'dun al] Dulaymi had his own approach to dealing with his relatives of the Dulaymi Federation. . . . It was the fact that we initiated the al Anbar Security Council, and the Security Council, I told him that we'd bring General Casey and the MOD [minister of defense] down because it was important to engage them, and it was about getting the forces that they needed, which is what we told them originally, "This is what you're going to need.". . .

Now, what we were able to do, there was probably a mixed metaphor of things going on here, but General Casey was kind of penning some notes, saying, "Okay, here's five principles that we ought to kind of build this thing around." Because ultimately we were using the base information of getting Coalition forces out of the city, but we've got to build the Iraqi security forces in al Anbar to do that, which meant they had to participate.

As it turned out, the parts of it had come to fruition fairly quickly, like the IPs [Iraqi police], the IP recruiting and all that. The weakness right now in my mind is still the army, because even though we're getting closer to doing the recruiting and things that we need to do, this meeting basically set the conditions around getting the al Anbar Security Council petition put together. Actually, at that point I had actually had a first draft, and then I added General Casey's five principles after I sent it back to him and he kind of did a little editorial work. And he did a little more editorial work, and then we incorporated them. That al Anbar Security Council petition, . . . that's a seminal milestone document because that is what is driving everything right now. . . . The al Anbar Consolidation Plan, which is the follow on to the petition, is the plan that will be used to roll out the fundamental pieces of the Iraqi security forces that will be recruited, trained, and deployed, the economics and governance piece, the detainee release program, so all of that will be driven by that. . . .

Acosta: What changes have you seen occur in the Multi National Force West AO [area of operation] during these two tours of duty here in Iraq, the big changes?

Williams: For AO Denver . . . when you only went from 32 Iraqi security forces here, and then a small FOB [forward operating base] in Fallujah, very small police, and a few highway patrol guys, to Fallujah's authorized somewhere close to 2,000. I think it's actually 1,900 police officers in the region. So we've gone from this sort of small footprint of Iraqi players to this larger footprint of, okay, well, we've got the two divisions out here now. We have roughly 13,000 troops from the Iraqi side, or at least that are assigned on TO [table of organization], but the fundamental change of that is that where we thought they were going to provide their life support, logistics, maintenance and all that business, that's all coming from us. That is a disappointment, because that doesn't allow you to get away. So part of the transition should be how do you get away? Well, right now, we've made ourselves indispensable, and then we also added MTTs [military transition teams], BTTs [border transition teams], SPTTs [special police transition teams], and PTTs [police transition teams]. We've got our border, special police, the police officers in general, as well as the military. So that is sort of the next leave behind in the AO, is that, well, as larger security forces pull out, what are you going to do with the MTTs, BTTs, and SPTTs, because they require support, and so our support won't go away. It'll just be a force of a different color. . . .

Acosta: What do you say were the key accomplishments for the 2d Marine Division during your tour here?

Williams: I would say, first of all, if you run along the lines of operation, in security, the expansion of the Iraqi security forces, without a doubt. It got them out of just being city centric to expanding across the province. The actual operations that all the RCTs [regimental combat teams] did, the BCTs [brigade combat teams] did, to set the conditions that allowed engagement to take place. . . . The metaphor of building a house—the foundation in this case is security. So if you don't have security, everything else sort of falls apart.

The next thing is really the engagements that we've done with the government, both at the provincial and the city levels are really expanding now. I mean, it's really starting to become the heyday of what could make this province really a significant player out here.

There are all types of challenges. One of the challenges for Iraq is that between the two rivers, the Tigris and Euphrates, the Turks can jam it up in Turkey for the Tigris, and the Syrians would probably do the same thing [with the Euphrates]. That essentially can create a major problem here. It's like, where do you think the next war is going to be? It's going to be over resources. It's not only oil resources. It's going to be over the principal resource, and that's water. So right now, there are plans on both sides of those borders to build dams, and those dams will choke off the water, and since the resource begins in the other countries, that's a kind of a dangerous place for them to be. So I don't know how that's going to work just yet.

I think as a challenge, the outside influences are always big challenges, but the successes are if you can work with the people on the periphery of the country, economic development of the people in Jordan, for example. In Saudi Arabia and Syria, if you can get them to successfully beat back the insurgents and the insurgent camps, I would consider that a success. Now, those are still yet to be had successes, but I think for I MEF [I Marine Expeditionary Force] coming out here, that will be the follow on. But I think hopefully between the operations that we've done we've set up a good hand off.

Interview 8
Intelligence Assessment in Late 2005 and 2006

Major Alfred B. Connable

Senior Intelligence Analyst/Fusion Officer
I & II Marine Expeditionary Forces

2005-2006

Major Alfred B. "Ben" Connable served as the Middle East desk officer at Headquarters Marine Corps Intelligence Department before being assigned to 1st Marine Division as a foreign area officer. In 2003 and 2004, he was the division's foreign area officer and intelligence operations officer. In 2005 and 2006, Major Connable was the senior intelligence analyst and fusion officer for both I and II Marine Expeditionary Force at Camp Fallujah. His final tour was as Marine and Naval attaché in Jordan 2007. Connable retired from the Marine Corps is working for the RAND Corporation as an intelligence policy analyst.

Major Connable was interviewed by Staff Sergeant Bradford A. Wineman on 26 June 2009 at Marine Corps Base Quantico, Virginia.

Major Alfred B. Connable: [In 2004], I was the FAO [foreign area officer] out there [in al Anbar Province], and my primary task was to come up with cultural mitigating factors and then also to deal with the tribal leaders. . . . This is where we planted the seeds for the Awakening movement, and I'm going to explain to you why nothing happened until 2006/2007. . . . I'm going to kind of touch on a central theme as I go through this, [which] is that we never really established security. We simply didn't have enough troops . . .

When we showed up, we were given a brief by the 82d Airborne [Division, USA] intel[ligence] folks, and we were given a tribal overlay, and they showed us where the major tribes were. And we looked at the tribal pattern as if it actually existed, the lines on the map as if they actually meant something. [What] we didn't really understand very well is that especially in the urban areas, the tribes were commingled. Lines of control really didn't mean anything. And then, of course, the tribal network itself, I'm not going to beat a dead horse here. Everybody's written about the damage that had been done to the tribal network in Anbar, in Iraq in general, by Saddam [Hussein], during the sanctions period.* But essentially, it was magnified in Anbar Province, where you had a lot of what they call fake sheikhs in charge of these tribes.

It took us awhile, but we slowly discovered that in the absence of security—as the fighting started to bubble up in February, March, and then through the summer [of 2004], where it got really bad—in the absence of security, when the Iraqis had really dug their heels back in a survivor mentality and really started looking out for themselves and their immediate family, even if there were legitimate tribal leaders, and there were a few, they really didn't have any positive coercive authority at that point in time. In the absence of security, the people, the tribal members—and of course every Iraqi is a member of a tribe—are not going to risk anything for anything other than their own self interest, and even then they are going to be extraordinarily cautious about what they risk.

We were saying in '04 all of the things that were being said in, I won't say '05, but '06 and '07 that really helped develop the Awakening movement. We were engaging with the tribal leaders on a daily basis across the province. We were engaging with them on a range of issues that I think reflected the range of issues that were being discussed during the Awakening movement period—reconciliation, reconstruction, development. We pressed the IO [information operations] themes home: "Hey, we're here to help. We want to make sure that we protect you from al Qaeda."

We promised a great many things, and of course we couldn't deliver them. And we demanded of them a quid pro quo. . . . We never got the fact that we were asking something from somebody who was incapable of delivering it. . . . So we would give things away to anybody that was willing to talk to us. We would promise things to anybody that was willing to talk to us. And we were often engaging with people that the tribe did not see as legitimate representatives.

---

* Iraq's tribal sheikhs trace their linage back hundreds, sometimes thousands, of years. During his leadership, Saddam Hussein appointed new sheikhs to better control Anbar and its business.

So it's a common refrain: "You were speaking to the wrong people." In some cases that was true, and in some cases that was pure manipulation by the Iraqis who were saying it. . . . We were suckers, essentially, because we were taking people at their word, people that were not in any position to give us an American version of a promise.

So any progress we expected to make in that time period was rather foolish. It was foolish on our part to assume that we were going to make any progress in the absence of stability. And if you read not only all of the counterinsurgency experts that have ever written anything about the first phases of a counterinsurgency operation, but also all of the insurgents as well—Mao [Zedong], Che [Guevara], and all the other folks—they all place a primacy on security. The insurgents attempt to disrupt security, and the counterinsurgents have to establish security. I think the 2006 version of the COIN [counterinsurgency] manual is kind of an accumulation of conventional wisdom on this subject, and it goes through, point by point, a list of things you have to do in order, and it says to establish security.

So of course in '04 we had done almost nothing to establish security. I argue that we had insufficient troop to task from day one. We did not really appreciate the complexity of the insurgency, the number of different groups, the motivations of the insurgents themselves. Of course, this is not a traditional insurgency in that it was a single or one or two, three, competing organizations with a political objective. Most of it was, in my opinion, an expression of social discontent. It was a method of expressing themselves. Violence is a method of expressing yourself in Anbar Province. We never understood that, and from March through the end of al Fajr [second battle of Fallujah] in November, the province was in essentially a chaotic state.

So any efforts we made during that time period—and we kept the same IO theme all the way through—but any efforts we made during that time period were essentially pointless. Anything we did, any money we spent was pointless, because all the reconstruction projects were corrupted. The money was simply taken away, and the schools would go up with watered down paint, or faulty concrete, or whatever. The overtures to the tribes to try to get them to establish some security and to get them to bring their tribal members to sign up for the police, or sign up for the ICDC [Iraqi Civil Defense Corps] at the time, or the Iraqi National Guard after that, all fell flat because we'd never accomplished step one. So in the absence of step one, in the absence of establishing security, the rest of it is not completely pointless, but it certainly is not going to further your operational and strategic objectives. And so we were essentially treading water at that point.

Now, it's important to know that we did maintain the same themes. A lot of people who have written a history of the Awakening to date have written as if everything started in the middle of 2006, and that's simply not the case. . . . We were saying all the right things, we were doing all the right things. We were trying to engage with people, but we had a very immature understanding of Iraqi culture. We had a very immature understanding of the authority and the power of the tribes, the tribal leaders. We had a very poor understanding of the divisions within the tribes, the fact that tribes are not monolithic entities, that there are subentities within tribes, and we didn't really understand how the insurgency overlaid onto the tribes, and vice versa.

For instance, if the Albu Fahad tribe exists as a monolithic entity, then you would assume that every Albu Fahad joins one insurgency, one insurgent group. Of course [that was] not the case, and the Albu Fahad is broken down into many subtribes, and clans, and families, and things, and you actually had an intra communal war in 2006 between Albu Fahad members.

So we did not see past that, or we did not see into it. But the tribal leaders we were dealing with at that point at that point, again, you had all these fake sheikhs that we were engaged with. That started to shake out—no pun intended—out at the end of '04. You started to see the very beginnings of the tribal system righting itself. And this is really critical to understand what happened in late '06 and early '07. In early '04, I'm going to argue that it simply was impossible, for three reasons. The security situation was a mess, the social situation needed to work itself out, and maybe as a codicil to that, but equally important, is the fact that the tribal system needed a period of adjustment before it could become an effective tool with which we could develop security, help develop localized security.

So that kind of sets the stage; '04 sets the stage. All the mistakes in the world, but even if we had done all the right things, I'm going to argue that we probably couldn't have gotten anywhere. And a lot of us saw back in '04 that this was going to take time, and all of us said five years. Oddly enough, here we are in 2009, and Anbar is past five, but we understood that it was going to take a long time, and we also understood that we weren't necessarily going to be given a tremendous amount of time. But a few of us saw that these things were going to have to shake themselves out, that the tribal system was going to have to shake itself out, that the fake leaders were going to have to go away at some point, and they were going to have to regain trust in their patronage, patron client networks, not even in the provincial government, but even just in their own social structure, their own informal social structures, which they really did not have back in '04.

So I left in early September in 2004 and went back to Headquarters Marine Corps. . . . I showed up [back in Iraq] in December of 2005, and we were just coming up on the elections. There had been the elections earlier in the year that had failed. Some of the tribal leaders at this point had shaken out, so you've started to see some tribal leadership emerge. You also started to see several former Iraqi general officers, military general officers, emerge who were prominent players, not in Syria, [but who] had remained in Iraq, had obviously been involved in the insurgency, but started to see the light, along with the tribal leaders. And what they started to see was that they lost, [that] they self disenfranchised in the elections earlier in 2005. Not every tribal leader saw that as a mistake, some of them did.

So at the end of 2005, towards the end of it, September/October time frame, you had a very senior, very well respected tribal leader who had insurgent credentials, a guy that I had spoken with in 2004 on multiple occasions, who would stare daggers into me and told me in no uncertain terms that he wanted me to leave and wanted the rest of us to leave and had absolutely no interest in negotiating with us. This is Nasser al Fahadawi. . . . The Albu Fahad tribes are very large tribal groupings, centered in the Ramadi area. Sheikh Nasser kind of saw the light towards the end of '05 and I think had gotten sick of all the violence, and I think he saw that we probably weren't going to be making any progress on our own. He was in direct contact with a senior insurgent leader with the 1920 Revolution Brigade. You could probably argue he was the leader of the 1920 Revolution Brigade, which was the primary, or the most effective, most well known nationalist insurgent organization operating out of Anbar Province, and they were a national group as well.

Mohammed Mahmoud Latif . . . had religious credentials but was also an insurgent leader. Latif and Fahadawi joined together and decided to support the December [2005] elections. And they started putting together a small coalition of other tribal leaders and of senior general officers, brigadier and major generals, . . . guys who were influential, guys who were fairly well known. And as we came closer and closer to the elections, they started to take an opposing stance to AQI [al Qaeda in Iraq]. . . . This was the Anbar People's Committee, [the] APC. This is Fahadawi and Latif and those other folks.

I showed up, and there was almost an immediate lull in activity in Anbar Province. It was if everybody was collectively holding their breath, and I think there was a shock that this had come off successfully, and nobody really understood what it meant. And when I say nobody, I mean I don't think the tribal leaders understood what it meant. I don't think the Marines certainly understood what it meant. I don't think that the people really grasped the meaning of a successful election, because again, they're not very well educated in electoral process. I know for a fact that the Iraqi central government was distracted and did not see the value of the opportunity that they had in front of them. And I also know for a fact that MNC I [Multi National Corps Iraq] and MNF I [Multi National Force Iraq] completely missed the fact that we had an opportunity at the end of 2005. Or, if they did see the opportunity, they completely misinterpreted.

So at the end of '05 you have a successful election. You have a tribal organization that has started to recover. You have legitimate, genuine tribal leaders coming to the fore. They're starting to have more influence over the people and their province, and this is really important also for the Awakening. The fact that a guy like Albu Fahad is going to turn against AQI reflects . . . that there was a broader grassroots discontent with al Qaeda.

So the parallel story you have here at the end of 2005 is that [Abu Musab al] Zarqawi had started becoming more violent, had conducted the hotel bombings in Jordan. That turned a lot of people off, including Iraqis, . . . the al Qaeda associated movements in Iraq to the point that it started to get away from him. A lot of the local Iraqi leaders were actually members of other insurgent groups that held none of the beliefs that the AQI leadership held. So you had guys that were in it because AQI was the biggest game in town.

If you go back to reading your counterinsurgency manuals and books and everything, if you don't have an ideology, if you don't have a political message, you don't have an insurgency. That's just the way it is. So by the end of '05, the people were starting to really realize at the grassroots level that maybe al Qaeda was not doing things in their best interest, and that maybe it was time to start shrugging off the al Qaeda yoke, because at that point al Qaeda was probably more powerful than any other organization in Anbar Province. And you started to get that sense, but they were still terrified. There was a murder and intimidation campaign.

Another thing that really turned them off, but also kept the people tamped down, was the fact that al Qaeda in Iraq criminalized as it Iraqified. So as it incorporated more and more Iraqis at the mid to lower levels, it absorbed low level criminal networks who used techniques that al Qaeda was using, hijacking of vehicles, kidnapping, et cetera, that had proved successful in '04 for pure self interest. They were threatening people, they were hijacking, carjacking, kidnapping, and doing all those things, but it had no political purpose behind it. It had no real value other than the value that it held to the people who were conducting the crimes, and the money stayed at the low level. . . . So if you're an Anbari at the end of 2005 and you're being not only intimidated by these guys but robbed blind by them, and you don't see anything, any value in their message, you don't have much motivation to support them, or at some point even put up with them. . . .

At the end of 2005, we had the successful election. Attack levels plummeted to an unprecedented lull in the province since 2003. I think they went down to 20 to 25 attacks per day, from 60, which was at that time almost a negligible number of attacks. You had an Anbari people who were holding their breath and were saying to themselves, maybe this is our shot at getting rid of AQI. Maybe there is something in this information operations message that the Americans have been preaching since day one. Maybe if we go against AQI and at least temporarily support some of the American initiatives, the Americans will leave and the insurgency will end. Not that they supported us, but that would be a way that they would achieve their goals, because they'd been asking us to leave since day one and we weren't.

That was kind of the framework at the end of '05. You had this, I don't know, almost like a blank canvas, where we could have repainted the while program, and instead of taking advantage of this, we flubbed it. Taking advantage of it would have consisted of sending in more troops to Anbar Province. It would have been an opportunity to establish genuine security. Again, your baseline state is security, and nobody was fooling themselves at the end of '05 that we had established security simply because attack levels had gone down. So if we had surged at the end of '05, you have the Anbar People's Committee waiting in the wings to fight against al Qaeda. You have a people who are ready, are sick of al Qaeda, and maybe are on the verge of reaching a culminating point, maybe not quite yet but are close to it.

Instead of that, General George W.] Casey [Jr., USA] at the end of December came out and issued a public statement saying that the next two brigades deploying to Iraq were going to be kept back as a reserve. So we did what we had been doing since day one in Iraq, which was to start withdrawing. Every time we had a minor success, we would start withdrawing troops, and each time we did that, we relinquished control of whatever area the troops had just left. We lost ground in the battle to establish security, and in this case, it proved to be disastrous.

Al Qaeda started to recover. When they realized, "Hey, Casey says now you're pulling out, the Americans are leaving, now we need to sink our teeth back in here." We held a recruiting drive in downtown Ramadi on January 5th [2006]. Several hundred people in line, it was the biggest turnout we'd had, hands down, in a long time. The guys who were on line seemed motivated. They wanted to be there for some of the right reasons, which was the first time that had happened. AQI detonated a suicide vest in the line, killed 30 to 60 people, depending on what source you believe. Now, two remarkable things about that. One is that a lot of the Iraqis that were there—even some of the injured—stood back up and got into line again. . . . That's a powerful signal, that they're willing to get back in line, to risk their lives, after seeing something like that and still having their ears ringing from the explosion. But it also signaled the reemergence of the al Qaeda in Iraq murder and intimidation campaign, and also their attacks on the civilian populace and their willingness to reengage us at the tactical level.

Very quickly after that, the attack levels started to rise, and within two weeks, I think 50 percent of the Anbar People's Committee leaders had been assassinated. I think it was January 18th that Fahadawi was murdered. He was killed by a member of his own tribe who was a member of al Qaeda. So an Albu Fahad killed the Albu Fahad tribal leader. That was the point where it all started to fall apart, and by the middle of February, early March, attack levels had really risen dramatically. Al Qaeda was completely back up on its feet, and new leadership had come in. The nationalist insurgents at that point really started to stumble and fall apart because al Qaeda was so dominant, and a lot of the nationalist insurgents were joining al Qaeda at a rather rapid rate, almost in a mercenary way, but were supporting al Qaeda or working with them, using the al Qaeda name.

The people were cowering from, I would say January through the summer. They were increasingly vocal to us about their discontent with al Qaeda, but increasingly frustrated in their inability to do anything about it. The story of what happened in Anbar between January and the summer of 2006 is fairly clear. I mean, the security situation fell apart.... So we had completely missed the boat on our one opportunity. The initial Awakening movement, if you want to call it that, or the first Awakening, was crushed by al Qaeda and the security situation collapse....

It was supposed to be the year of the police, 2006. We had made several fitful starts in developing police forces, and I don't need to go into all of the failures there, a lot of fake numbers being thrown out, a lot of really shoddy training, and people joining the police who were not motivated for the right reasons, and most of whom were insurgents at one point.... If you had gone after this holistically and established security and had a year of the police, maybe you would have made some progress there in the beginning of '06, but we did neither. So not only did we not establish security by not providing additional troops, ... but we put very little additional effort into building the police force in the beginning of 2006.

I saw almost no communication that referred to the year of the police coming out of Baghdad at any time, and I was sitting in the MEF headquarters.... I was aware of what was going on, and I can tell you that almost 90 percent of the focus of effort was put into destroying al Qaeda through high value target attacks—raids. In essence, the 1st Marine Division, or the MEF at that point, was seconded to Special Operations Forces, who were going after high value targets.... We didn't see any effect other than an increasing level of violence. So as we focused more and more on manhunting, the level of violence steadily increased from February, when we had the Samarra bombing, all the way up through the middle of the summer, just a steady increase in violence, and through the end of the summer, actually. Attack levels went from 25 a day at the end of '05 to something like 90 a day in the March, April, May time frame, so essentially a tripling of the volume of violence in the province, and a lot of it focused in Ramadi, but also Haditha was falling apart, Zaidon, Amariyah, a lot of the other areas....

General [Richard C.] Zilmer realized that we needed to secure Ramadi, and I'm going to say it was the end of March, early April, he organized an operational planning team . . . to come up with a plan to secure Ramadi. This is the other story that doesn't make it into the modern history of the Awakening movement. For about a month, a group of us put together a very, very well constructed, very detailed plan to secure the provincial capital. . . .

We were going to do this in the absence of any tribal awakening. We realized at that point that the tribes were not ready. There were very few tribal leaders, we felt at that point, that had the ability to do any positive coercion, because again, tribal members were not ready to do anything positive. The glass factory bombing on January 5th set a tone for recruiting, and the murder and intimidation campaign set a tone for tribal leaders. So at that point, it was essentially a Coalition effort to establish security. Now, we included our Iraqi partners in that. The Iraqi army was going to play a very big role in helping to secure Ramadi. . . .

Ramadi is split in two places by the [Euphrates] river. The terrain varies dramatically. Even within the urban area, you have an industrial area, you have a semi open commercial and industrial area. You have the heart of the city, you have the suburbs, and it blends out into farmland that is fairly well populated. But you can't really control it. There are ratlines everywhere. There are easy ways to cross the river, many, many ways of getting in and out of Ramadi proper, let alone the edges of Ramadi. So [it was] a major task, requiring a significant number of troops to secure not only the city, but necessarily the area around the city, and understanding, of course, that Ramadi sits on Route Michigan and Route Mobile, which is the main artery going into Baghdad from Syria, from the safe haven in Syria. This had strategic implications outside of the fact that we were going to secure the provincial capital. This should have been a pretty big deal.

At the end of April, May, I think Ramadi, if you looked at the color tone map of all the cities that were good, bad, and ugly, Baghdad was yellow. Ramadi was orange going towards red, as in the deeper the color, the worse it gets. So Ramadi, according to

MNF I, MNC I intelligence experts, was the worst city in the country, in that time frame, in the time frame that we were developing this plan. One would think that the worst city in the country would receive some sort of assistance, especially if we had gone to all the trouble of coming up with a plan to secure it.

The planning, and I want to give you a little bit of detail on this, because it's important to understand that we came up with a good plan. We went inch by inch over the imagery of the city. I knew the city first hand from 2004, and I was helping plot from an intelligence perspective where we were going to put each checkpoint, where we were going to put each police station. We had built police stations out of Conex boxes [Container express military shipping containers] that we were ready to just drop in and provide security for with mutually supporting stations, mutually supporting fires from the Marines. We had a very, very solid, methodical plan to build oil spot zones of security and build out from there. We knew that there were areas in the southeast of the city that were no go for us, essentially. We knew where the rat lines were. We knew how they were coming across the river, and attacking the government center every day, and coordinating their attacks through the mosque loudspeakers. We knew what was happening. We knew what needed to be done to fix it, and we knew exactly how many troops we needed, or thought we needed.

The plan called for an overlap of the two brigades. In order to establish the security in the city, we were going to overlap the arrival of the new brigade with the departure of 2/28 BCT [2d Brigade Combat Team, 28th Infantry Division (Pennsylvania Army National Guard)] by a month. . . . We were going to surge in Ramadi and overwhelm the lines of communication and then use that opportunity to set the police, the first few police stations, and really just kind of get the ball rolling. . . .

I'm going to do some informed speculation here about what went wrong at the strategic level in early 2006, and why the first Awakening failed, and why things got so bad towards the middle of '06 that the scene was set for the second Awakening. Essentially, everything had just been thrown up against the wall. From day one,

General Casey and General [John P.] Abizaid [USA] believed—I think incorrectly, although not cynically—I think that they believed it genuinely and I think they believed it with good intention, that we were the cause of the insurgency, that our presence was the disease, was the foreign body that was causing the antibodies to activate, so to speak. And they never really understood the fact that it was really the underlying social conditions in the country that were creating the insurgency, that the insurgency was not just a reaction to American presence, that it was an expression of Iraqi discontent across the board, and that led them to both pull us back into the FOBs [forward operating bases]. When we did that, we lost our intelligence collection opportunities, human intelligence. We lost our connection to the population. Again, Counterinsurgency 101. We lost control of the lines of communication, and this happened between '04 and early '06. So we basically did everything you should not do in a counterinsurgency campaign. We disconnected for the populace, we pulled back from our efforts to establish security, and every time we had an opportunity to capitalize on a success, we withdrew troops.

The bottom line is that we were told point blank, very clearly, that we weren't getting any more troops. Now if you recall the public statements by senior general officers and secretaries of defense, all the way through the war, our commanders will get what they need. If they ask for more troops, they'll get them. So obviously, that was not true. That was a blatant lie, to be perfectly honest with you. . . .

Colonel [Peter H.] Pete Devlin was the G 2 for the MEF, and he can give you a really good insight of how 1/1 AD [1st Brigade Combat Team, 1st Armored Division, USA] adopted our plan, modified it, and then was successful. . . .

By the middle of '06, Ramadi essentially looked like Stalingrad. We were dropping shells in the middle of the city. . . . It was a disaster at that point. I argue that mid 2006, the population had recovered from the blow of the destruction of the first Awakening, and they had reached their culminating point with al Qaeda. They had reached the point with al Qaeda where they had had enough. So now you had, at a very broad level, the people—not everybody, but the people, a majority of the people in Anbar were ready for a change. A lot of them were ready to come in our direction, and you saw a change in rhetoric, and I got this because I was reading all the traffic every day and engaging with people. Guys that in 2004 were saying, "Get out, get out of the cities. We'll take control of everything," were saying, "You need to secure the cities for us, and then leave." You saw pockets of resistance against al Qaeda. You saw an intra tribal fight in the Albu Fahad tribe sometime in the middle of '06. You saw all sorts of indicators that they were done with AQI. So the conditions, the social conditions, had been established, and what we needed at that point then was security.

What 1/1 AD did was come in and do two things correctly—and of course the Marines, too. I mean, 1/1 AD seems to love getting the credit for this stuff, but they managed to establish security while simultaneously taking advantage of the shift in social conditions on the ground, which meant taking advantage of the growth, or the rebirth, or the correction of the tribal lineage system, the tribal power structures. So there were tribal leaders at that point that were capable of positive coercion, of getting people to join groups. The people were ready, and the tribal leaders were ready, and so everything kind of neatly fell into place in '06. You had that culminating point. You had the tribal leaders ready to go, and even though we didn't get all the troops we asked for, you had an active duty Army brigade that was very competent, had just come out of a very tough area and was getting a fresh look at a problem, and did a very good job executing a security plan. . . .

By late summer, early fall '06, Colonel Devlin—and this is unclassified now, I mean, the damn thing's been released—Colonel Devlin sent me an e mail. I was back at the Marine Corps Intelligence Activity, where I was the head of the cultural intel program. And he said, "Here's a PowerPoint brief on the state of the insurgency in Anbar. Turn it into a paper." I agreed with just about everything he said, so we wrote the 2006 state of the insurgency paper that was leaked to the press, to [Thomas E.] Tom Ricks [of the *Washington Post*] in particular, where it was twisted, misquoted, and taken out of context. And Colonel [Sean B.] MacFarland [USA] cites that leaked version of the paper in his article in the *Military Review* article that's so widely quoted for the Awakening. . . .

What was left out of the equation there is that at the end of the paper, we also made some recommendations, so it was not a purely negative paper. Tom Ricks did not portray it that way, and that was how it was consumed by the general populace, and also by a lot of military people. So it was misconstrued, it was taken out of context. The Marines had not given up. That's absolutely absurd. It was a couple of intel guys making a point, and nobody was reading the intel traffic for a year before that that led up to the writing of that paper. It was a good example of what happens when you leak intel reporting, the negative consequences for leaking intel reporting.

Okay, and then specifically why was Sheikh [Abdul] Sattar [Abu Risha] ready to go? We, collectively, the Coalition, had kept him on the sidelines for quite some time. Various people had been engaging with him informally, but he had never sullied himself by engaging with Coalition openly and directly. He had insurgent credentials, he had smuggling credentials, and he was enough of a kind of criminal vagabond, these kind of suave criminals that became so popular in western Iraq during the sanctions period. He was one of these well respected criminals, and he still had a little bit of an aura of mystique about him. So he was the right guy at the right time, and he was able to capitalize on the fact that a lot of other tribal leaders were ready to go. . . .

Staff Sergeant Bradford A. Wineman: In the Awakening process there's the dynamic of two forces, the Iraqis and the Coalition. How much do you see the Iraqis doing this under their own power, and how much do you think is this being genuinely driven by U.S./Coalition forces in sort of the '06/'07 time frame?

Connable: Insurgency, any civil violence, whatever you want to call it, revolution, rebellion, civil war, uprising—all the terminology— it's about social conditions. I mean, at the heart of it, you get to the root of the problem, and it's about social conditions, whether it's land reform, whether it's political repression, or lack of human rights, or whatever it is. And you cannot effect legitimate change in the absence of a shift in those conditions.

Now, did we change the social conditions in Anbar Province? That's really the question here. No, no we did not. Things happened naturally over the course of time. What we did do was provide a poorly run; no, not poorly run, [but] a poorly supplied resource, a poorly resourced stabilizing element. So we were basically, and I've used this analogy before in an article I wrote. We were like the control rod in a nuclear reactor. The control rod was about halfway in, so we gave them a kind of semi protected environment in which they could work out a lot of their own social problems. They worked a lot of them out against us, obviously, but they also worked them out against each other. They had to reach the conclusion that the Awakening was the way to go on their own. You can't force feed this stuff. You can't convince people that it's in their own best interest to do something when they know damn well that it's not. . . . You cannot make this happen through coercion. So all of our recruiting drives, all of our IO [information operations] messages, we basically were giving them the mechanisms to take advantage of the shift in social conditions.

So okay, "we're here to help; al Qaeda's bad." That was our message, essentially, our theme. And they didn't believe it, they didn't believe it, they didn't believe it, and finally they said, "You know what? We're getting pretty sick of al Qaeda. Maybe that is true." And then the whole time we're saying, "We want to help you establish an army and a police force, and we want security." And they didn't believe us, they didn't believe us, they didn't believe us, and now so they didn't want to do it, essentially, because they didn't believe us. So they're not going to take advantage of the structure we provide because they don't believe in the message.

So they get to the end of all this, all of these things happened, all this cathartic activity takes place. They start to see Iran as a greater threat than the United States, because of all the stuff that happened in early 2006, and they see the criminalization of al Qaeda and all of these things, and then they say, "You know what? Maybe joining the police force or whatever, maybe we take the Americans up on their offer." So being consistent helped us.

I think that consistency and the persistent presence paid off in the end, but it didn't make it happen. You can't make an insurgency end. If you make an insurgency end by killing people, then you really were fighting a terrorist organization. You weren't fighting an insurgency.

Wineman: Is there a misunderstanding you wish you could correct about the concept of the Awakening?

Connable: It's a process, not an event. This is not something that happened overnight. This is not something that was created by an American unit, or a series of American units. This was not something we did. This is something that happened over time, that we helped set the conditions for, and so you've got to understand that counterinsurgency operations take time. There is no miracle cure, no surprise negotiation with the right guy that's going to turn the whole thing around. That happens only in very, very few cases, and I would argue even in those cases [that] the social conditions have to be right for that to occur. So you've got to take away from this, it's a long process. It's the social conditions, it's the root causes, that matter at the end of the day.

2006
Counterinsurgency and the
Roots of the Awakening

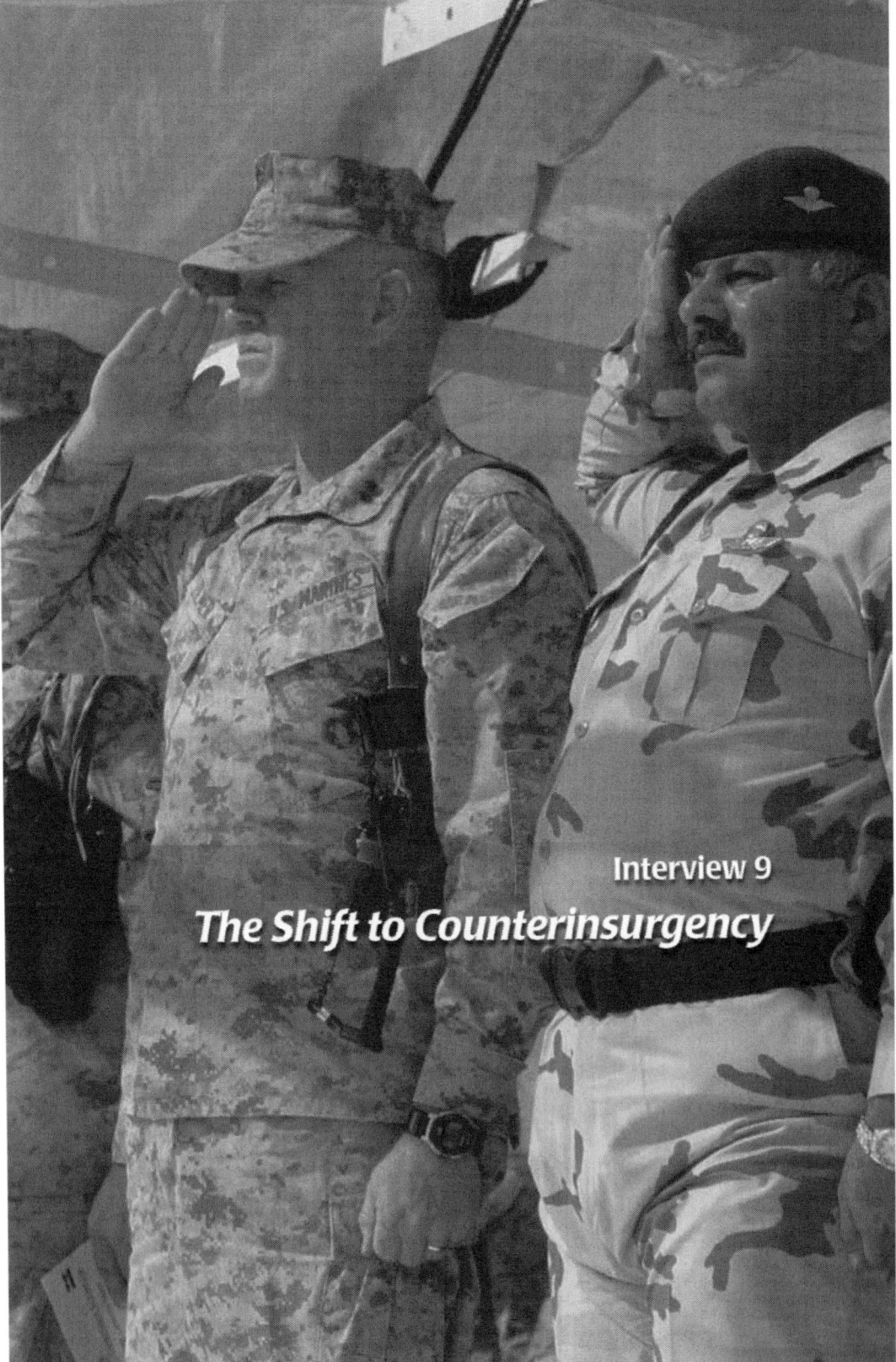

Interview 9
The Shift to Counterinsurgency

Major General Richard C. Zilmer

Commanding General
I Marine Expeditionary Force (Forward)
Multi National Force • West

February 2006 to February 2007

Major General Richard C. Zilmer commanded the 1st Marine Expeditionary Brigade in 2005 and served as the commanding general of I Marine Expeditionary Force (Forward) [I MEF] in Iraq from February 2006 to February 2007.

In this interview, Major General Zilmer describes the goals and progress of I MEF during its tour and the significant improvements in the Iraqi security forces in 2006. He discusses the Awakening and its impact on improved security, as well as Coalition efforts to improve the economy and self governance in al Anbar Province, especially as a partner and mentor to the provincial governor. He notes the importance of cultural understanding in the success of military and police transition teams and the need to balance engagement of tribal leaders with support for the elected government.

Major General Zilmer was interviewed by Lieutenant Colonel Kurtis P. Wheeler on 1 January 2007 at Camp Fallujah, Iraq.

Lieutenant Colonel Kurtis P. Wheeler: Sir, a year ago as you took over I MEF [Marine Expeditionary Force], what were your key priorities? What were your objectives?

Major General Richard C. Zilmer: The key priorities when we got over here were really to focus on Ramadi. At that time, a year ago, the operations out west up in Husaybah, al Qaim, River Gate, those operations had been pretty much concluded at that point. They swept most of the western Euphrates River Valley, had some hugely successful operations up there with II MEF and RCT 2 [Regimental Combat Team 2]. And we were still in the aftermath, if you will, of al Fajr and Fallujah, so in one sense we thought we had two bookends that were reasonably secure. No one would have thought that in one short year, the progress that has happened out west in Husaybah and al Qaim would have been as great as it's been. That's been hugely successful and a very, very pleasant surprise to see that area rebound from being inundated with insurgents to rebound to the point now where they have a police force, they have a city government, they have Iraqi army forces out there and the economy of the town has come back. That has been a truly remarkable good news story.

Fallujah. We got here a year ago [February 2006], barely 2,000 police in the entire Anbar Province, most of which were in Fallujah, which was a good story. You had a city council there. You had a mayor there, so Fallujah was doing very well, and we saw the beginnings of the emergence of the shopkeepers. That sort of economy was beginning to get traction again, and every day that you drove down ASR [Alternative Supply Route] Fran or Michigan, it almost seemed by the day you could see more businesses. There would be more fruit sellers out there, there would be more auto shops opened up. There would be more, just the shops that are important to the Iraqi economy, and particularly out here, out west. So we thought we were pretty solid on the ends, but, at the end of the day, Ramadi is the key to Anbar Province.

Ramadi, at the time, just by design, by necessity, was an area that we did not have firm control on. While I would say our forces could go anywhere in Ramadi that they wanted to—I mean, any fight we got into we would win in Ramadi. The fact is, we saw the population decreasing. It was the provincial capital of Anbar Province. The governor was a one man single point of failure. The provincial council still does not meet in Ramadi. They did not meet then. There is no mayor in Ramadi. There is no city council in Ramadi. Yet because it's the most populous city, about 400,000, in Anbar, and because it is the capital, you aren't going to secure all of Anbar until you take Ramadi. So our focus coming out here was to zero in on Ramadi. That was the main effort, in terms of our security operations, was to focus on Ramadi.

That needs to be seen in a larger context. While I MEF Forward, and II MEF before us, were the lead in the counterinsurgency fight in Anbar, the long term plan—strategy of success—was to transition that fight to the Iraqi security forces. So when we got here, our mantra was to make as many police as we could possibly make, train properly, as well as increase the size, the capability, of the Iraqi army. And 2006 was supposed to be the year of the police, and in the grander strategy, the Coalition force was the windbreak, if you will, to allow the Iraqi army to come behind us, and then behind them, as we built the police force, to turn over to the police force, the city security to the police. All those things would contribute to Provincial Iraqi Control, or PIC, and that was a measure of security that would allow the governor [and] the division commanders out here the ability to address security emergencies and essentially provide for their own security without the help of the Coalition. That's what we're trying to do: put Iraqi army in the lead and really enable the Iraqis to do it themselves. So that's what we set out to do, coming here.

When we came here, there were slightly under 2,000 police in all of Anbar Province. After a year, we've got about 8,500 trained Iraqi police. Our ceiling that we're working under is 11,300 police, so we are still below where we need to be. The original timeline was to be there by December. We hit some months in March, April, May, where we were not able to generate any young men from Anbar to join the police or the army. Of late, meaning since October, that trend has just gone straight up. We are now able to recruit almost all the police we need to recruit, and right now I would say by about March [2007], possibly as late as April, we should be able to achieve that figure of 11,300 police, and that's for all of Anbar. That's Fallujah, Ramadi, Husaybah, Haditha, Haqlaniyah, Barwanah, all those cities will have a police force of their own. . . .

The inroads that we've established in terms of trying to create a province that has confidence in their ability to generate an economy, I think we've made tremendous progress there, mainly through the efforts of General [David G.] Reist and his efforts to attract investment from outside of Iraq and Anbar. He's maintained a very aggressive relationship—I mean that in a positive sense—with the expat community that lives in Jordan. Most of the intelligentsia, the affluent Sunnis from Anbar left. They went to either Jordan or Syria, or other places. And his experience in the last year was [focused on] trying to attract them to come back in. We've looked at international support to attract investment. He has bridged to the secretary of defense's office to bring in economic transformation specialists in the form of Mr. [Paul A.] Brinkley to come in here and examine some of the state owned enterprises— a glass factory, the cement factories—and what could we do to help transform those businesses, state driven businesses, and have them now take on a more profit generated, profit incentive development. And, again, these are new concepts. . . .

The work we've done to establish the central services—electricity, water, sewage, trash, employment—I think we've established a foundation for those things to work. Trying to get, the Iraqis out here in Anbar, who have been suppressed for the last 30, 40 years by a state driven economy, to now ask those people to look at a capitalist view economically is a major change. It's a sea change for the people. So through a series of meetings, conferences, conventions, we've been able to bring a lot of people who have some ability to influence what's happening here in Anbar. And you look at the natural resources, this place abounds in natural resources. The one natural resource that Anbar lacks is petroleum— oil—but there is wild speculation that out west there are huge natural gas fields that are out there, awaiting to be developed.

Anbar is largely an agrarian province. Estimates are that the agricultural production is only at about 30 percent of what it could be. The Euphrates River Valley is a hugely fertile area. It could easily feed this country, if not most of the Middle East, but trying to take a 19th century view of farming and accelerate that into an industrial farming mindset is a big change. So there are a lot of resources out here, not the least of which is the people themselves. I think they have always been tied to Baghdad with petrodollars, and it's the fear of the unknown, breaking away from Baghdad, because of that support network that the petrodollars always provided. Oil is still the biggest producer of cash in Iraq, and it probably always will be, but trying to get the Anbar people to have confidence in the other things that are here has been, that will take more than a year to do that. So those are the things I'm very optimistic about.

Watching the governor [Mamoun Sami Rashid al Alwani] grow, the governor was—again, he's still a one man band—but watching him develop, sending him off to workshops to teach him how healthy bureaucracies work in a provincial government, training him, taking his staff with him, that has been very rewarding. We've watched the governor grow from being very uncomfortable with his position as the governor to the point now where he can go into meetings. He acts like a governor. He acts very authoritative, in a positive way. I've watched now mayors come up and acknowledge his presence as a governor. A year ago, no one saw him as the governor of Anbar Province. So he's grown into his position.

He's become more influential, and he's taken a very active role in the development of the economy of Anbar Province. He's all over the businesses, whether that's trying to get microfinancing up and working, whether that's, again, returning essential services, banking. It's a lot of work that remains to be done, so the governor has seen, I think, a very, very positive improvement in his capabilities. . . .

Wheeler: What have you seen as the key hurdles with Iraqi army recruitment nationally? That is a national issue.

Zilmer: Nationally, it's not a problem. The problem is out here in Anbar Province, where 90 percent of your province is Sunni. There is absolutely no problem with Shi'a. Shi'a soldiers, or *jundi* recruits, are very interested in joining, so the problem out in Anbar is that we can continually infuse or have *jundi* soldiers come out here, but we'd like a better mix with Sunnis. And trying to entice the Sunni young men to come out and join the army, that has proven problematic for us.

Many of the kids out west cannot pass a literacy examination, which is a requirement to join the police and the army. We think that a literacy program and waiver needs to be established to allow these kids to join the army, and during boot camp, or recruit training, or after some period of time, that there is a national program that teaches these young men how to read. In our view, that would be hugely successful in helping them come along.

But again, total numbers across the country I think are pretty good, but we're after Sunnis out here to join, and we've had checkered success on that. Now, what's changed all of that in the last three months, at least with respect to Ramadi, is the emergence of the tribal sheikhs. They have taken a much, much larger role in the security for their communities. They have come together in Ramadi to resist al Qaeda, and in so doing, they've been able to chase out the young men to join the army, join the police most notably. We've seen great interest in joining the police, and, of late, in the last month and a half, we've had this organization sanctioned by the Ministry of Interior, called the Emergency Response Units, three battalion sized units, about 750 Iraqis, or soldiers, or policemen, per battalion. So we've been able now to get our numbers swelling in terms of Iraqi police. I'd say in the year that we've been here, that's probably the biggest positive change we've seen.

So the key there was trying to get the sheikhs and the tribes that they lead to take a larger role in their own security, and I think that's come together for a combination of reasons. One, I think they've watched the success of the Coalition forces and the Iraqi army forces out there in their communities. We've been persistent there. In most of these communities that we're operating in, we remain a stable entity. In other words, we continue to be there. I think that's the trust that they were looking for, but that's been important. But what has also been important is the brutal murder, [the] intimidation that al Qaeda practices on a daily basis has absolutely—before this—had smothered the tribes and some of the other groups. So I think they finally hit a point where they said, "Look, we're not going to survive this way, we're not going to progress this way."

So you have a couple of those things all come together at the same time, and then you get a couple of key personalities, like Sheikh [Abdul] Sattar [Abu Risha], and that's what we're looking for, this middle class leadership to emerge and bring the people together. We've finally found some of that in Ramadi, and we're hoping that phenomenon [the Sahwa or Awakening] will spread throughout Anbar. But there are some parts of Anbar where it won't work. The tribes are strong in Ramadi. They're strong out west. They're less, though, as you get closer to Baghdad, so again, that same phenomenon may not take place in other places that are in our area of operations. . . .

Wheeler: How does the Coalition plug in to the [Provisional Joint Coordination Center (PJCC)]? We're enablers, we're mentors?

Zilmer: Absolutely. We are advisers to the PJCC. Again, eventually we want to be able to extract ourselves from that, but, in the meantime, through our MTTs, our military transition teams, through our PTTs, our police transition teams, through our governance support teams who work out of the governor's office in Ramadi, through our advisor role, if you will, and our ability—frankly, we still have a lot of capability. We have a lot of enablers that the Iraqi people still need, whether that's the army or the police, so our involvement helps to facilitate the process, but also, if there are capabilities or enablers that only we have at the present time, then we can reach back and do that. But I think there's a great, at least in our experience out here, there has been I think a very, very strong relationship has developed between us, the police and the army, and the governor. We travel frequently with the governor. We spend a lot of time with the governor, now at the government center. We're joined as advisor teams with the army and the police, so I think for the most part they are very, very comfortable with us. They do trust us. They believe in what we're trying to do, so there is not an issue of us not being there. . . .

Wheeler: Has the Marine Corps had to shift their way of doing business to a more patient approach in al Anbar?

Zilmer: Well, patience is certainly a virtue out here. I think we do recognize it, as a service, as a Marine Corps. We recognize that dealing in a counterinsurgency in the Middle East, or in the Arab world, requires a fundamental understanding of the culture, which gets back to some of the things we're now doing as a Corps in terms of identifying our officers, core areas where they will become experts, they're expected to become experts over the course of their career, whether that's in the Western Hemisphere, or the Middle East, or the Pacific region, or Europe. We've gone to great lengths to develop our cultural center that works out of Quantico [Center for Advanced Operational Culture Learning]. Mojave Viper ... all the Marines would go through a four hour session of cultural training with Dr. Barak [A.] Salmoni, and he would go through the cultural nuances of how Arab people live, how they act, and understanding that cultural difference. And so we've applied a lot of that. We spend a lot of effort to get our Marines sensitive to that. It's hard to do in a four hour class, to make you an expert on Middle Eastern culture. You just won't be there. But I think if we at least make our Marines and sailors coming over here, walking into a new culture, a new society, and these are the sort of norms, these are the sort of things you're going to have to do, and making sure that they have realistic expectations of what they will see happen, I think is important.

When I brief all the new MTTs, military transition teams, I talk to them specifically about that: is this an unrealistic expectation? They are not Western, and they have a certain style and methodology that is unique to their culture, and we ignore that at our own peril, and we set ourselves up for frustration. We want to see things happen—[snaps his fingers] boom, boom, boom—just the way Americans are, and it doesn't work over here. But if you look back at where you were two months ago, and two months before that, that's when you see the progress. If you want to see what changed today from yesterday, you're going to go nuts. But if you allow yourself to work through and then say, "Ah, two months ago, remember, we couldn't even do this before. We didn't even have this two months ago." That's where you see the success, and almost without exception, every Marine that I do talk to that finishes an advisor tour will tell you that this has been the most challenging, and yet the most rewarding, assignment he's ever had.

Like I said, it's not the guy who finishes number one at The Basic School. It's not the guy that finishes number one at EWS [Expeditionary Warfare School] or Command and Staff. It's not the guy that is six feet, two inches, 300 PFT [physical fitness test] guy. The people that come out here, their greatest gift is communications, and if they can't do that, if they can't immerse themselves with the Iraqi people, they can't communicate, they will not be effective. Almost any Marine can come in here, with the skills he brings with him, if he has the ability to communicate, he will be an effective advisor. I mean, he certainly has to have a certain basic combat skills, particularly weapons employment, that sort of thing, but he doesn't necessarily have to be a combat arms guy to be successful in this role.

And the more senior they become, the more apparent that is, and I would use the example of our division MTT leader, Colonel [Juan G.] Ayala, who is a logistician. The requirement calls for a ground combat guy to be in that job. For a variety of reasons, we picked Colonel Ayala, and he has been wildly successful as an advisor, and he has just fit in so well here that they absolutely trust him to always shoot straight with them, and they will follow his lead. They will ask for his advice, and he will force them to work. So that's been a beautiful example, I think, of how the guy with the right skill sets can be a successful advisor.

Wheeler: You talk about this acknowledgment of Iraqi culture, Iraqi ways of doing things. Do we also acknowledge and bring in the nonelected, traditional leadership in places like Ramadi? What lessons have we learned?

Zilmer: Well, I think the biggest lesson we learned, you can be told a lot of things, but until you stick your finger in the fire, you don't understand what hot means, and then you understand not to do it again. And I think probably the biggest thing that we learned out here was the importance of the tribal engagement. Tribal engagement, in my view, at least for the near future, without tribal engagement, without tribal involvement, to include in the government, we're going to have a tough road. They are absolutely essential to the social fabric of the people in Iraq, and specifically in Anbar Province. And they must be part of everything. They must be part of everything that we do. That's probably been the single biggest lesson I think we've learned here. I think understanding what democracy is, again, it's easy for Americans because that's all we've ever known, the only thing we've ever lived under. And every American, every kid who's graduated from high school, has a working knowledge of government and democracy.

That just did not exist here. So you're asking here for the Iraqi people to place their faith, and trust, and confidence in something that they don't really understand, because they've never had the opportunity. It's not because they're not smart enough. They are clearly smart enough. They may not be book smart, but they are very, very intelligent people. And it takes time for them, when you're trying to ask them to place trust and confidence in a government, a network, or a system of elected officials who may not necessarily have a tribal rank, that is foreign to them.

I think the votes were good, the elections were good, the people came out, there was a certain novelty to that. But I think then we start sitting down, okay, well, what does that mean, particularly the elected officials? Okay, all right, you are an elected official, these are the sorts of things that elected officials do. And when you resort to votes over and over and over again, whether it's a vote in a committee or a vote in a council, those are the pieces of democracy that I think are new for the process and that will simply take time to do. To make those city councils, provincial councils, to make them successful, there's going to have to be a strong buy in from the tribal sheikhs. That is the custom, that is the most important social feature, I think, of the Anbar people, is that tribal sheikh relationship, and I think we had to learn that. And we've seen now, with the development of the Iraqi response units, the Sahwa Anbar, or the Awakening, that is purely being driven by the tribes and the sheikhs.

Wheeler: Sir, is there in any way a tension between supporting the sheikhs? Is there a danger of that undermining the elected governments?

Zilmer: Absolutely. We saw some examples of that where some of the sheikhs would go straight to Baghdad, and they would have an audience with the prime minister, or any of the ministers. They would curry favor with the ministers, who would bestow authorities unto them, would empower them to do things that completely circumnavigated the provincial governor. And so in some cases where it got them an immediate gratification, it was something that was maybe good, but long term it just undermines that ability of the governor to be the spokesman, if you will, for the province. It's like a chain of command. When you now allow these people to go straight to the top, you marginalize the capacity of the governor.

So yes, that potentially can be destructive to that provincial government you're trying to establish here. . . .

Our problem set is being driven by al Qaeda. That's the common enemy to everybody out here. With a common enemy like al Qaeda and some of these Sunni extremist insurgent groups out here, there's been a lot of common ground that we've been able to have between us, whether that's the Iraqi army, the Iraqi police, and Coalition. Our enemy is a common enemy that we all are sworn to defeat, so I think that's enabled us to do that.

So I think we've been able to have entrees into these teams. Every one of our transition teams is embedded with their battalion, brigade, division. They are embedded. They live there with those units. Many of these units still have partnerships with our battalions, meaning their companies live with our companies inside the combat outposts. We have that relationship, which doesn't always exist further east of Baghdad. Because of that, we've been able to build this trust and confidence, and I can go places with my division commanders. They can come up here and meet with me. I can go down there and visit with them. We can travel together throughout our areas of responsibility. They are TaCon [tactical control] to us, so they freely acknowledge that relationship.

The last thing that makes it easy to work with them, going back to this historic gulf that exists between Baghdad and Anbar—Anbar Province has never, ever been close to Baghdad. The real cynics out here would tell you that Baghdad has no interest whatsoever in seeing Anbar Province succeed, for any number of reasons. So we have in many cases become the champion of the Iraqi army and Iraqi police. We advocate for them, we fight many of the fights for them in Baghdad, whether that's Ministry of Defense, Ministry of Interior. We become the advocates for them, and in may cases, when the Ministry of Interior or Defense fail to provide sustainment, we provide that sustainment at a price. So we are always there, and so that's why I think we have a relationship out here that is different than other parts of the country, and for the most part, it's a very, very solid relationship.

Interview 10
Enabling the Awakening, Part I

Brigadier General David G. Reist

Deputy Commanding General (Support)
I Marine Expeditionary Force (Forward)
Multi National Force • West

February 2006 to February 2007

Brigadier General David G. Reist is a logistics officer who commanded 1st Transportation Support Battalion (redesignated Transportation Support Group during Operation Iraqi Freedom) from 2002 to 2004 and Combat Service Support Group 11 during Operation Iraqi Freedom II. He was the commanding general of 1st Force Service Support Group (redesignated 1st Marine Logistics Group) from 2005 to 2007 and served as deputy commanding general (Support) for I Marine Expeditionary Force (Forward) from February 2006 to February 2007.

In this interview, Brigadier General Reist discusses the relationship between security and growth in the economy and self governance in al Anbar Province. He describes the economic potential of al Anbar and the role I Marine Expeditionary Force has played in helping Anbaris to tap into that potential. He notes the relationship between key leaders who remained in al Anbar amid the violence and those who were outside Iraq in places such as Jordan. He concludes with a description of the overall progress in al Anbar and it potential to reach a "tipping point" toward rapid improvement.

Brigadier General Reist was interviewed by Lieutenant Colonel Kurtis P. Wheeler on 3 January 2007 at Camp Fallujah, Iraq.

Lieutenant Colonel Kurtis P. Wheeler: Sir, when you stepped on deck, what did you see as the priorities, and what were your key goals during your tour?

Brigadier General David G. Reist: First of all, the focus obviously was economic and governance. And of the five LOOs [lines of operation] that exist, we kind of viewed it that the economics and governance would be the decisive effort, but not the point of main effort on a daily basis. So it's kind of that silent hand that needs to happen that will turn events and will offer the things that will prove to be the tipping point. But on a day to day basis, realize that the security situation is going to drive everything around here. And that has proven very true.

One of the things when I say that, though, is a lot of people always ask, how can you sit there and have economic growth when you've got a security situation, [with] violence that doesn't, or would not be perceived that it would allow that? A recent article said that the GDP [gross domestic product] grew somewhere between 4 and 17 percent here in Iraq in 2006. A lot of folks went, "But how can that be happening? That's a country at war." Discounting that probably most of that growth comes from the Kurdish section, there are some things happening here. The unfortunate thing is it's not like measuring the GDP back in the United States. Their housing starts aren't monitored, the things we see on the news, but there are some things happening. It's touchy feely, though. It's when you're out riding around and you see more people on the street. You see shops open. You see students on the street that you haven't seen in a long while, going to school and carrying their books. Those are indicators. Can you put it in a win loss column and come up with an arithmetic formula? No. And that's the frustration sometimes, and quite honestly, I don't know if we want to do that. I don't know if we want to turn it into a total metric so that you'd put it into some algorithm and you'd come out with, "oh my God, here's exactly where you're at." The economics is slow, too. I mean, it's literally like watching paint dry.

Now on the government side, looking at things when we got here, once again, watching paint dry, but even slower drying paint, because there is some frustration as we sit here on the ways the Sunnis view Baghdad, the way they see the national government as nonsupportive, the way they look at the government in that nonsupportive role, on the perception that it is a Shi'a led, Iranian backed government. Now whether that's true or not, it doesn't matter, because that's what they perceive. That's manifested in that they don't get their budget, that they don't get reconstruction funds, they think they see other people getting some things. It just adds to the fray.

How do we overcome that? The governor and I, we go to Baghdad probably once a week [to] lobby with some of the ministries. Our provincial council happens to be in Baghdad. And that's not a perfect situation. It should meet in Ramadi. When we first got here, it was meeting in Ramadi, but the security situation—going back to that—did not allow that. So what we've got, and I know this is a long, twisted thing, but you've got the five fingers of the LOOs here, the lines of operation, and you'd like to be able to slip them into a nice form fitting glove, and each finger being equally important. Boy, I gotta tell you, this is something that you take maybe two steps forward every day, and some days you only take one step back, and some days you take three steps back. Then you wake up the next day, and you look where you can make some progress and bolster success, watch to keep failure from happening too much in one area. The most challenging thing I've done in 28 years, the most exhilarating thing I've done in 28 years. . . .

Wheeler: How do you balance, on a daily basis, the subtleties of something like tribal engagement versus enhancing the elected government, which are, to some extent, at odds with each other?

Reist: Good question. First of all, I'm not going to pretend that there's a cookbook for this. There might be people who have done this their whole life who understand it and know the complexities. For a lot of us that get put in a billet like this—I don't say this flippantly—but we make it up every day. Yeah, we have a plan, we have a goal. But that goal is framed from engagement and listening to different people at all levels.

We're engaged at Amman, Jordan. Why? Because there's a number of expats, there's a lot of very, very wealthy men that are there who are of Sunni origin, and Amman is a trading hub for this part of the world. So we go there, and we listen to some things that are happening there. We bounce it against some things that we hear from the RCTs [regimental combat teams], bottom up and top down, and we bring those things together. We had an economic conference, bottom up, from the city of Fallujah in Amman in May [2006]. We did a thing with the sheikhs, top down, in Amman later. . . .

Occasionally those folks cross a border, a border that exists for us on a map, a border that really doesn't exist for them. But these men are in touch, and they feed off each other. They are shaping things. They are probably determining who's going to be the winner in this. They're looking for economic gain. . . . Very wealthy men are looking at the situation for how they can exploit the economic gains that are going to come down the road. . . . What we've tried to do, I'm not sure how well, but you put the pieces in the same room and let the puzzle kind of come together, don't try to force the puzzle together, because forcing it will have a U.S. flavor on that force and probably not be as productive as the way the Iraqis will do it. . . .

Wheeler: If you could, connect back—and this is an additional complexity, or perhaps a benefit—when you're dealing with these businessmen, they can also influence the security situation because of their influence on the people. How does that all fit into the equation in terms of IP [Iraqi police] recruitment and things like that?

Reist: When we first started involvement, yes, we did tell them that we would love to have seen them—"gentlemen, can you influence this?" That's a dynamic that's been explained to me as follows: there's guys on the inside and there's guys on the outside, and guys on the inside are the guys that stay. The guys on the outside are the rich guys that either always had a business in Amman, or, because the security situation and maybe they were threatened, they left. Some folks have estimated that there are as many as 500,000 al Anbaris that have gone to Amman, Jordan. So what you've got is, with this inside outside dynamic, there's a little bit of friction there. If you're one of the guys who stayed, and you're fighting through it, and you're having a little bit of success, . . . you're the guy whose friends have died, and now there's that feeling that the rich guy, when everything settles down a little bit, is going to come back in and reestablish either an economic foothold, a traditional tribal relationship, this that, and the other, and we're dealing with that.

What we've done is we've tried to put these guys in the same room and let them work it out, because there are traditional tribal entities that exist out here that they will sort out. For example, if you were always the sheikh of sheikhs of the Dulaimi Federation, even though you're in Amman, you're still recognized as the sheikh. There might be somebody inside al Anbar that stayed that went, "You left them. I'm the sheikh now." They've got to work through that. I don't think we're in a position, both from enforcing, or cultural sensitivity, or knowledge wise to know the nuances of who was doing what to whom within the tribe.

Now you get back to what you just asked, and where I kind of hinted at the start of the answer, can they influence things in Amman? Yes, I believe they can. I think they can influence it for two reasons. The first is the traditional, tribal nature of al Anbar, and even though some of them have left, there is still that, "I am a member of the Dulaimi Federation," and 88 subtribes—about 15 prominent ones. It's there, though. That will not go away. Three years of fighting, four years of fighting, I don't think that will disappear.

The other thing, and the other aspect, is [that] there [are] very wealthy men in Amman. And money talks. Follow the money sometimes in life, and usually you get to where you're going. Those two things together are very important. . . .

The success in the police and the army appears to come, though, from the inside to date, not from the outside. That's provable at this point in time. But who knows what the subtle influence and that silent hand can do from the outside. It might be a call, a gesture, a meeting that we don't even know about that's happened. That's why we continue to engage, because those subtle nuances can make all the difference in the world. . . .

Wheeler: Sir, what have you seen in terms of refugees? There's been a lot of publicity about people fleeing al Anbar, but what are we seeing recently in terms of people actually coming into al Anbar from Baghdad and other places?

Reist: I don't have a count for you, but I've heard this, just talk on the streets and talk from people. It's kind of ironic that people are coming to al Anbar for refuge when you would think that everybody, if you listen to the news, you would go, "Oh, I'm not going to al Anbar, that's the worst place in the world." That's not the case. Fallujah is a city that is known, that is accepting refugees from Baghdad right now because of the killings that are going on. Around here, it's done where families take in families and matters such as that. Are we seeing growth? Yes, we are. That's why economic growth is even more important, because we will have extra people in the province. What we need to do is we need to create as many jobs as possible so idle hands don't find other work.

The governor, just before Christmas, got his first allocation of reconstruction dollars from the federal government, and it equated to just under 40 million dollars. He'll get another 30 million dollars here, hopefully, in another couple weeks. And there are projects that are starting as he distributes that money to his mayors that will do a couple things. It will be a physical sign for the people that, "Wow, projects are starting, my community is getting a little bit better"—a success breeds success type thing. This is a slow ball to get moving, though. Once that happens, though, then possibly with some AQI [al Qaeda in Iraq] getting pushed out, with the tribes taking control, the synergistic effect of several of these things happening all at once, that's what we're looking for.

And what are we waiting for? The tipping point. What will that tipping point be, as [Malcolm] Gladwell put it in his book? I don't know. Will we know it when we see it? Probably not. Will we be able to look back and hopefully say, "That was it"? I hope so. And that just like Gladwell describes in his book, *The Tipping Point*, it's there. Do some of us feel that we're in that area in some areas? Yeah, we do, because al Qaim is a relatively good area right now. A combination of increased police across time, tribal entity, Coalition forces all working together after AQI was pushed out last year under II MEF's offensive campaign out there. So good things [are] happening where good things can, once again, based on the security situation. But that doesn't mean that good things can't happen where the security situation isn't pristine, either. I mean, there's economic growth in some bad areas all over the world. It just happens. . . .

Wheeler: On that note, sir, in Ramadi, which many people consider the worst of the worst, talk about some of the progress there in terms of improving security and how that's leading to improved status of governance and economic growth.

Reist: The way Ramadi's kind of been done is it's been a clearing effort that Colonel [Sean B.] MacFarland [USA] out of the Ready 1st Combat Team has done from west to east across the city, and that's in process right now. But in the areas where there's been a persistent presence, increased IP, things like that, there is where we look at the atmospherics for a few more shops open, more kids on the street, things like that.

I can give you an example. Right around the government center, there were some buildings that had been just absolutely destroyed. ... Those buildings were dropped, and they were dropped because they could not be repaired. There was a contract to remove the rubble. It took a lot to even get a contractor to go in there under the auspices of a safe enough umbrella to do the rubble cleanup. But that's the sort of thing that just started right before Christmas. Then, okay, you're a local citizen, and you see your community starting to be cleaned up, that's one of those visible signs that we hope link towards the tipping point of, "Geez, they're picking up my city." And commerce is just starting to show. Even if they see traffic on the street in a positive way, as opposed to a bomb going off.

I'll go back to Gladwell's *The Tipping Point*, when [Mayor Rudolph W. L.] Giuliani cleaned up New York City, one of the things that Gladwell emphasizes is, he painted the subway cars to keep 'em clean, and just kept painting them every night, so when somebody sprayed graffiti on them, repaint it—clean it up. ... I think there's a basic thing in every human being that they just want things to be a little bit better. They want a little bit more money in their pocket. They want a little bit more food on their table. They want their neighborhood to be a little safer. And there's a basic understanding that when they see that, they will want more. And that will continue to take off. That's a very, very long fuse that's hard to light. But we hope that once it's lit, that fuse will really burn faster and faster as it gets closer to the nice boom at the end—a good boom, not a bad boom.

Wheeler: Sir, on the concept of the provincial capitol, what have been some of the thoughts behind the decision to stay with the traditional government center despite the fact that it is in ruins versus building, moving to another location that might be more secure and more . . .

Reist: The government center is not in ruins. . . . The governor works in there, he's got workers there, Civil Affairs does some business out of there, we've got a company of Marines living there, for example, so the building itself, no. . . . Is it a fortress right now? Yes. I don't think anybody would deny it. . . . I guess a translation into an American analogy, it's kind of like the Alamo. If you leave that, you're saying you've given up. And the governor is adamant about that. . . . He told me a story once about walking by the government center as a young boy. He's from Ramadi, so he has seen that as the kind of central hub, the Alamo, since he was a kid. Even departing for a short time while things get better, he pushed back hard on that. . . .

Wheeler: The road ahead, sir—your last few weeks here, as you turn over to II MEF, what's going to be your advice to them—where to focus their energies, where do we go from here?

Reist: Keep pressing a lot of the economic things. We've got a business conference in Dubai. The governor is going there. Why are we going to Dubai? We're matching up businessmen from inside Iraq with folks from the Middle East to attract investment, not just in al Anbar, but there's a couple other provinces that are participating with us. We initiated this here, though, and we're working with the governor. And these are the sort of things you need to do. This is the sort of thing I think the governor needs to do. He needs to look internally at some things, but he needs to look outside. That's why going to Amman, look outside, and bring some things in.

The wireless local loop [telecommunications system]—we need to get this thing up and running. It's going to be huge—tips hotline, voice and data capability. The world runs on the Internet today. These folks need to open up their horizons. And the Internet will do that for them. I'm not talking about subverting the Muslim religion, or the culture, or anything, but just think of what that's going to do. They're going to get online, and they're going to be able to expose themselves [to more ideas and information].

I've met some of these folks; they are extremely well educated. I meet with one guy who's got his college degree from USC [University of Southern California] and his master's from MIT [Massachusetts Institute of Technology]. He's smart; he's a lot smarter than I'm ever going to be. Some of these guys get it. And they're just looking to get it more.

Interview 11
Enabling the Awakening, Part II

Brigadier General Robert B. Neller

Deputy Commanding General (Operations)
I Marine Expeditionary Force (Forward)
Multi National Force • West

February 2006 to February 2007

Brigadier General Robert B. Neller served as the deputy commanding general for operations of I Marine Expeditionary Force (Forward) in al Anbar Province from February 2006 to February 2007. He was promoted to major general in 2007 and assumed the presidency of Marine Corps University in September 2009.

In this interview, Brigadier General Neller describes the significant improvements in the Iraqi security forces in 2006 and the transition of battlespace those gains have allowed. He emphasizes the role that tribal engagement has played in the growth of Iraqi forces. He discusses the resiliency of the insurgency and the lingering level of violence despite enhanced Iraqi and coalition force capabilities. He also details the success of the Marine air ground task force in 2006 2007 despite the loss of some forces to stem the sectarian violence in Baghdad and comments on the role of the media in the conflict and the impact of information operations.

Brigadier General Neller was interviewed by Lieutenant Colonel Kurtis P. Wheeler on 23 January 2007 at Camp Fallujah, Iraq.

Lieutenant Colonel Kurtis P. Wheeler: Sir, if you'd begin by going back to the beginning of the tour, as you took over the operations in this area, what were your key priorities, key objectives, as you came on deck for the year?

Brigadier General Robert B. Neller: Before I even arrived at I MEF [I Marine Expeditionary Force] in the summer of 2005, I MEF had already put together a planning team and had done a detailed mission analysis and COA [course of action] development and had written a mission statement that said that their task was to focus on development of the Iraqi security forces [ISF] and then conduct counterinsurgency operations. So we felt that our success here was going to be our ability to develop Iraqi security forces, the idea being [that] as we developed them and transitioned, we would then transfer authority to them and transfer increasing levels of responsibility to them, and that we would reposition our forces into those areas where we had not yet been able to do that. Conceptually, we thought that was going to happen, basically from the east to the west, or an inside out approach. That was the plan.

As it's turned out, we have focused on ISF development. I know the Iraqi army is not any larger in number, but capability wise, they're better trained. We transitioned a significant amount of battlespace to 1st Division. The number of police has gone from somewhere in the neighborhood of 2,000 arguably trained, and whether they're going to work or not, and I'd say anywhere between 8,000 and 10,000 police.

The effect that we wanted is taking place more in an outside in, or west to east, flow. In other words, the level of violence in the west has decreased faster than the level of violence in the center. Right now, the level of violence in the eastern portion of the AO [area of operation] is much higher than it is in the center or the west. So we've transitioned the battlespace of the force and repositioned forces in the west because of the level of the Iraqi security forces, particularly the numbers out west that we plan on transitioning the battlespace. So we executed the plan, yes, maybe not in the way the operational design was, but I think we executed the plan, in some places faster than we thought, in some places not as fast.

It seems to be the type of fight you really can't measure progress in days, or weeks, or even months. You have to look at it over a longer period of time. We've only been here three years, going on four, and that isn't a long time to conduct this type of a fight. How long will it take is another question. The other question is how much time do you have, and I don't know really the answer to either of those.

Wheeler: Sir, the deviations from the plan you just described, or things turning out differently than anticipated, has that been driven more by the uneven development of the ISF, enemy action, or a combination of those things?

Neller: I think it's a combination. I think we were surprised early on that we were unable to recruit men from al Anbar to join the army. I look back at it now, and I think we were probably naive. The people out here, being Sunni, and a very large retired army crew, they do not view the army as their army. They were very reluctant to, particularly out west, join the army at first. The mayor in Fallujah promised us 5,000 recruits, [but] we've gotten basically at the end of the day a very small number. So that said, people have been willing to join the police. However, the police are subject to murder and intimidation since they live out in town, so there's the disadvantage. So it's a mixed bag.

We've had really great success with the police out west and now with the police in Ramadi, because of tribal engagement and civic support. When we got here, there were police in Fallujah, and there was the beginning of police in Ramadi, and maybe a few guys in al Qaim. Now there's police, some form of police force, in every city of the province except for Rutbah, and we think that that may turn here soon.

I think the thing that we really didn't understand or appreciate to the extent that we do now is the importance of tribal engagement—engaging the different tribes, tribal support for the people joining the army and joining the police. We also didn't think that we would have issues with literacy, joining the army or the police. We believed the almanac that Iraq had a certain percentage of literacy. In the far west and out in the country, it's a rural area. Going to school out there, particularly for men, is not, the academic situation is not real good.

We've tried, unsuccessfully, to get the Iraqi Ministry of Defense to waive the literacy requirement, and they haven't done that. We tried to get them to start a reading and a literacy program; they haven't done that. Over the last month, we finally did it ourselves. We actually took guys out of an Iraqi army division, set up a division, and set them up in Camp Habbaniyah to bring guys who couldn't pass the initial screening for reading and teach them—in effect, teach them to pass the test. That was a real missed opportunity for the Iraqi government, to have a national literacy program. It's difficult to have a democratic society when people can't read or be employed in a lot of areas. This society is one which is not based on literary communication. It's based on oral and visual communication. You see it on TV or you hear it from your friends, or your tribe, or the sheikh, or from the imam, and then passing it in verbal information. That's the way they communicate.

Wheeler: Is that cultural difference why you think you got the push back, or the lack of action, on setting up the programs?

Neller: I don't know why we got the push back. Honestly, I don't know. I think it was just another thing. We didn't have anybody to champion it, so we championed it ourselves. We've found that in several cases, we've had ideas of things that we thought were good ideas, and there's a lot going on, everybody has needs, and so we ended up being our own advocate.

Wheeler: Sir, when you look back over the tour, what have been the greatest challenges that you've faced in the operational realm and, subsequently, how have you overcome them?

Neller: I think a lot of what we've done has proved to be much more difficult than what we thought. Life support and administrative support of the Iraqi army and the police, the simple pain, the Herculean task, spent a huge amount of energy on that. Life support, even in the army, getting them their gear, we're giving them all that stuff. That's really not an issue anymore, but it was something that took some effort on our part. I think trying to figure out what was the right operational design for each area, whether you should berm an area or restrict movement, or whether you should give or not give certain support, find out who the sheikhs were, who were the real sheikhs that could influence the action.

I think we were surprised to some degree about the resiliency of the insurgency at the beginning, and that's probably the most discouraging point. We have killed a very substantial number of these guys, and yet the level of attacks has continued to go up. So we can attribute that to the fact that we've gone in areas where we weren't located before, and we've dispersed the force, and we've got more surfaces for them to contact against. Or that they're just, that the insurgency is very resilient and they're able to regenerate. We know they're very, very well financed, and again, it's a vicious circle of, "Why can't you hire people, why can't you put people to work?" Well, if you try and it comes from the Coalition, then they get murdered, or threatened, or intimidated, or killed, and therefore there's no work. So when there's no work, they can take money to participate in the insurgency. There is a certain level of zealotry involved in the insurgency, but there's also a certain level of "it's just business" and a way to feed my family.

Wheeler: On the other hand, looking back over the year, what have been the greatest successes the MEF has achieved in its time here?

Neller: I think all those things surrounding the ISF. I think we increased the number of police and the proper provision of administrative support, life support, base support, putting the support on the army and the police, facilities, communication, setting up a joint coordination center for the city and the provincial joint coordination center in Ramadi.

Repositioning forces. If you looked at the battlespace geometry of this AO and put it on a time lapse photography, it would appear to be a moving, amoebic like force as people have repositioned, moving on, adjusted for maybe the loss of forces or reduction of forces and repositioning of forces. We operated at a deficit almost from the day we got here. We lost 1st Battalion, 1st Marines, had to go to Baghdad and support that, and then soon after that was over, we lost the Army battalion that was out at Rawah, so that one was never replaced. When the 2d of the 28th [2d Brigade Combat Team of the 28th Infantry Division (Pennsylvania Army National Guard)] were replaced by the Ready 1st Combat Team at the very, very last minute, we had a net loss of a battalion. So the weapons, and combat power, and the ability to generate presence have diminished ever since we've been here, until the MEU [Marine expeditionary unit] came aboard. We mitigated that by repositioning forces and taking risks in certain areas and also positioning or developing the ISF. We're having them assume greater responsibility for certain areas, which allows us to reposition with our forces and the Iraqi army. I'm very proud of the flexibility and the planning process that took place that allowed us to keep this thing going. . . . This has been I think very innovative, very flexible, very aggressive, very much taking calculated risks in order to try to improve the security environment. The downside is that we haven't been as successful as we would like to have been in reducing the level of violence.

Wheeler: You mentioned a couple possible explanations for that in terms of causes. What would be the one that you would point to, that you think is the leading cause, for why the violence has not decreased, despite the successes in many areas?

Neller: I think when the Samarra mosque was bombed, that changed the whole calculus for the violence. That let the sectarian genie out of the bottle, and all the violence, the increase in violence everywhere has been fed by that. Anbar is a—with the fighting that goes on in Baghdad, the Sunni Shi'a—Anbar, because of the demographics, is a friendly place. You remember that the insurgents, they have families here, they have tribal connections here, and the people, even though they may not support them, they're not going to rat them out. And because of the empty and wide spaces out here, it's very easy to hide in plain sight. It's just another tent in the desert, another Bedouin sheet tent. So I think the level of violence has gone up everywhere, to include here, and I think the level of violence here is directly related to the level of violence in Baghdad.

Wheeler: To what extent do you think the violence is caused by us pressing into neighborhoods where at one point the insurgents operated freely, and now they're being . . .

Neller: I'm sure that's some of it. If you don't want to have any violence, all you've got to do is stay on the FOB [forward operating base]. If you don't want to have any engagements, or any contact, or escalation of force, just don't go out. The downside to that is, I think we've seen in areas where we haven't been, or where we were and then subsequently left or repositioned, the insurgents will move immediately back in and establish themselves. This hasn't happened 100 percent of the time. In some places where there were police, or when the citizens will stand up and they didn't get killed, that hasn't happened.

Understandably, the majority of them don't want us here. Their answer is, "If you leave, all this would stop." Well, no, it wouldn't stop. It would stop what is happening now. And Baghdad certainly wouldn't stop. What might stop is them fighting us, because there wouldn't be anybody there to fight. And I think very clearly that the al Qaeda led insurgents would very quickly overwhelm the nationalists, or what's sometimes called the legitimate resistance, and make them be subjected to the will of al Qaeda, and they would do what they have said they're going to do, which is to establish an Islamic caliphate, or Islamic state of Iraq, based out of al Anbar.

Wheeler: Could you assess for me, sir, the strategy, the berming, and the enhanced security in the various cities across the province. Where has that worked best? Where is it still ongoing? Discuss that overall strategy.

Neller: One could make the argument that one of the bases of this fight is population control, and that we want to have some control so that we can provide security for the population, and I think the insurgents in these areas want to have some control. Keep the insurgents out, keep the good people in, and be able to provide them a secure environment so that they're confident in the security forces, and they'll also tell us when the bad guys move in on them. You can do that with entry control points to the city, you can do it with the barriers, the berms, and the badging of people, like Fallujah has a Fallujah city badge. You can do it with biometrics, all those things, providing population control, driver's license, if they had drivers' licenses—if they had a driver's license, if they had a national ID.

Where has it worked best? Well, it works to some degree everywhere. It's not perfect.

As far as physically berming of the city, the engineering effort to get it done is substantial, so if it's a large city, it's much more difficult than a small city. Geography plays a role. Are there any natural barriers, like railroad tracks or rivers or something which gives you somewhat of a barrier, so that the amount of engineering work that you have to do is less? Like every other obstacle you put in, you're going to have to figure out how to overwatch it and cover it by fire.

So the most successful berming has been normally on smaller cities, although the Haditha Haqlaniyah Barwanah berm has almost 25,000 meters of berm. That was substantial. Sometimes you can berm inside the city, you can put barriers, like Jersey barriers or Hescos filled with dirt to block off certain streets so that people can only enter a neighborhood through one way or two ways in. . . . I think the berming up at the triad of Haditha, Haqlaniyah, Barwanah was very successful. I mean, you can see the day it was done, the level of violence just dropped right off, because none of the bad guys wanted to be caught inside the city. Now, some of them have made their way back in, and maybe even through the ECPs [entry control points]. But we do census operations, and we get biometric data on everybody, and it will become more and more difficult to move around without having somebody be looking for you.

Wheeler: Could you compare then, sir, the two alternative strategies. In most of the cities, we've tried sort of an outside in approach with the berming. Ramadi is almost a different approach with the "inkblot" strategy. How is that approach?

Neller: The first wave with Ramadi, we went outside. We isolated the city by using the railroad track as a berm, using the river, using ECPs on main roads to block the roads. So we did isolate Ramadi, probably not as effectively as we had hoped, and we then started to move from west to east in the city, tried to keep the Coalition forces in the front, followed by the Iraqi army, followed by the police. And we were delayed in that effort because there was a period of a couple of months when we couldn't recruit any police. That's changed, so that strategy now, we kind of push our way into the center of the city, and I would say the east southeast portion of the city is about all that's left.

Wheeler: So that was really a modified form of the same strategy? It was just driven by geometry?

Neller: Yes.

Wheeler: Looking back on the tour, sir, are there any anecdotes, things that you've experienced out here that you think capture the essence of what the story's been like for you and for the MEF as a whole?

Neller: I think you asked me what I'm frustrated with, and I'd say when you do information ops [operations] and everybody opines and wrings their hands about why aren't we winning the operation with information ops. I think the answer is very simple. The Western media is the most powerful information operations tool in the world, and they tell the story they want to tell. We try to get them to tell our story, but they get to choose. Whereas the insurgency, al Qaeda, the Arab street, most of the media outlets that cater to that particular clientele tell their story rapidly, quickly, immediately. We timed it the other day. We had a tank attacked with an IED [improvised explosive device], and it caught on fire, and an hour and 45 minutes later it was on Al Jazeera. A couple hours after that it was on video. Now, why is that? Because that's who they cater to. They cater to Arabs who feel that the West has been unjust to them, and [that] the Israeli situation and Palestine situation is a great injustice to the Arabs, and that the invasion of Iraq is unjust and unfair, [that] this is all about America wanting to steal their oil.

To counteract that, we can set up our own media outlets, but nobody's going to listen to that. They certainly aren't. So I guess the question is, how do you get either the Western media or the Arab media to tell our story, the story that, hey, we came here. You can argue about the reasons we came here, but we're here, and we're trying to do a good thing. We're trying to improve the life of the average Iraqi, trying to give the average Iraqi an opportunity for choice and for economic development. We're not going to be here forever. We are going to leave. We don't want your oil. We're here to help you. Why do you continue to persist in this fighting when all it does is delay the reconstruction of your country? They watch the TV, whether it's Al Iraqia or Al Arabiya or Al Jazeera, and all they see is IED after IED strike after IED strike after IED. The message is [that] the insurgency is doing great things, the Web pages, they cue them for donations all over the world.

And yet the Western media, and I know that they're required to remain balanced in their reporting. One could argue whether they maintain that balance. I mentioned, before we deployed, I went to a course at Carlisle [PA, at the U.S. Army War College], the

CFLCC, Combined Forces Land Component Commander Course, and they're like, "It's a media battle." One of the four members of the panel was from Al Jazeera, and I said to the guy, after they gave their little introductory talk, I said basically the same thing I told you: "Hey, we think we're doing a good thing. We think we're trying to help. We don't understand why they're trying to kill us. We're trying to rebuild their schools, fix their power, fix their water, fix their streets. We can be out doing this, but these guys just can't get away from the fact that they feel like shooting at us and killing us. How do I tell our story to the Arab street, through your TV station? How do I tell that story?"

He goes, "You don't."

I said, "You don't?"

[He replied,] "You know I can't say that. If I printed that, nobody would watch my show and I would lose all my advertising."

Okay, you're like, "All right, I got it."

I'm not whining at the media for any of our failures, but I guess I would pose the question, what if the media really wanted us to be successful? How would that change their reporting? And I certainly think they do want us to be successful. I do think they want democracy, I do think they want economic opportunity. I do think it would be difficult to discern that from their reporting.

Wheeler: When you say media, Western or Arabic?

Neller: Any. It is somewhat ironic that on the Arabic media, you watch, and [they have] very attractive young Arabic women announcing the news, [yet] when there is an Islamic caliphate, they'll all be home, burka'd up, having children. And they can't see that.

Wheeler: Given all that you just described, sir, is there an answer in the IO campaign?

Neller: I don't know. I think you just try to reach out, like we've tried to reach out aggressively with the media, to try to tell your story, try to get them to be balanced and fair. It's the way you report. I had a reporter with me, and we went out and saw the police out west, talked to him about all the increase in police and how many there were. We went to a police station, and obviously they had concerns. It's a young police force. And I thought it was a great story, and, hey, al Anbar police are increasing by X thousand. All he wanted to talk about was one guy said he had a pay problem. That's all he wanted to talk about in the whole article. Very discouraging. But that's the risk you take. They're going to see the world from where they sit. . . . So that was a teaching point.

Wheeler: And in the end, obviously, he printed the story that focused on the negative as opposed to the . . .

Neller: That was my opinion. He would probably disagree with that. And the next day, he wrote another story which was a little more positive. We're not Pollyannaish out here. There are good things going on, good things for the Iraqi people and the Iraqi nation. You don't hear that that often. There's certainly enough problems that you could keep busy reporting on that, if that was your propensity to do.

Wheeler: Is there more that we could be doing to try to shape that? As you said, you can kind of show both sides, and they're going to pick what they're going to pick, but is there more that we can be doing from an IO standpoint to steer that?

Neller: I don't know. We put out all the IO messages and flyers and public pronouncements. If no one's going to pick them up, and no one's going to print them, and no one's going to read them, they don't have the effect they should have. If you put them on your own TV or radio station, and no one watches it because they think it's propaganda, you're not having effects.

Wheeler: You mentioned before, sir, that the primary medium in the Arab world is verbal. Some would argue that the greatest IO tool that we have is the individual Marine out on patrol, talking to people in the neighborhood. Has there been a broader effort to focus that as an IO tool, from your perspective, . . . to harness the power of all those individual squads out there?

Neller: That's part of why you have to go out on the streets. You have to put a face on us. You have to put a face on the occupier. If all they see is guys driving by all buttoned up in Humvees with machine gun turrets, and everybody's got their sunglasses on, it just fulfills that perception. But our inability to speak really hurts us. There's risk when you go out and talk to the local people. I wish we did more of it. I wish we were down at the al Anbar University teaching a class on civics, but unfortunately, that hasn't been achievable through security.

The most effective tool we have is the kindness, and the compassion, and the discipline, and the courage of Marines and soldiers and sailors. But unfortunately, most of the time they're doing operational things where it's kill, capture, do another op.

Interview 12
*Partnering with the
Tribes in Ramadi*

Colonel Sean B. MacFarland, USA

Commanding Officer
1st Brigade Combat Team
1st Armored Division, U.S. Army
Multi National Force • North

January 2006-June 2006

Multi National Force • West

June 2006 to February 2007

Colonel Sean B. MacFarland is a career Army cavalry and armor officer who served in Operations Desert Shield and Desert Storm. His 1st Brigade Combat Team, 1st Armored Division, the "Ready First," spent six months in west Ninewa Province as part of Multi National Force North before moving to Ramadi to serve under the control of I Marine Expeditionary Force (Forward). Colonel MacFarland's brigade had a battalion of Marines (1st Battalion, 6th Marines), a Marine boat unit (Dam Support Unit 3, 1st Platoon, comprised of Marines from 4th Light Armored Reconnaissance Battalion), and a Marine detachment from 4th Civil Affairs Group under his command.

In this interview, Colonel MacFarland describes the changes during the brigade's tenure in Ramadi associated with the Awakening movement. He discusses the strategies employed to develop the Iraqi security forces in his area, as well as their growing independence. He also describes the joint nature of his command and the successful collaboration between elements of all services.

Colonel MacFarland was interviewed by Lieutenant Colonel Kurtis P. Wheeler on 13 December 2006 at Camp Ramadi, Iraq.

Lieutenant Colonel Kurtis P. Wheeler: Once you assumed control of the battlespace, what was your focus, initially? What were your first objectives in AO [area of operation] Topeka?

Colonel Sean B. MacFarland: When I got here, my first priority was to complete the isolation of the city.* There were still too many ways into the city for insurgents. And shortly after we got here, Abu Musab al Zarqawi was killed, and we decided that we would jump over the next phase of the operations, which was shaping, which was developing the Iraqi security forces and growing them, and go straight to decisive operations, which meant installing combat outposts throughout the city with what Iraqi army and Iraqi police we had, which at the time was not a lot.

So it became a matter of necessity being the mother of invention, where we were kind of deliberate and seized one neighborhood at a time rather than seizing numerous combat outposts in one fell swoop. Of course, the limiting factor there was availability of barrier materials, material handling equipment, and engineers to install all these COPs [combat outposts]. But in June [2006], we began that process, and then we just basically did shaping operations in parallel with our decisive operations. General [George W.] Casey [Jr., USA] and General [Peter W.] Chiarelli [USA] came down here, and we were able to make a good case for retaining five maneuver task forces in Ramadi.

We were able to maintain that momentum, which is a good thing, because the fruits of those operations are only now just being realized as, one by one, the local tribes are beginning to flip from either hostile to neutral or neutral to friendly. And that's been probably one of the most decisive aspects of what we've done here, is bringing those tribes onto our side of the fence. That has enabled us to massively accelerate Iraqi police recruiting, from 20 to 30 a month to routinely 700 guys will show up, of whom we'll take 400, because a lot of them are illiterate or have bad ID cards. But they'll come back the next month with the right ID cards, and they'll get in the next month.

And then the tribes have formed a group, called the al Anbar Rescue Committee by some. They call it the Awakening, the Sahwa

---

* Initiated under 2d Brigade, 28th Infantry Division (Pennsylvania National Guard), at the direction of I Marine Expeditionary Unit (Forward).

al Anbar. And this group has initially begun actively targeting al Qaeda in their tribal areas while sending off their military age males to serve in the Iraqi police forces and have now begun integrating themselves into the provincial government. So that's all been very exciting, and we've been working with them.

They've also begun forming Emergency Response Units, which we're still grappling with the support issues, and command and control, and a whole host of questions. But it's the kind of problems that you want to have, because now we have more friendly forces than we almost know what to do with. When we got down here, we were kind of alone and unafraid. So we have an embarrassment of riches, so to speak.

Wheeler: How does that pose challenges in itself, sir, almost controlling some of these newfound forces that you have, who aren't necessarily 100 percent on the same sheet?

MacFarland: Well, one of the things, like I said, shaping operations, we had to do in parallel with our decisive operations. And up north I was responsible for the entire 3d Iraqi Army Division, partnered with me, plus a brigade of border troops. So I had four brigades, plus a division, that I was working with up there. And we had a number of programs in place up there to train their officers, develop their command and control, and their division level troops, and provide kind of finishing school type training for their junior officers, actually all the soldiers and police. What that gave them is the ability to stand up and fight a little better than the average Iraqi army soldier or Iraqi policeman. Iraqi police come back from Jordan trained, but not trained to fight in an urban environment, in a paramilitary role. So we give them that training, and we have not had a single Iraqi police station or Iraqi police squad defeated, overrun. In fact, they routinely destroy suicide VBIEDs [vehicle borne improvised explosive devices] at standoff distances. I'd venture to say that the Iraqi police have killed more suicide VBIED drivers than suicide VBIED drivers have killed Iraqi policemen, since we have been here.

We transported a lot of those programs down here. We run our own training camp here on Camp Ramadi, called Camp Phoenix.

And we put about 100 or so either police or soldiers, Iraqi army soldiers, through it each week. It's run by my artillery battalion. Over time, they've trained up a cadre of Iraqi army NCOs [noncommissioned officers] who actually do most of the hands on training for both army and police, which is good, because that builds up police army cooperation from jump street. And then of course we've reached out to the 7th IA [Iraqi Army] Division and the brigade MTT's [military transition teams]. And we have a number of embed programs and combined targeting meetings, and so forth and so on, which has really built up the partnership at the command and control level.

More importantly, when I put out a combat outpost, it's never—well, I shouldn't say *never*—but it's usually a U.S. company with an Iraqi army company living in the same buildings, eating the same chow, and operating side by side. And that has tremendously accelerated the professionalism of the Iraqi army, when you have a one to one partnership experience like that. It's almost one soldier, one Marine, per *jundi* [Iraqi soldier], in some cases more than one soldier or Marine per *jundi*. And now it's sometimes soldiers and Marines, *jundis* and *shirta* [Iraq police officer]—police, Iraqi army, and U.S., all living under the same roof, operating together. That really mitigates any challenges that I might have had with dealing with the Iraqi army because they're living cheek by jowl with my own soldiers, who I have very good control over. So that's one of the ways that we've done that.

Over time, we have turned over a number of these combat outposts to Iraqi army control and then have turned to purely Iraqi police control, once we have beaten down the enemy resistance to the point where the army alone, or the army with the police, or just the police alone, can handle it all by themselves. So they go through a confidence building period, and then we move out. And in those combat outposts, we have well established leadership, and there's never really a problem with controlling them.

Wheeler: What do you see as the next phase of that type of approach here in Ramadi?

MacFarland: Well, we'll just continue doing more of the same. We have the ink spot strategy. All of the ink spots haven't connected up with one another yet and completely covered Ramadi, like the Sherwin Williams commercial, where the paint covers the globe. We're working toward that end state, but as the tribes come over to our side, more and more, they want to stand up some sort of security force presence in their own tribal areas, to keep al Qaeda out of there. And so, over time, what I expect is because of the great acceleration we've had in Iraqi police recruiting, is the city of Ramadi will be predominantly patrolled by Iraqi police, with Iraqi army really only in selected locations, mostly outside of the city. Then outside of the city, we'll have army and police working together, wherever al Qaeda tries to establish a safe haven. And of course our role will diminish over time.

Wheeler: Is there a problem, or is there a gray area between tribal militia and heavy tribal recruiting of IPs [Iraqi police]? Have you sensed any . . .

MacFarland: There was a crossover point. When the tribes began to work with us, they began sending their young men off to Iraqi police training. The first combat outposts, or IP stations we stood up were in the tribal heartland so that the IPs that were going off to Jordan for training didn't have to worry about the safety of their loved ones while they were serving as police. After they sent off about 600 or 700 guys to training, they said, you know, we need to take a knee for about a month until some of these guys start coming back from training, because it's about a three to four month turnaround, because they needed to keep enough of their tribal militia folks around them to secure their families. Once we had that crossover point, which I think was in September [2006], we were back up to 400 recruits being shipped per month, and there's been no turning back since then. So we're up to about two thirds of our quota here of police, and we'll keep on pressing. The tribal militias, to an extent, have been absorbed into the Iraqi security forces, which is what we wanted, either the Iraqi police or now the newly established ERUs [emergency response units] are really what used to be tribal militia.

Wheeler: Could you describe the capabilities of the ERUs?

MacFarland: I wish I could. They're just still standing up. Very limited weaponry. They seem to be well disciplined, but they just don't have a lot of equipment at all. I mean, as you would expect. These guys are just kind of right off the farm.

Wheeler: Sir, as you look back on your experience here, what are some of the most vivid memories you have, throughout your tour, but especially your time here in AO Topeka?

MacFarland: Well, we've had a couple of interesting days here. One of them I would say would be the 24th of July, which was the first and really only massively synchronized counterattack that the enemy was able to mount, where we had I think 20 some attacks in less than half an hour and all five maneuver battalions were in contact at the same time. The enemy paid a price for that. We killed about 30 of them and lost two of our own, but that was probably the most significant resistance that we've met since we've been here. Since then, enemy resistance has been on a steady decline.

Another very memorable thing was the day that I went into Sheikh Sattar's house, where they were kind of holding their "Philadelphia convention," writing their manifesto, and forming the Awakening. I felt like I was kind of on the ground floor of an historic moment there.

Another memorable day, which unfortunately I was traveling back from R&R leave—it was very frustrating—was the day the tribes in the [Jadellah] Sofia stood up to al Qaeda and we had to rush to their assistance. And since then, we've been very active up in the Sofia area. But I know I'm not going in chronological sequence here. Also, the very beginning of our operations, where we, the first thing we did was we opened up the railway bridge on the south side of Ramadi, and pushed a company across there, and established our first combat outpost [COP Iron]. It felt a little bit like crossing the Rubicon. There was no turning back at that point.

Lots of memorable days, a lot of good ones, some bad ones, [like] when I lost two officers and we lost six soldiers and Marines in one day on the 5th of December. We were in contact right up until midnight, all across the AO, and I think almost every battalion task force had a KIA [killed in action] that day, with the exception of 2/37 [2d Battalion, 37th Armored Regiment, USA], so that was pretty memorable. Having some of our important visitors, like General Casey and General Chiarelli, come down here and suddenly realize that Ramadi is not an unrelenting source of bad news, that there really is progress being made here, and watching them experience that revelation. That's pretty interesting and rewarding. From that, we've been able to get the resources that we've needed to continue to make progress down here.

Wheeler: Along those lines, has it been frustrating to you to be doing so many positive things here and not see very much of that show up on the network news back in the States?

MacFarland: I don't care if it shows up on the news or not, as long as the newsmakers understand what's going on, the higher echelons, the chain of command. It's amazing how little of our story gets out as far as Baghdad. Our higher headquarters in Baghdad, I think the commanders understand when they come out and they see it, but so much of what we're doing here is being filtered at the staff level that it gets lost. I had a reporter in here earlier today, and I was explaining to him how we're flipping these tribes one by one, and I said the thing people don't understand in the States, and you see it in the Baker Hamilton Report, is this underlying assumption that Baghdad is Iraq and that the [Shi'a] are monolithic. Well, Baghdad is an important part of Iraq, but they are no more representative of the rest of Iraq than New York City is of the rest of New York state. You can have a totally different dynamic outside of Baghdad than you have in Baghdad. There's no sectarian violence here. There are no sects. There's one sect— Sunni—so where is all the violence coming from?

We had sectarian violence when I was up in Tal Afar. We had Sunnis and Shi'as. There, my biggest problem was keeping the Sunnis from killing the Shi'a. Here, my biggest problem is to keep al Qaeda from killing the IPs. The IPs are absolutely the center of gravity here, and al Qaeda recognizes them as their greatest threat, so they tend to go after the IPs, which is why I invest so much in training them. And I'll tell you that, as a nation, we've invested far more in the training of the Iraqi army than we have in the Iraqi police, and 2006 was supposed to be the year of the police. Look at the Iraqi army MTT [military transition] teams, headed by full colonels, lieutenant colonels, 11 guys per battalion. When I got out here, the provincial PTT [police transition] team consisted of one U.S. Army major, Chemical Corps. He wasn't even an MP [military police], with really no staff. And again, an entire police district like Ramadi, we put one MP company, headed up by a captain.

And really, we're authorized as many police here, almost as many police as we are army, over 3,400 police in Ramadi. And where are all the full colonels, and the lieutenant colonels, and the majors, and the captains that are supposed to be lining up with these Iraqi police brigadier generals and major generals, like we do with the Iraqi army? They're not here. They're nowhere. We never really put our money where our mouth was on the Iraqi police, so we have formed out of hide some PTT programs and teams that have, I think, borne some fruit. But if you don't do something like that, you're not going to really make any headway on the police side. So it's painful, it's out of hide, and all that kind of stuff, but it's been worth it. . . .

Wheeler: Your command, sir, this is a great example of a joint enterprise. Can you talk a little bit about some of the joys and challenges of that experience?

MacFarland: Well, I'll tell you, first of all, it frustrates me somewhat that this is not recognized as a joint unit. We work for a Marine headquarters [I MEF]. I have a Marine battalion [1st Battalion, 6th Marines]. I have a Marine boat unit here [Dam Support Unit 3, 1st Platoon, comprised of Marines from 4th Light Armored Reconnaissance Battalion]. I've got Marines on my staff. I've got Navy on my staff. I've got Air Force on my staff. I've got Navy doctors. I've got a Navy Catholic chaplain. I've got a Marine PAO [public affairs officer] and a Marine now S 9 [engagements/governance officer] to replace the Army S 9 who was killed [Captain Travis L. Patriquin, USA]. . . .

But because there's no JMD [joint manning document] for this brigade that authorizes a certain service for a certain position, it's not considered a joint organization. We have [U.S. Marine] ANGLICO [air naval gunfire liaison company] on the staff. You walk around, you see the mix of uniforms everywhere you go. We have [U.S. Navy] SEALs that work with us. I call them Army SEALs because they wear Army combat uniforms and they're so well integrated, living with us out at the combat outpost, and we work so well together that I've adopted them. They like it. But it's been great. We've got SeaBees [U.S. Navy Construction Battalions] working with us. We had an Army engineer company commander putting in COP Firecracker for the Marines. He had three platoons out there. He had an Army engineer platoon. He had a SeaBee platoon and a Marine sapper platoon out there working together on that project. That's "joint" at the lowest possible level. We have Army tank platoons attached to Marine companies, and Marine companies attached to Army infantry battalions, and on and on and on, and Marine ANGLICO guys working as JTACs [joint tactical air controllers].

So it's been great. The Marines and Army each bring their own capabilities to the table, and the Marines have helped me out with some kit that I don't have, and I've helped out the Marines with some kit that they don't have. It's been a very fruitful partnership.

Interview 13
Counterinsurgency in Central Ramadi, Part I

Lieutenant Colonel William M. Jurney

Commanding Officer
1st Battalion, 6th Marines

Assigned to 1st Brigade Combat Team
1st Armored Division, U.S. Army

I Marine Expeditionary Force (Forward)

September 2006 to May 2007

Lieutenant Colonel William M. Jurney assumed command of 1st Battalion, 6th Marines, in October 2004, ultimately commanding the battalion for nearly three years, including a tour in Fallujah following Operation al Fajr. During its September 2006 to May 2007 deployment, 1st Battalion, 6th Marines, served in central Ramadi under the U.S. Army's 1st Brigade Combat Team, 1st Armored Division, which fell under I Marine Expeditionary Force Command as part of Multi National Force West.

In this interview, Lieutenant Colonel Jurney describes the mission of 1st Battalion, 6th Marines, and the focus on three primary lines of operation. He details the battalion's approach to partnering with Iraqi security forces and the use of augmentation teams in addition to military transition teams and police transition teams. He outlines the battalion's strategy to protect the government center area and the role of security stations in the area of operations as well as the critical role of information operations in creating a perception of stability in the city.

Lieutenant Colonel Jurney was interviewed by Lieutenant Colonel Kurtis P. Wheeler on 17 February 2007 at Camp Hurricane Point, Ramadi, Iraq.

Lieutenant Colonel Kurtis P. Wheeler: As you arrived here for your second tour, what did you see as the mission for 1/6 [1st Battalion, 6th Marines] in this area of operations?

Lieutenant Colonel William M. Jurney: Overall, our mission was to improve the security and stability of the area we were responsible for, so that's what I perceived as our mission. By doing that, we would then facilitate the continued progression of both the Iraqi security forces taking greater responsibility and control along with the local leaders in the area and their appointed and elected officials and the government's role.

Wheeler: So, taking that broad mission, how did you begin to marshal your resources and forces to accomplish that?

Jurney: Well, across the board, I think we focused on what I would call three lines of operations in our battalion. First and foremost is to neutralize those criminal and terrorist threats that would choose to do us harm. You can do that by killing or capturing them. Second would be a focus on not so much training, but employing the Iraqi security forces. And employing is training to us. So we're not running a boot camp type of rudimentary training regime here, we're employing right along side with the Iraqi security forces, and that's both Iraqi police and Iraqi army. And third was conducting those operations in support of civil affairs units, CMO [civil military operations], that not only provide for essential services for the people, which brings their life back to a sense of normalcy, but you also want to do those in such a way as to give you a tactical advantage, which leads back to neutralizing the insurgency and, more importantly, also supporting the elected and appointed officials and the Iraqi security force in that you want the populace to gain a new found trust and confidence in them.

So the objective here is, . . . the key terrain is the population and in securing that population, i.e., improving the security and stability. We're gonna focus our attention on those three lines of operation. We say that we execute those concurrently, not in a linear sense. We talk about clear, hold, and build. I will tell you that we don't specifically follow clear, hold, and build. I mean, you can conduct civil military operations which set conditions for kinetic neutralization of the insurgency. It's one street, one block at a time. What's interesting in that respect is that it's in different degrees. We think you pursue all three lines of operation concurrently, not a step at a time.

The difference is understanding that it depends on which area you're in. In one area of our AO [area of operation], you may be conducting a significant amount of civil military operations and getting a lot of success out of that. In another area, you may simply be discussing with key leaders future projects, economic and social development. But I don't think you should give up on any line of that operation. No matter how bad the enemy threat is in a particular area, some people might argue, well, you gotta go in and clear those enemy [insurgents] out first, and then you can begin rebuilding. I would argue against that. I agree that the security situation may not allow contractors or SeaBees [construction battalions] to actually go in and repair a water main, or a sewage line, or something of that nature. But that would not prevent me from engaging local leaders in that particular area in a discussion about how we're going to do that, and what we need to do in order to achieve that, and what benefits to them and their *wasta* [respect, clout] and the people around them are. That's my policy on how we were going to approach improving security and stability in our area of responsibility as we saw it. . . .

Wheeler: One of the aspects that's impressed me as I've travelled across your AO is the degree to which your ISF [Iraqi security forces] are partnered with, working with, living with your companies, your forces out in the battlespace. How have you gone about creating that circumstance, and what's been your approach there?

Jurney: It was a stated mission essential task that we undertake actions to accelerate, expand, employ the Iraqi security forces. We don't want to come back. So if we're not going to come back, we're going to have to get them stood up, moving forward in greater degrees, taking responsibility for their own security. It's an order, first and foremost. How you go about doing that? I think you'll probably see varying approaches to it. Our experience has been that if you live with, plan with, execute with [the Iraqis], you stand a greater chance of success—success being defined as their progressive increase in responsibility and leading to independent actions. So that's the end state.

A lot of times, it's built on relationships. I mean, I get my Iraqi counterpart to extend his responsibilities or undertake actions that quite frankly are dangerous, that he would prefer not to do, sometimes simply because he doesn't wanna let me down, or because we've become friends. And he doesn't wanna do it, but he's gonna do it. I mean, I'm not opposed to their being repercussions with milestones, and I'm not talking on the political level, but when an Iraqi unit has the capability to take the next step, there are many times when they will look at you [and say], "I don't want to." I mean, why should they do more? Why should they put themselves at greater danger? Why should they work harder and impede their leave, when they know we're gonna do it? So quite frankly, as we're absolutely partnered with them, I give them the shirt off my back. And when I say, "Now I need you to do something," I expect them to do it. And if they don't, then there will be repercussions. I'll call off support to 'em.

I've never asked an Iraqi soldier to do something that I wouldn't or couldn't do, or my Marines themselves. I mean, they can see right through that. It's simply [that] you wouldn't ask another Marine unit to go into harm's way in a situation that they're not capable of handling. And we all do that. I move Iraqi soldiers around the battlefield under the same protection as Marines. We eat the same chow, attempt to live together. So we're building this together. I show them the same respect as a lieutenant colonel, or colonel, or whatever their rank is. We openly discuss options for moving forward.

The other part of this is we're taking advantage of a strength here. As we pursue our lines of operation, I mean, you would no sooner attack the old hill without the proper fire support planned in advance, so why would you approach this situation without taking full advantage of all the strengths? Iraqi police who are Sunni, and live here, and can see a terrorist a mile away, who have there own ability to do indigenous R&S [reconnaissance and surveillance], which we have them moving around in plain clothes, undercover, coordinated, validating targets on a regular basis for us, where no American could go or uncover the information that they are. I mean, you should take full advantage of that.

In order to do that, your operations have to be synchronized with them. Some people will argue there are risks associated with that. I agree, there are risks. There is some high value targeting information that we do not share with them. But there is other intelligence information that we do share, that there are risks of the target getting away, or risks to our Marines. But you're never going to move forward if you're not working in a combined sense with their operations and intelligence sections. So that's been our approach to it, in addition to, we say we're a combined action battalion. You hear about the old CAP platoons [combined action platoons] of Vietnam. We are a combined action battalion. . . . We provide an 11 man MTT team, you know, military transition team. That was an "A" team we put together. All those guys were on the last deployment with us.

If I could invest $11 in the stock market and get nearly $500 back, that would be a pretty good investment. So for providing 11 quality Marines and a sailor to our MTT team, in return I've got an Iraqi battalion of about 550 personnel who can now be effectively—or more effectively—employed. That's a pretty good investment, or bang for your buck. So we did that. Secondly, when people ask what else are you doing to support the Iraqi security force—"have you put any more people with your MTT team?"—I would say "yeah, about a thousand." Everybody in this battalion, if you look at my original intent, no one says "no" to the Iraqi police or Iraqi army unless there is a damn good reason for it because that's why we're here.

We partner down, you have to partner down to the platoon level. A MTT team is 11 guys. It's set up to advise a battalion staff. Now when you assess the battalion that you're partnered with, it may require partnership down at the company and the platoon level. A MTT team is not manned to provide that. And when you piecemeal two guys from the MTT team, and you put them down at the company level, now you've hurt your opportunities for developing the logistics, sustainment and C2 of that Iraqi army battalion when you do that. So it's the responsibility of the partnered U.S. battalion to pick up that relationship, training, and deployment. Or that's our sense of it.

So for that reason, you see Iraqi companies co located with Marine companies, and there is a partner relationship that exists company commander to company commander, platoon commanders to platoon commanders, you know, *jundi* [individual soldier] to our team leaders and lance corporals. And pretty soon, the training that is occurring is nothing more than mimicking. You see how it is to be done correctly from pre combat checks and inspections to execution. Pretty soon you then can transition to supported and supporting relationships. For example, in Alpha Company is the supported company, and the Iraqi army is supporting them in a raid or a cordon and search. A month into it, you should be able to change that relationship, and the Iraqi army company is now the supported and Alpha Company is supporting. So that would be a progression.

That may have been more than you were interested to hear about military transition teams and training. I'm pretty disgusted when I watch TV and I hear people say, "We need to do more to train the Iraqi army." I want to ask them to define it, define what training is. What the hell are you talking about? These guys are absolutely capable, the ones we are working with, to conduct security operations. Now, do they need specialized training if you want them to develop EOD [explosive ordnance disposal], boat, special ops? Sure. But day in and day out, they can conduct security operations. Their greatest limitation right now is manning. I mean, an Iraqi battalion is about 850 people. It's only manned at about 550. And then when you take that 550, and you send one third of it on leave at any one time, you're only working with about a 300 man unit. [With] 15 guys in an Iraqi platoon, there's no way they're going to assume battlespace. And then when you send another third on leave while they're swapping out, two thirds of that Iraqi undermanned battalion is gone. No way they're going to achieve any level of independence until they overcome the manning issue. . . .

Wheeler: What types of functions are being performed by your augmentation teams down with your Iraqis? What types of tasks are you asking them to do to be a force multiplier, to make the Iraqis more effective?

Jurney: The short answer is, they're there to facilitate employment—operational and employment focus. That's what our augmentation teams are there for. Typically, a PTT team [police transition team], those guys, they've got a [lot] of paperwork they've got to do. They're accounting for gear, they've got higher headquarter reports. . . . And what's most important to me? Employment and operational focus. And it has to be synchronized with all the other efforts that are ongoing in the battlespace. The police force that operates in this AO, the police, the Iraqi army, and the Coalition force all have to try and work as one element. So that augmentation team there is the focus on that employment piece of it. So he's not necessarily inundated with those other tasks. More importantly, I will tell you, in the police, we have eight Marines who live in the police stations 24 7, which didn't happen beforehand. When there's time sensitive information that comes into a police station, which it does, there is a fleeting target of opportunity. Typically a police force couldn't move on that because they'd be afraid they'd get shot by Coalition forces, at night, moving around. . . . Now with Marines living there 24 7, you know they're going to pick up.

I sat down with the police chiefs with the Iraqi army and said, "all we have to do is coordinate. We're all three trying to do the same things. Sometimes we're going to do them together, sometimes we're going to do them independent. But every time, we're going to do them, and they're going to be coordinated so we don't shoot each other." Pretty simple stuff, they all understand that. They say, "Very good, we don't want to do that. You're right, this has been a problem in the past." So now they just pick up the radio [and] my augmentation team chief says [that] the police want to go to this sector to execute this mission. I'm able to provide him with up to date intelligence; "okay the route's clear, there's not an IED [improvised explosive device] there," or there is one there. I'm trying to protect them just the same I would a Marine unit. What does the police chief need? Does he need casevac [casualty evacuation]? QRF [quick reaction force] support? I've got fixed wing overhead. I'll provide you up to date information on what our ISR [intelligence, surveillance, reconnaissance] assets are seeing, all of which enable his mission to be successful, which at the end of the day, if we're capturing and killing bad guys, it's a win for the whole team.

So that's what our augmentation teams are doing on a full time basis down there. They have the trust, and respect, and friendship of those that they work with because they live there 24 7. And those relationships facilitate expanding and accelerating that particular ISF element's employment. You just can't show up every now and then and expect to get anything. I'm not some cultural guru, but it just doesn't work that way.

Wheeler: The next question I have is how you, basically, evolved this battlespace during the time that you've been here. You fell in on a situation where most of the preceding battalions' forces were focused here on the western side, closer to Hurricane Point. Talk about how that's changed over time from the initial layout of your forces to what it is today and how that's happened.

Jurney: You always go back to "think like the enemy." Operations have to be enemy focused, not reduction of internal friction. If I were the enemy, you have the provincial government center of all al Anbar Province in the middle of our AO. If I were the bad guy, every other day, if I can go down with only two insurgents, empty a magazine and shoot at the government center, then I get great press out of that. And the press is, "Al Anbar Province is defunct, the government center is under siege, there is no progress, there is no stability." What an economy of force for an insurgency. To be strong everywhere is to be weak everywhere. I don't have to be strong all over al Anbar Province, I just need two guys to shoot at the government center and it looks like I'm kicking everybody's ass in al Anbar Province. So that was my assessment. If I'm here to facilitate eventual provincial control—Iraqi control—then you've got to be able to go to the government center without getting blown up.

Having said that, a deliberate operation was not going to happen in one week or one month. You can't rush to failure given the threat of IEDs and sub surface IEDs. So we started one block at a time, and then basically we just started clearing from west to east. You provide for your own secure LOCs [lines of communication], and when you clear an area, you stay there. If you go in and you wreak havoc for two or three days and you leave, well, the bad guys are just going to come back. People aren't going to help you. Everything is driven by information. The first question the people are going to ask you is, "When are you leaving?" You've got to show them you're not going to leave. I mean, if they tell you things and then you leave, they're going to be dead. So it's got to be based on permanent presence.

So we started clearing areas, seizing terrain. We established a secure facility. That secure facility enables introduction, full time, of Iraqi security forces. It all builds on itself. Iraqi police and Iraqi army don't have the enablers to put up Jersey and T barriers in a hostile area, so they're going to sit out on the periphery and never go down where it's dangerous. I happen to believe that there should be shared hardship and shared danger. This is their country. But in order to move them into that portion of battlespace, they [should] take part in a combined operation to clear it. They take part in a combined operation to build the facility, fill the sandbags, build the positions, and then they live there with you.

So we've moved basically from west to east in that clearing evolution. It's all conducted, like I said, consistent along all three lines of operation. . . . We coined the name "security station" because a "combat outpost" don't sound like things are getting back to normal. So we told people we were building police stations. Our permanent positions are future police stations. And so we called them security stations. So now they're combined security stations, some of which will, in fact, be police stations. They're obviously manned by police now. Soon thereafter, you want to start providing for essential services in and around those security stations. I mean, "okay, that's great, you just came in, you ran off the bad guys, I appreciate that. Now what else is in it for me?" And that's where, as we were conducting these operations, CERP [Commander's Emergency Response Program] projects, CMO, economic development, opportunities for jobs and improved essential services closely followed to the tune of almost $3 million worth of projects now that are ongoing. So pretty soon, you have people on the other side of town going, "When are we going to get some of that?" Well, as soon as you start taking an active role in helping us help you, then as you can see, good things and good opportunities start presenting themselves. So now you're leveraging CMO. Even though you may not be building, you're still leveraging that line of operation to neutralize the insurgency. . . .

Wheeler: As you've moved from west to east, right now, the sort of forward edge, as you mentioned before, the enemy's FLOT [forward line of troops] has been pushed out now to the Qatana area. What's next on the horizon during the remaining time that you have here?

Jurney: Well, as you know, we were extended an anticipated 60 to 90 days, but I think it's only going to be about 45. I'll turn the clock back just a little bit. When we first got here, our advanced party was composed of myself, my company commanders, and my primary staff. We came on the advanced party because once you TOA [transfer of authority], you need to be in the execution mode, not the find your head from your ass mode. One of the things we did is we established a 120 day plan, called a four block plan, which had some significant milestones set against time, although they were conditions based and event driven. It was our glide path to accomplish the things we just talked about, which led us up to about January the 12th. And all of the things we've discussed were on the plan and were, quite frankly, were achieved.

When we received notification of the extension, we sat back down as a staff and with the commanders, and we were determined not to slow roll this thing. We're going to treat it completely as a new deployment, because for all intents and purposes, it was. We put together another four block plan of what our milestones and goals were, and there were several things that were part of that. At this juncture, each one of the company commanders has a different set of circumstances in his battlespace. So I had him develop along our three lines of operation what he saw as the primary initiatives he thought should be undertaken relative to neutralizing the insurgency, employing/expanding the ISF, CMO, and IO [information operations]. If you've noticed, everything we do is relative to those three things. . . .

Just off the top, I would say that one of the major initiatives that's a part of this will be to increase the Iraqi security force, and I say ISF because that includes both IA [Iraqi army] and IP [Iraqi police]. We're going to increase their taking the lead by at least 25 percent. And I think that's absolutely doable in really what is the three fully operational months that we have available before we start turning over battlespace. So that's our focus. You basically have to take a month to socialize that plan. I mean you can develop a plan, you develop it with the Iraqis, you've got to let them think about it, it's going to take two weeks, and then you're going to implement it. You're going to develop, socialize it, plan for it—that's going to take you a month. I mean, things take time. Then you're going to implement it. And then once you implement it, then what's real important to us is to basically, as always, you're assessing and revising. It's constant; it's never ending. It's a thinking man's game. But we have to assess and revise that plan so that it's steady state, more of an enduring task for the ISF before our replacement gets here. In other words, we're not going to implement a good idea right before our replacements get here and go, "Hey, check out we did. Why don't you go ahead. We set you up for success, you can go ahead and smooth this out." We want it to be smoothed out, fully functional, kind of the expected, the norm, prior to them getting here. So that's probably the major initiative that we're undertaking.

Wheeler: How do you measure that 25 percent shift to ISF lead?

Jurney: Well, you can measure it by the operations and the enduring tasks that are ongoing. It could be as simple as, at this particular site, for example, if you have 25 percent less Marines standing post, that's pretty measurable. If you have the Iraqi army conducting 25 percent more dismounted patrols then they were previously, that's very measurable. . . .

Wheeler: The last topic that I wanted to inquire about specifically is your IO piece. What's driven that? What you're doing is fairly unique in the AO. How did you conceive that and carry it out?

Jurney: I think the IO piece that you're speaking to is the broadcasts approach that we're utilizing. I think we all recognize that you can be doing great things and changing the security and stability of an area, but what really matters is what people perceive, what they think. If they don't know things are improving, then it really doesn't matter what you're doing, because their behaviors are going to be driven by what they think. The question we posed to ourselves was, how do you get the word out? How do you communicate with the populace? We simply took a look at what means were available to us, which were, you have your standard paper products, your flyers, and things of that nature. You have your standard TPT [tactical psyops team] broadcasts that go out. And our experience has been that those are not very good. So we started trying to look at other mediums that we could influence.

We have a nonkinetic effects working group here in the battalion which is headed up by the battalion XO [executive officer, Major Daniel R. Zappa]. They sort of coalesce not only the 2/3 side of the house, but an IO cell, our CMO efforts, because again, those things can achieve making the enemy less effective. So that group was tasked to basically analyze other ways in which we could do this. Amongst that meeting, we recognized, we were tasked with monitoring mosque broadcasts. Our brigade tasked us to monitor mosque broadcasts to see what messages they're putting out. And we said, holy cow, why don't we broadcast our messages? I mean, people are already conditioned, that's the way they receive information. We can do this. And so there are some systems, public announcement systems that are out there—LRAD [long range acoustic device], TacWave— we inquired about getting some of those, but in the interim, we just went to a local contractor, went to Baghdad and bought a big PA [public address] system. Our three target audiences for that are both the Iraqi police and Iraqi army, which strengthens their resolve; obviously the population; and the insurgents.

You have to make this credible, and the way we felt we could make it credible was that these broadcasts would only come from locations in which police were actually located. We created a basic cover story, which was this is the voice of Ramadi coming from the Iraqi police. Initial broadcasts were basically to desensitize the people to hearing it. They hear the national anthem, local music, we take credible information of things they are interested in off the BBC [British Broadcasting Corporation] and Jazeera, and we say thank you for listening. For several weeks, we play that, and people get used to hearing it. It's coming from a police station—this seems okay.

Then soon thereafter, we start wickering in our own PsyOps [psychological operations] products, which cause reactions by the enemy and influence the people. In addition to that, we start including the police chief, the governor, local officials to make their own announcements, which then further makes this a credible medium for transmitting information. The whole time we're doing this, it's almost like conducting marketing. We're taking focus groups, we're getting feedback, what they liked, what they didn't like, what their reactions to it were. And we're slowly modifying this to reach out and touch more people. And we expand the speakers across every fixed position where we have police, so that now we're reaching a larger audience. And the feedback we started getting was, it was well received. They said, "This is how we used to get information." We didn't even realize that they used to do more of this, so they perceive a sense of normalcy. We now have leaders coming to us wanting to make broadcasts on this system. So now it's really just taken on a whole life of its own.

We're not really having to drive, I mean, they're saying the things that we want the word to get out about in terms of areas which are secure, areas they're having trouble with and they need the peoples' help in getting rid of folks. We're also having reactive messages, which are off the shelf. If there's a firefight, it's ongoing, that says, you need to go inside for your children's safety because the insurgents are at it again. It's always turning things back onto the insurgents. You wouldn't believe the number of incidents which occur in which the people think we did it because everything works off of word of mouth and rumor and we weren't breaking into that at all. . . .

It matters what people think, what they perceive. They just started believing their area was getting safer, even if nothing changed. Now contractors started working. Shops started opening. Schools started opening. Yeah, this area is safe now, the police are here. And I'll tell you, nothing really changed. But it changed in their mind. It developed its own momentum. It's become a key tool in driving a wedge between insurgents and the population. Again, we're all after the same target. The insurgents are after the people, and so are we. They can't exist without them and their ability to blend in with them. So we're all after the same thing.

Interview 14

Counterinsurgency in
Central Ramadi, Part II

Major Daniel R. Zappa

Executive Officer
1st Battalion, 6th Marines

Assigned to 1st Brigade Combat Team
1st Armored Division, U.S. Army

I Marine Expeditionary Force (Forward)

September 2006 to May 2007

Major Daniel R. Zappa served in Iraq as the commander of Company A, 1st Battalion, 6th Marines, in Saqliwiyah, outside Fallujah, during a tour in 2004 2005. He returned to Iraq from September 2006 to May 2007 as the battalion's executive officer. The 1st Battalion, 6th Marines, was assigned to the U.S. Army's 1st Brigade Combat Team, 1st Armored Division, in support of I Marine Expeditionary Force (Forward) in central Ramadi.

While Major Zappa's commanding officer, Lieutenant Colonel William M. Jurney, concentrated on building Iraqi security forces and overseeing the battalion's kinetic efforts, Major Zappa played a key role in the battalion's engagements with Iraqi leaders and its non kinetic efforts. His work with Sheikh Abdul Satter Abu Risha and Sattar's confederation of tribes at the outset of the Awakening laid the foundation for U.S. Army Colonel Sean B. MacFarland's engagement and support of the Awakening movement.

In this interview, Major Zappa describes taking part in meetings with local sheikhs. Although 1st Brigade Combat Team, 1st Armored Division, under Colonel MacFarland took the lead in engagements with Sheikh Sattar, Major Zappa met frequently with other local sheikhs, including Sattar's brother, Ahmad Abu Risha.

Major Zappa was interviewed by Lieutenant Colonel Kurtis P. Wheeler on 17 February 2007 at Camp Hurricane Point, Ramadi, Iraq.

Lieutenant Colonel Kurtis P. Wheeler: Two of your nontraditional roles that I've heard about in my travels around the battalion are, one, chairman of the non kinetic effects working group, and second of all, a pretty significant role with sheikh and local leader engagement. Can you talk a little about each of those roles?

Major Daniel R. Zappa: I think the non kinetic effects piece is important for counterinsurgency operations. . . . It's an operations function, but it's not going to get a lot of attention unless we put someone over the top of it, and the OpsO [operations officer] has got too much to do when it comes to kinetic operations, and managing battlespace, and assets, and things like that.

So really, what it entails is once a week I get the key personnel in the non kinetic world together. It's all based off of how we can gain tactical advantage. How can we further our abilities or our influence in our battlespace? When you're doing counterinsurgency operations, the population is the terrain. So how [do] you identify what the people want, how [do] you address that, how do you solve problems together effectively and attack the perception that you are an occupier?

Our goal is not to solve all the problems in the world, but it's to make things a little bit better and to promote the Iraqi government and the Iraqi security forces, specifically the army and the police. The key is the police. It's been that way, we've seen that it's what the people respond to. It's the return to normalcy. If you're standing on the street corner in your home town, and three vehicles role by, United States Army or National Guard, you're going to get up in arms, and it's going to bother you. You're not going to have a very warm feeling about that. But if you see a police car drive down your street, it makes you feel secure, it makes you feel comfortable. You probably know that guy or have at least seen him before if it's a routine local policeman. So we promote that.

[When] we got here, we went from zero. We had no pending projects. We had no points of contact in the town. We had no civil military operations tracking. If you talk to Major [Scott J.] Kish, he'll tell you how he basically started at ground zero when it came to contracts and points of contact, who was going to get things done. So we pulled him, we pulled the intel [intelligence] officer, humint [human intelligence] officer, information operations was our Arty LnO [artillery liaison officer], the attached tactical PsyOps [psychological operations] team, public affairs, staff judge advocate, and operations officer. Those are really the primary players in this. And we just talk about the opportunities and the threats that we face in the battlefield. How are we going to address the threats to us? What are some things, outside the box things, that we can do to further our agenda? That's kind of the long and the short of it.

From this group, we'll cover the kinetic operations that are coming up and how can we support them with information, how can we let people know what we're doing? Because too often we'd see destruction in town that the insurgents could turn around and pin on us, regardless of if we caused it or not. An IED [improvised explosive device] destroys a vehicle and causes civilian casualties, it's easy for the enemy who is on the site there and speaks the language, is part of the culture, can turn that on us and say, "Well, the Americans blew up that. They blew that up. That wasn't something we did. They plant the bombs on the streets." And in this world, in the Arab world, in the Middle East, and here in Iraq, it's the rumor in the street, it's what everyone listens to. The word on the street gets out quickly. Our biggest challenge was how we addressed that, how we fight that. What do we have in our arsenal that we can put against that? One is to co opt the locals and pass the word through them. We don't have an effective telephone or Internet or television station capability here, so we had to go back to 100 years ago, 150 years ago in technology and just ask what could we do to increase the word of mouth, the good news.

We've got ECP's [entry control points] that we control. We can pass the word through the Iraqi police and the Iraqi army at the ECP's. Technologically, we've got the LRADs [long range acoustic device] that we can use and we can post information. Captain [Sean P.] Dynan, the H&S [headquarters and support] company commander, had the idea of putting big white boards at the ECPs where the Iraqi security forces can write information as it occurs up on white boards, to impact people as they drive and walk through the city. They're going to see that, and that's going to get information to them quickly.

The other thing we're attacking is perception. I mean perception of this being the most violent city in Iraq, the provincial capital is controlled by insurgents. I'm sure everyone has read about that. We did before we got here. In March and April when we were reading blogs about this place, we thought what are we getting ourselves into? They're pinned down there, and you can't do anything. Then you get here, and you realize a lot of that has to do with perceptions . . . enemy perceptions, friendly perceptions—people's perceptions. And that's what we're battling here.

So we try to manage our own information flow. How do we talk about Ramadi? How do we . . . this goes right down to the articles your PAO [public affairs officer] Marine, your corporal is writing about 1/6 in Ramadi. He doesn't write about, you won't see, the articles on the sniper engagements—even if we win the sniper engagement, even if we kill five guys with snipers—you won't see articles about 1/6 like that. You'll see articles about we met with the mayor, or we're engaging the sheikhs, or personality sketches on Lance Corporal Smith from Arkansas. You're not going to see a lot of kinetic stories coming out of here, and that's for a reason, because we're managing perceptions. I think that's pulling the curtain back a little bit on what we do. Some people might say public affairs is not information operations, but I take the other side. And I think there are a lot of people that would agree. You spend a little bit of time here and you see how important that is to shaping people's perceptions.

Wheeler: What was behind the battalion's thought process with regard to the speaker broadcasts? Where did that come from, when did you start doing it, what are the effects you've seen from that?

Zappa: Well, it was something we developed during our skull sessions in September, October, November [2006]. We really couldn't get past how do we beat the word in the street, about what's going on, how do we get information to people? And we had certain things in our arsenal, that the military provides, the loudspeaker systems, the LRADs. But we talked about it at the table. I don't know whose idea it was specifically; I know Major [Tiley R.] Nunnink pretty much picked it up and lent a lot of time and energy to shaping what the actual procedure to producing it. But it was pretty much a team effort. . . . When we were banging our heads on the table with how do we do this, I don't know if it was me or if it was somebody else who said, "Why don't we just buy the same speaker systems that they use on the mosques?" Buy the same PA [public address] systems that they use and put those up on the stations that we own, on the fixed sites that we own. And so we did. And people take to it very kindly.

The implementation and the way that it has been used to not only provide information but to effect the enemy's OODA [observe, orient, decide, act] loop by, he's now looking over his shoulder because when we put in the broadcast [things like] "thank you for your continued support of Iraqi security forces," "thank you for using the tips line," "thank you for reporting information on insurgents." The insurgent is now looking over his shoulder saying, who's reporting on me? Who's doing this? And we can tell we're having an effect with it. And by the same token, you're impacting the friendly audience and your neutral audience, conditioning them to be familiar with hearing it, they hear the Iraqi national anthem, they hear familiar voices, they hear things that people have to say to them. It's about this place getting better, the mayor, and sheikhs, and governor, and police chiefs—people who are on their side—and it gives them a little bit more faith, hopefully, in their government and in their security forces, which is all we're trying to effect.

Wheeler: The other piece that is very encouraging here is just seeing the central role which civil affairs and CMO [civil military operations] play in your battalion's overall strategy. Where has that come from?

Zappa: It comes from the boss. He makes it a priority. He outlines [that] we're going to do three things: we're going to neutralize anti Iraqi elements, we're going to train and partner with Iraqi police and Iraqi army. And when I say train, I don't mean little academies where you're teaching them to point their weapons in the right direction, they already know how to do that. I'm talking about partnership—living with them, operating with them, getting them operational. And the third thing would be to pick up and support any civil military operations, any civil operations that contribute to that return to normalcy or that construction or that impression that things are going forward and getting better. Those three things, they come straight from the boss, and that's from his vision as part of where he wants to operate. And those three lines of operation have worked, I think, for us in a good way. It also tempers a lot of things that Marines are trained to do that you can't just do wantonly in this town. You can't just be all about kinetics and killing and shooting people and talking about it, which is what we, as a culture, value.

So when you make a priority out of civil military operations, you made that a priority, you're conditioning your Marines, too, to avoid incidents that will hurt you more, and hurt you strategically. You're now sharpening the edges and taking some of the rough spots out of potential serious liabilities that impact far beyond our own AO [area of operation]. He's got a friendly audience as well, you've got several audiences he's working on, and that's one of them. I think that's part of the reason why we've been so successful. It's not just blanket leadership that keeps people from doing that, from doing bad things, or stepping outside the lines. You have to make them aware how important it is to have that right mentality, that mindset that you're not in al Fajr here, that we're not conducting the Fallujah assault. Although there are times when we are, and it goes full kinetic. And that's been evident by the statistics. We did our operations in December, in January we're like in a mini al Fajr in the middle of the city with the number of caches found, with the number of contacts, the amount of attacks, our success, the numbers of enemy killed and captured. You can look at those and say, on a microcosm, that's pretty tense. And it still is intense. That's the long answer.

Wheeler: Many battalions have spoken, during my interviews with them, about their frustrations with the "catch and release" program, and [your commander] credited a lot of your lack of frustration with that with the fact that you've just plain old killed a lot of the bad guys and the detention piece hasn't been as big.

Zappa: I think HVI [high value individual] pursuit, I don't personally, from where I sit, I don't see the results as well as some other people do, or I don't lend a lot to that. I think, especially these days, you need to empower the local population, you need to empower the policemen to take out and capture the bad guys. They know them a hell of a lot better than any of the task forces that we have do. I'm sorry to say that, but you aren't going to kill or capture every bad guy and flip this thing on its head. But you can help the Iraqi people and help the Iraqi security forces by going after maybe the key individuals or leaders, or flushing them out of the AO. Just by putting their picture up, you're impacting them. Putting them on the loudspeaker, "we're after you," is just as effective as killing them or capturing them. That's why I don't think we stress too much about that. That's my own personal feeling. You can't kill enough bad guys. I mean, we killed the number one bad guy over here, and what happened? Nothing. It got worse. You aren't going to chop the head off the snake. He's just going to sprout a new head, or maybe a couple. So that's not the way you win here. And I think that's evident in the way we do business here.

Wheeler: Is there anything else that I haven't asked you about that you think may be important to get on the record about your role here, about 1/6's approach to this battlespace, about 1/6's experience?

Zappa: I think we have great relationships with our higher headquarters. We're here with 1/1 AD [1st Brigade Combat Team, 1st Armored Division, USA] and I MEF [I Marine Expeditionary Force]. We have a lot of assets and the ability to bring things to bear materially that the Iraqi people don't, the [Iraqi] leadership doesn't. They can't get fuel, they can't get certain food items, so we go and get it for them. . . . Because of our relationship with the sheikhs, and more importantly, with the mayor—even though he is a brigade partnered key leader, he falls in our sphere because he works in our AO—we own the center of the city. We can identify, we can partner with him most effectively and most frequently, and I think because of that, we can identify needs and operate quicker. You know, if you're at the brigade level, you might not check in with the mayor every day. You may check in with the mayor once a week, maybe check in with him a couple times a week. We have the ability to do that every day, and we pretty much do.

Wheeler: You mentioned the key local leaders. How is it that you've become one of the key people, interacting with local leaders?

Zappa: It was an accident, really. The first time this happened, the JCC [Joint Coordination Center (between Iraqi army and police and Coalition forces)] is in town. There was a meeting that was allegedly going on between some tribal leaders at the JCC. The CO [commanding officer] didn't want to become involved with the tribal leaders himself, he's more along the lines of the legitimate government, you know, governor, mayor—[that is] if there is one, because this was before we had a mayor. So he sent me to link up with them. It ended up being at the Sheikh [Abdul] Sattar [Abu Risha] compound, where he and his brother live, which is not in our AO, it's on the other side of Camp Ramadi. And we ended up going there to this meeting, and we were the only Coalition forces there. There were dozens and dozens of sheikhs and important people in it. I'd been here before, and this is the most impressive group of men I've ever seen gathered in one spot. Very businesslike, there wasn't a lot of smoking cigarettes and glad handing; it was all business.

They were frustrated. They had organized, and they had decided that they were going to fight al Qaeda, and they just needed someone to start telling them that they were going to be listened to and they were going to be supported. Major Kish and I were there, [and I was] just kind of like, okay, sounds good to me, I like it. Maybe you're not talking to the right people. And brigade ended partnering more with that. But we recognized that as a spot where we could go and we really set it up with Sheikh Sattar's brother, Sheikh Ahmad [Bezia Fteikhan al Rishawi]. We said, hey, we like talking with you guys, and we think we can do business. He said, every Monday, come back. So we did. That was in early November, and we basically go there every Monday or so. Even if we don't have a lot of business, they get used to seeing us there.

One of the things it yielded is there is a multi million dollar rubble removal contract in the middle of the city of Ramadi. In front of the government center, down on Michigan, they demolished a bunch of buildings that were providing the enemy with cover and concealment to attack the government center. To deny it, they knocked all those buildings down, and there was a contract to remove all that rubble. It was in our AO, so the MEF asked us to supervise it. Well, the contractor never did anything. So we recognized that the sheikhs—Sheikh Sattar, Sheikh Ahmad—had a contracting business, and we said, hey, we might be able to get you a piece of this, and eventually, long story short, they got the whole contract. It's a difficult place to work. You're working in a former impact area, in front of the government center. But these guys have worked slow and steady and really made a dent in it down there. So that is something that we think is a small victory.

We also, we've asked them for interpreter support because we, everyone across the AO, it's difficult to find good interpreters. Based on my relationship with a guy, with an engineer who works with them, . . . he brought a guy to meet me, this former teacher, he's out of work, he lives in Fallujah, he's one of our interpreters now. . . . Because he's local and we want to protect his identity, we put him in a place where he's working just with Marines and Iraqi army. But he's making money now, because Titan [defense contractor] is paying him, and he's freed us up to continue to work with the Iraqi army and . . . with Marines there. Now we don't need an interpreter dedicated to that spot, so everybody wins. I just view this as another way to strengthen the ties with these people. It's little things like that that kept us going back.

We've also partnered with them. Through them is how we got very close with Sheikh Raad [Sabah al Alwani], who is the leader of the Abu Awan tribe, who lives in our battlespace and really has done a lot of good work. Contract wise, he finds people who will get work done, not just people who will sign the contract, take the money and run, but people who will actually do the work, [like] remove burned out vehicles from the city, which is another small cosmetic thing which increases the appearance and takes away some of the everyday IO [information operation] reminders. If you've got burned out vehicles from VBIEDs [vehicle borne improvised explosive devices] lying all over the city, that's a loss on IO because it's a reminder every time people walk by or drive by [of] who's running the town. We contracted through [Sheikh Raad] to get all those removed and clean things up around here.

Plus it's a security issue, you get those things cleaned up, there's not going to be something concealed in them. So he's turned out to be a very important, very valuable leader. And really he has done a good job, he's been very courageous in the fact that he's assumed that sheikh leadership. He's not really the senior man in that tribe, [but] the guy who was was too afraid to lead the tribe anymore, so he's basically ceded it over to Sheikh Raad, who's done a good job.

Wheeler: Is there anything else I haven't asked you about that you think would be important to get on the record here about your experiences, about 1/6's experiences?

Zappa: Be persistent. Don't rest. You're only as good as your next visit. Your relationships need to be maintained. They can't just be left to rot. People expect to see you frequently. Learn a little bit of Arabic. Learn some things beyond hello. Learn to say a couple things that they will recognize, and it will go a long way. Personal relationships are really important with working with them.

But don't forget the big picture. When it comes to dealing with the tribes, you can't sell yourself all the way on them. You have to remember that there's an elected government, there's a legitimate government, and however the two sides may fight over joint forces, you, at the end of the day, need to remember that you're on the side of Iraqi government, so they may or may not be as effective at leading the people. But the tribes have to be subordinate to the governor and the mayor.

2007

The Awakening Turns the Tide

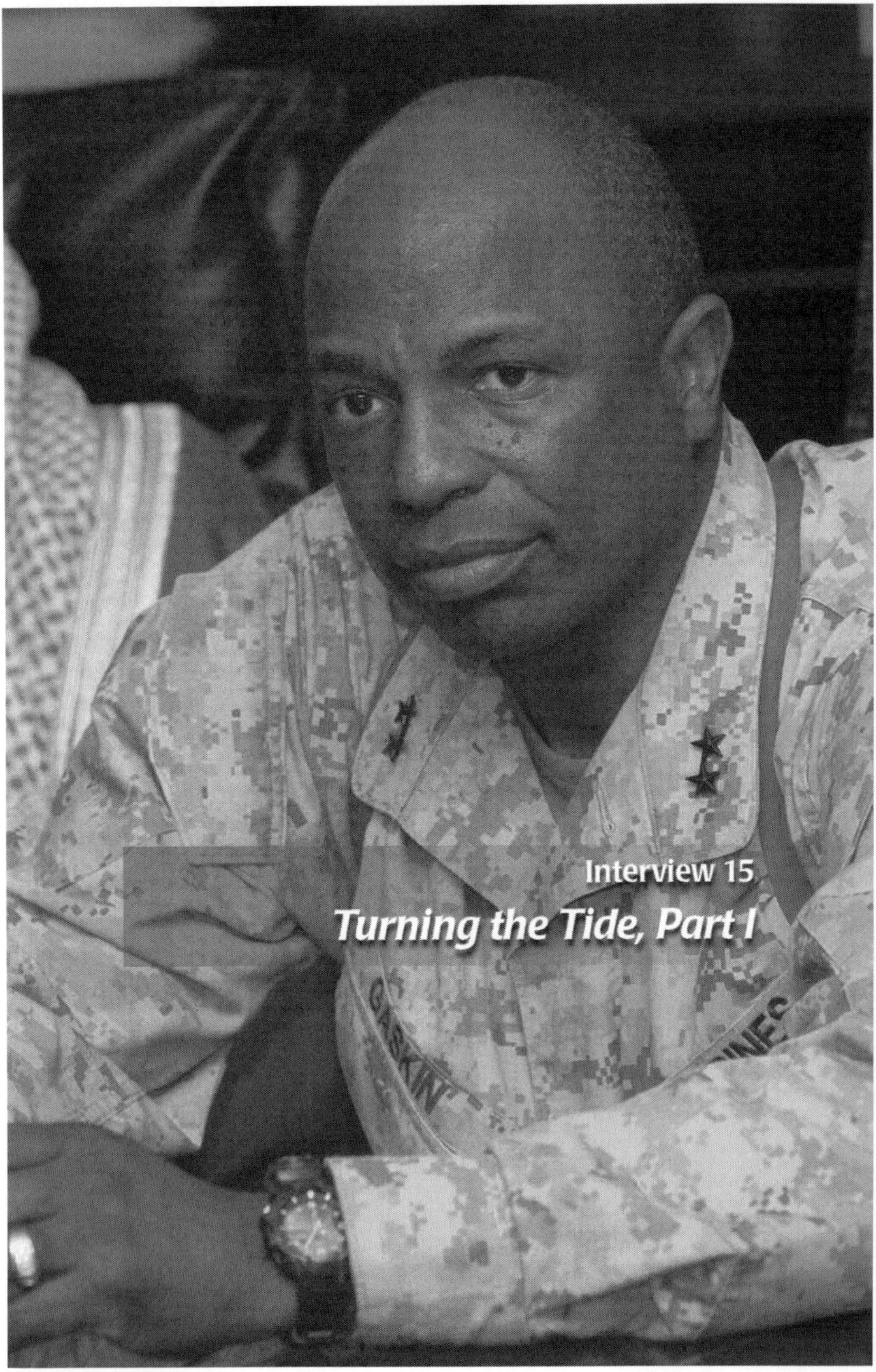

Interview 15

Turning the Tide, Part I

Major General Walter E. Gaskin Sr.

Commanding General
II Marine Expeditionary Force (Forward)
Multi National Force • West

February 2007 to February 2008

Major General Walter E. Gaskin Sr. took command of the II Marine Expeditionary Force in June 2006 and deployed to al Anbar Province in February 2007. This interview, conducted near the end of the tour, details the progress during that period and is a follow on to one conducted with the general the previous year. Major General Gaskin describes continuing operations and the success of taking back population centers from al Qaeda, economic governance development efforts, the drop in kinetic action and transition to counterinsurgency, and helicopter governance.

Major General Gaskin was interviewed by Colonel Michael D. Visconage on 11 January 2008 at Camp Fallujah, Iraq.

Colonel Michael D. Visconage: If you look at that period from late June [2007], when we spoke last, and today, how would you characterize what you have seen as the key operations initiatives, evolution of the fight out here in west?

Major General Walter E. Gaskin Sr.: I think what you'll see is a continuation of what we discovered from right at the beginning of March through June, and that was the taking back of the population centers from al Qaeda, pushing them out into the hinterland north of the Euphrates River, east of Lake Tharthar, and south and down into the wadis, and into the areas toward the route and the MEF's [Marine expeditionary force] security area. We believed then that we had—as we are seeing now—we had to have a single focus of both our kinetic effect toward removing al Qaeda, but followed very closely, we had to have economic development, a sense of development of governance, and the building of capacity of the Iraqi security forces.

So the first thing that kind of grabbed this thing, we were right at the beginning of our contribution from the "surge." What really grabbed us is that as we were able to take the population centers back. The incidents, whether it be IEDs [improvised explosive devices], small arms fire, indirect fire, dropped precipitously, so the enemy realized that we were really onto something. But it was not like we had done before, because we had fought in al Qaim, we had fought in Fallujah, we had fought in Ramadi. But this time, what we did differently is we backfilled, so there was a persistent presence with the Iraqi police.

When I got over here, the year 2006 was the year of police, but I would now characterize 2007 as the actions of the police, because they brought to the table familiarity with their communities, loyalty from their community, respect from their communities, being one of them. Their agreement to provide a rule of law made them a very viable force for eliminating what we discovered was the TTPs [tactics, techniques, and procedures] of al Qaeda, and that is stifling, intimidating, and murdering the folks within the cities. This is a classic COIN [counterinsurgency] operation, separating the enemy from the people.

We made the people the center of gravity, and there, when we saw these [things] happening, the discovery was, as we got into the city, not only did we gate up the city by dividing it into precincts or districts within the city and establishing a joint security station that had Iraqi police in charge, in number, but also engaging the populace in the support, engaging the mukhtars, who was the civic leader for that community and also bringing in Coalition forces, along with Iraqi forces together as a team in that. But clearing that out, al Qaeda out, putting in those security forces and immediately bringing some relief to the people.

When there was humanitarian aid, or some claims to fix things that were broken during the actual fighting, . . . we started having the civic government looking at bringing the services back to the folks. Immediately, once they got some security, they wanted these services: electricity, water, sewage, trash, rubble removal. All of those items were very meaningful to them. Rubble removal meant clearing away places for their kids to return to school. It also meant day labor for hiring those young folks who were kind of thrown out and caught in the middle of fighting or because the state owned enterprises were closed. There were no places to work. So not only this hiring of these Iraqi police meant meaningful work for somebody in the community, it also meant that for us, stability and security so other people can work. They can open up their shops, and they could participate in the day labor program that was pushed throughout the community.

We saw this moving throughout the major population centers, whether you're talking about Ramadi, Hit, Baghdadi, al Qaim, Rutba, or Fallujah. It's the same process that was working, so we watched the Iraqi police grow from about 11,000 up to its current state of 24,000. We also knew that we had to train those Iraqi police, professionalize them, and make sure that they were working within the rule of law. But, instantly, we discovered that because the people believed in those indigenous personnel working in the cities, the tips came in. So we created our own HumInt [human intelligence] pool that actually provided information to us about those who shouldn't be there, and those who were passing through that were foreign fighters, because they have a different accent or facial structure. They knew all of that, we were glad to see.

Discovery of cache finds went up exponentially, and we got through, like I said, the incidents just dropped down, so the cities became instantly calm places to live, and you saw the bustling marketplace. I think that we were onto something. We discovered how al Qaeda operated, and they operate near a mosque. That's where they did their recruiting. They had some type of chop shop or place to make IEDs, whether that be vehicles or just the kind that they buried or shoved out in the road, those pressure plates. They had a safe haven where they could actually hang out and have meetings. We discovered that they were very closely located, and they used that to intimidate the police and the leadership in the community. Once we found that out, we would even engage the imams, as far as their leadership and helping to rebuild a mosque. We would not go into mosques. The Iraqis go into mosques. They appreciate the respect for their culture and their religion that we brought with this.

Visconage: Since we spoke in June, what has been the continued growth of governance and economic pieces?

Gaskin: I think it's tremendous. As a matter of fact, probably one of the best things we did in the organization was having the deputy oversight over the economic development portion and the tribal engagement, so the governance, economic development, in addition to those members of the G 5, and as well as the CAG, civil affairs group. All of that came with oversight. . . . From the staff perspective, [this engagement gave us] the ability to understand what was happening and how the Iraqis felt at being disenfranchised and separated from their federal government, and even most of those separated from their provincial government because of a boycott of an election in 2005.

So it ended up fairly consistent, and most of them are now experiencing new principles of democracy that they had never had before. They were very, very used to it just being pushed down to them—this is what you get, this is all you get, shut up and be happy. And now, in order for them to get anything, they had to find the means to pull it out of a government, a government that they didn't really trust, because it was now run by Shi'a—Shi'a from a political sense, and influenced by Iran—so they figured that the government failed them.

We started at the grassroots level; there were some sparkles of hope out there. We had a Governor Mamoun [Sami Rashid al Alwani] all those years from IIP, Islamic Iraqi Party. He was still a very brave person, and he never gave up the governorship. His life was [nearly taken] 35 times, but he came to work every day, and on the vehicle, got put on a vehicle, but he believed that that was the seat of government, and that if he ever left that, he would leave the government. The provincial council was meeting in Baghdad, and there was no city governance at all. They were of course in the hiding because of the murder and intimidation campaign that al Qaeda took against anybody expected to be leadership, other than the implanted emirs that they put up.

So once we were able to remove al Qaeda from the cities, each one of these cities started setting up their own government. They appointed a mayor, they had a city council. They were explained the rules that city councilship means, that each one on the city council is subdivided into sections, the sections have technicals, and there are so many technicals, meaning a professional person. You have so many seats for sheikhs, and you have so many seats for the party membership or political membership. But what you are beginning to see is representative membership.

Once we started getting those formed up, we then can explain to them [that] in order for you to get money from the governor, you've got to prioritize projects, and that includes some of the rebuilding, the electrical power, the fuel, all these services that you want. You have to also understand that your government, very, very stovepiped as it goes from the director generals of each level right up to the central government under the ministries, and that you have a governor, and we have a mayor, and you have that line.

So we found that it took time to train them on how to plan city planning, how to run a city, and how to develop a budget, because they've never had a budget before. We did some classes up in Irbil, where we got the leadership sitting down and doing "Governors 101." We did it in Jordan. We had the leadership come together and say this is how you plan a budget. Here's your budget that you had that we can't really have any transparency of in the 2006 budget, but here's what we know we have in 2007, and this is how you've got to administer, how you expend that, and the cost of that expenditure. They were able to go back and petition the prime minister for a supplemental, and they were the first one to get a supplemental budget of $70 million because we could show how we were expending the $107 million that was given, so that [helped].

Then we had a thing called helicopter governance, and that's where the DCG [deputy commanding general], General [John R.] Allen, was absolutely phenomenal. He was able to put the governor on a helicopter, along with the precinct chair, the provincial police, some of the DGs [director generals], and some of the members of provincial council, and they would go out and see the constituents around Anbar. In Anbar, we talk about the tyranny of distance. When you're talking about an area the size of North Carolina or

New York, it's an all day drive to go there. When we put them on a helicopter, and they could actually fly into these municipalities and actually do what they are supposed to by their rules—in other words, when the provincial chairman goes in, he validates that city council. You can tell them, "Yes, you've got so many of those representatives on here. Yes, you've got that, and, okay, what projects have been council approved?" The governor meets with the mayor and accepts the mayor's papers: "Yes, you've gone through the proper vetting, and you have been nominated by your provincial council. I now say that you are the mayor, and, oh, by the way, I'm Governor Mamoun," because some of them had never seen him before. They'd heard about him. He's over there in Ramadi. And you've got the provincial chairman.

We discovered that, by their own method, Anbar is divided up into 10 police districts. We were trying to divide them up, but then we said, "Wait, they know what the districts are. Let's just send over the districts." And it turned out they've got 10 districts. The district of al Qaim includes [Ubaiti], Husaybah, all that. Haditha has a triad, like we thought, but we found with Hit, it had Baghdadi and Husaybah. . . . He goes out and he meets with the police, district police, and talks about hiring orders, training, criminal enterprise, and those things that you would expect the chief of police to do, and responds to the provincial chief of police. And they would do this, and, of course, the government will then take their petitions of what they need to bring it back and prioritize for the province based on funds that he has available. He had $107 million, and he looked at all the things people needed, and it exceeded the capacity that he had, so that's what drove him to do that. But [in] the major cities around Anbar is where he did helicopter governance.

The other part that governance is, is that this whole country, this whole area, is tribal, and if you understand how important and how fundamental the tribal society [is], and the influence and the position of the sheikhs, then you begin to understand how everything works. They will tell you that they were tribal before they were Muslims, and they will always be tribal. You can ignore that fact if you want to, but it's to your own peril. They will also tell you that nothing happens unless the sheikhs agree to it, and they'll tell you, too, that the sheikhs are the ones that say fight, and the sheikhs are the ones that will say don't fight. The sheikhs are the ones who said don't participate in the election. So understanding why they do what they do, and who the power brokers are, as far as the sheikhs and their influence, and seeing how the sheikhs are grouped together.

We were very fortunate that the sheikhs happened to be, just like we had our areas of operation grouped together, so we had the Fallujah sheikhs, the Ramadi sheikhs, and everybody to the west, the western sheikhs, and, frankly, that's what they called themselves, too: the western sheikhs. And then we'd have a number of sheikhs who were expatriates. They were living in Jordan or Syria. Five of them have come back. Five of the major sheikhs have come back, five out of eight. But there's a real misunderstanding if you believe that these sheikhs left and deserted their people. It was all the other way around, with people who sent their sheikhs off. Sheikhs are so important in this society that when they are killed, as al Qaeda had done to sheikhs, it was devastating. It was like losing the patriarch. You just lost the head of your existence. You actually lost your connection up through the tribal ones through Mohammed, or through Moses. I mean, these guys trace their history all the way to Adam and Eve, and they can tell you, one sheikh talked to me 21 grandfathers ago. So when you lost these sheikhs, who were the keepers, who were the protectors, who provided for them, they said, "No, we can't handle that," so they sent them out of the country.

They'd never lost influence; they were always sending word to whoever they designated to handle it while they were gone. So being able to engage with those sheikhs, and talk about the future of Anbar from a position where, it's that you've got to realize that the Shi'as are in charge—get over it. Get over the fact that the Shi'as are in charge, and connect what that government is going to be with security [people]. So our thing that we want to do with the engagement with the sheikhs is use them in the connecting and the reconciliation that has to occur between the government and the province. That's what we did, and I think that was the major movement that connected together. The sheikhs approved the leadership. The leadership used the sheikhs' council, as they have always through history. I mean, right out in the government sector, for example, there is a sheikhs' room, because of how the sheikhs meet, and they remind you that [Iraqi Prime Minister Nouri Kamil Mohammed Hassan al] Maliki, or any of the leadership in Baghdad, belongs to a tribe. They understand. . . .

They understand exactly what we're saying, and they'll play this political game, but they understand the influence, and we will not be ignored. The sheikhs believe that they are the foundations of reconciliation that will occur out here. But there will be ways to do this to forge genuine relationships with the sheikhs. So I talk about Sheikh [Hamid], and when I talk about Sheikh [Hatoum], or Sheikh Ahmad, or Sheikh [Kheba], I'm talking about guys I know. We sit down and eat goat together and talk about the issues of the day. It's not someone who I just send a note to, who actually [generally] understands.

The two things that I think have brought about our relationship with the sheikhs that are very, very important, [are] trust and respect. If you trust me, then when we talk, we can talk very candidly. I can tell you when I fought you, why I fought you, and why I won't fight you again, and why I hate al Qaeda and I'm not ever going to turn again on you because you helped me kill al Qaeda, and I have a blood feud with al Qaeda, and it takes six generations to eliminate a blood feud, so it's permanent. The other thing is respect. I am not somebody running around the fire with a loincloth on. I am a man. I am a very educated man—and a lot of them are. I have a sensing of my country, I have a history, and a respect for my history and meaning means a lot. So I don't expect you to talk down to me, at me, or by me. So when you get that, it's like you aren't the only one with good ideas. You may be in a better position to use your ideas, but I have good ideas as well. And that professional interchange, built on trust and respect, allowed us to get further along, and I'm convinced faster than we ever dreamed possible for creating stability and peace out here.

They prefer to call us brothers rather than friends, and I used to ask, "okay, are we a friend? Do you call us friendly forces?" Friendly forces are colleagues, but a brother is family. So with friends you can get mad with and lose. Brothers, you can get angry with your brothers, but that passes because you are bound by blood. So that's the relationship that we sought, and that's what we had in the makings. That relationship has been started a long time. It wasn't just II MEF Forward coming out here, but the relationship had been started. These Marines out here, there's something about these Marines, and their ability to see that we were sincere in it, whether we were out in al Qaim or in Fallujah.

So when they hear us talking about leaving, they're concerned, and I have got several examples of what they think about leaving. One, I was talking to the mayor of Haditha. He says, "Are you leaving?" I said, "Well, eventually." He said, "No, are you leaving? Because the last time you left us to go fight in Fallujah, they lined us up in the soccer field and shot some of the leadership of the city. So we just need to know if you're going to be here with us until we can get up on our feet and be able to defend ourselves." And I have promised him that we would be here, and we're still here, and we have built the capacity of their police. But as [one sheikh] says about leaving, you can't take the cake out of the oven before it is done just because it smells good. He believes that. He was talking about us moving out of the city. He was talking about the IPs [Iraqi police]. He said, "These IPs are training. They're going to be very good one day, but what the Coalition forces do for them is give them professional training and allow them to be able to do what they're put there for. That is security, and that's a lot to them."

Visconage: What do they say when you talk to the tribal leaders or the governor? What is their metric for knowing when it will be time for us to leave?

Gaskin: The first thing we have to learn is, talking about culturally, an awareness of what they need and how they go about making decisions. . . . They come to the meeting for the formal part of the discussion and probably eat. So if you go in there thinking that you're going to get a decision, you'll get a lot of talk, a lot of back and forth, and if you witness it, you will see a lot of arguing back and forth. But they're only talking about the issues that they didn't get to discuss before they got to the meeting, because it's already decided. [Decisions that were made ahead of time.]

So they have already decided that we are their guests, and like guests, we have to stay forever. You're here for a different purpose, and so they wanted us to very candidly and openly state what our purpose was, because they remind us that there is no land in Iraq that doesn't belong to the sheikhs. You can't buy it. You can't come out and build a house on it. There's only a few ways to get land. It is hereditary. You get it through the government taking that Saddam [Hussein] used to do, or you get it through conquering.

Well, [they want to know], "what are you doing?" When they hear that term "occupation," their connotation of occupation is in the conquer mode. "You're here to take my land. But if you help me get rid of those who mean me harm, then you're obviously my friend, and if you fight along with me and shed your blood, you're my brother." So they think that we're going to leave eventually, but they didn't want us to get caught up in the political implications of leaving that they hear, and they're very astute as far as that part. They didn't want us to leave until they were able to stand up on their own independently.

Interview 16
Turning the Tide, Part II

Major General John R. Allen

Deputy Commanding General
II Marine Expeditionary Force (Forward)
Multi National Force • West

January 2007 to February 2008

Major General John R. Allen was responsible for governance in al Anbar Province for Multi National Force West and II Marine Expeditionary Force (Forward) under Major General Walter E. Gaskin Sr. Since his return to the U.S., he was promoted to lieutenant general and became the deputy commanding general for U.S. Central Command. In this interview, Allen, provides a concise description of his tour while providing additional insight from the vantage of his position at Central Command.

Lieutenant General Allen was interviewed via telephone by Chief Warrant Officer 4 Timothy S. McWilliams on 23 April 2009 at Central Command, Tampa, Florida.

Chief Warrant Officer-4 Timothy S. McWilliams: In a series of recent interviews with Iraqis, former Iraqi ambassador Sa'doon al Zubaydi described meetings between Iraqis and Marines in Bahrain and Jordan in 2004 and suggested that there was an opportunity that could have prevented two years of conflict. Could you address that statement?

Lieutenant General John R. Allen: Sure. Let me comment on that first. I need to qualify what I'm going to say as not attempting to disparage the person who made that comment, or to disparage Arabs. But I need to make this comment. First of all, before I left Anbar, the provincial council made me an honorary Anbari, so I really do consider myself somebody who has an affinity for the tribes and Arabs. However, people who want to aggrandize their positions, to ensure that they get credit—within the tribal system, it's all about power and never giving up power—will make statements like "had someone listened to me in 2004," or "if I had been listened to when we did talk in 2004, I'd have saved you two years of war." I've been down that road a thousand times with people who never were called upon to deliver on the things they say they could have. Consequently, they live in the world of the possible.

I'm sure there were conversations that occurred in 2004. The difference between 2004 and 2006 and then 2007 was really on the battlefield and security. In many respects, we, the U.S. [United States]—not we, the Marines—had created a perfect storm in Anbar. We had dismantled the military, and Anbaris in large numbers were the security forces. There's a great martial tradition among those tribes, to be in the army. We had de Ba'athified the government, so everybody who was a member of the Ba'ath Party, and it required you to be a member to have any real status in that society, and when I say status, I mean be a director general within the province, representing the ministries from Baghdad. So a director general of electricity would be the chief guy for electricity in this socialized system in the province. And if you were a Ba'athist, you were out of a job [after de Ba'athification].

Now, not only were you out of a job, but the guy who runs electricity is now no longer a player inside the province. I mean, you've got all kinds of problems. And then the third thing we did is we closed down all state owned enterprises. So a lot of people were looking for anything they could do to put a little food on the table and make a little money. And so an awful lot of folks entered the business of fighting United States Marines and soldiers, and in 2004, it was starting to get bad; 2005, it got worse; 2006, we killed about 1,700, almost 1,800 al Qaeda, put another 4,500 of them in Bucca and places like that, and the violence levels doubled. So we were really in a very serious security situation, where you can have all the discussions you want in Jordan, and they're not going to play out in a meaningful way in the battlespace. So, when folks make those kinds of comments, I am always a little skeptical, because if it were a perfect world, then we wouldn't have gone to war there to begin with.

McWilliams: Can you describe the engagement and reconciliation efforts prior to your tenure?

Allen: I absolutely will. We had a lot of success in '07. In fact, I think it created the conditions, ultimately, for the complete turning of the province, which General [David H.] Petraeus [USA] has said "what began in Anbar spread throughout Iraq" [in a letter to the troops, 28 December 2007]. So people who were there in '07 should be very, very proud of what they've done, but I want to say this up front, and I want it to be very clear, that the MEF [I Marine Expeditionary Force] that was there before us, and all the MEFs did a great job. But the MEF that was there before us, I MEF, led by General [Richard C.] Rick Zilmer and [Robert B.] Bob Neller and [David G.] Dave Reist, the work that they did—I'm absolutely convinced of it now that a couple of years have passed—the work that they did during the darkest hour of the violence in the Anbar Province, which was in the latter part of '06 and into the first three months of our tour, they set the stage for our success. I absolutely believe it, from the engagement that they did.

For example, the young Army colonel who commanded the brigade in Ramadi, a kid by the name Sean [B.] MacFarland, who has since been selected to general, he took a chance on a coalition of sheikhs and tribes, small tribes, around the northwest of Ramadi, and that chance paid off in very, very important ways. The history is starting to shape up that the MEF didn't support him. That's not true at all. General Zilmer was very supportive. In fact, General Zilmer, on a number of occasions, with General Reist and Colonel MacFarland, sat down at the table with the sheikhs and the provincial government and refereed the sharing of power and the balance of civil governance with tribal activity. So I MEF, from roughly the summer of '06 until our handoff in February of '07, I think that of all of the occasions where reconciliation was initiated and paid off. It was under General Zilmer and Dave Reist and Bob Neller's general officer leadership where the seeds were planted, the shaping occurred that ultimately permitted us in '07 to cash in on that. In essence, they did the blocking, they opened the hole in the line and we ran the ball down the field. That's how I view it, and that's how I want history to understand it. Those guys had a hell of a kinetic battle. At the same time, they were putting steel on target in terms of real, valuable, long term reconciliation, and we capitalized on it.

McWilliams: Could you describe your engagement in reconciliation efforts in 2007?

Allen: When we got there, we were already talking to the tribes. What happened, though, was the tribes really had not made final decisions with respect to aligning themselves with the Coalition. There were isolated large tribal areas that had made the decision they were going to come with us, but there were other substantial segments of the tribes that were on the fence. As in any counterinsurgency—this is not my term, it's a term of the art—"the peasant waits to see what the government can do or will do about the insurgents before the peasant will come off the fence." At the time we got there, there were still a lot of folks on the fence because it was uncertain that the provincial government and the government in Baghdad would ever be able to build sufficient power. . . .

It was not certain in their minds that this government would ever have enough power to really be a factor for the good in their lives. And as long as al Qaeda was a nightmare in their lives every day if they appeared to be aligned with the government, then they were on the fence. So what we did was to do two things. We empowered the sheikhs, because there really wasn't a government functioning. It was the governor in his government center. He was basically a government of one in a building protected by a Marine rifle company. And we did all we could to empower the sheikhs in the short term, to give them back the power that had been taken from them by al Qaeda, and we did that both in terms of a kinetic alliance against al Qaeda, but also supported the sheikhs in affecting projects in their tribal areas to the good of the people, turning on water treatment facilities again, reconnecting the electricity, paving the roads that had been blasted by years, now, of IEDs [improvised explosive devices], repairing bridges, helping merchants to get their shops open again. All of it we funneled through the sheikhs, and all of it in the end empowered the sheikhs again, when al Qaeda had done everything it could to marginalize the traditional tribal leadership. So that was our first step to get governance going again in the province. Thereafter, we worked very hard at the provincial and district levels to get those governments functioning and in alliance with the tribes, which is always a bit of tension in a tribal society.

But ensuring that the two of them knew that we weren't going to favor the one over the other— we weren't going to favor the tribes over the civil government, but the civil government couldn't function unless they incorporated the tribes. We worked that very, very hard, and we began to see, we had a lot of kinetic fighting. In fact, the highest violence levels of the entire war in Anbar were during the first three months that we were there. We began to see this drop off significantly when the third factor started to play on the battlefield, and the third factor was—first factor being the tribes, second factor being the civil governance—the third factor was Iraqi security forces. We were training and employing and getting them out to the field, and partnering with them as much as we possibly could. And when we cleared Ramadi in April, roughly, of '07 and made it—while it was heavily supported by Marines and soldiers—made it appear to be a police action, that was what really began the turning. And once Ramadi began to quiet down, we then turned our attention to Fallujah and did the same thing in Fallujah in the summer, which was to make it a police action.

We moved the Iraqi army out of the cities so that the cities didn't appear to be occupied cities by the Iraqi army, and [we] continued to build and empower the police force. And we went from about 3,500 police that we could find on any given day when we got there, and I got there in mid January of '07, to about 29,000 police, all totaled, when we left, and they were pretty well trained, on the whole. So the three legs, if you will, of the reconciliation, we worked them concurrently, because we knew we had to. We were not stumbling around, figuring this out. We knew what we needed to do, so we empowered the sheikhs, we connected them to the civil leadership, and we supported them with indigenous Iraqi security forces, and then we provided the security top cover through constant conventional and special operations throughout the width and breadth and depth of the province.

McWilliams: From your perspective now at CentCom, have you had an opportunity to see how engagement and reconciliation efforts have continued since you left?

Allen: Well, I think that the successive MEFs, and we're now in the second MEF since I've been there. I MEF has gone back and returned and now II MEF is on the ground. I think that they have been clearly just as dedicated to engagement and reconciliation as we were, but the problem set simply just evolves and changes so that points of emphasis and objectives and outcomes change. I can't speak for how it's going right now, although in fact I do stay in touch with a number of the sheikhs. They surprisingly have e mail, and they find somebody passing by that can write English, and every now and then I'll get an English language e mail from these guys. The current MEF that's in there is getting very high grades for maintaining this close relationship to the tribes, and to some extent the brilliance of the Marine Corps approach with Anbar really deserves a lot of credit in the history, and that is, General Petraeus is trying to do it right now in Afghanistan.

You send the same units back over and over again and, guess, what? They know the ground, they know the people, and they know the enemy, and the people know us. Not long ago I was in Afghanistan, meeting with national legislators, and the national legislators from the Helmand Province had gotten wind that American troops were coming, and they said, "Please send the Marines to the Helmand Province, because when they were here before, we had a decent quality of life and the Taliban were not factors." They call it the darkness. The Taliban were not a factor in creating the darkness in our lives. So Anbar Province was a place where Marines went back to all the time, and your battalion may not have gone, may have gone to Haditha one time and al Qaim another time, but as big as the province was, you were still going to meet people that you'd served with before.

So I think the Corps deserves, in the annals of history, a lot of credit for the wisdom of sending, first of all, maintaining unit integrity to the maximum extent it can, and it could do that with seven month tours. And, number two, sending the same units back over and over again. It's still going on, . . . and it's still successful.

McWilliams: How do the Marine successes in al Anbar fit in the greater picture of Iraq?

Allen: The Sahwa [Awakening] was a phenomenon, and while the idea of the Awakening was a tribal idea, it could not have gotten off

232

the ground if it hadn't been supported by the Coalition forces. So it started in Anbar, with a fellow by the name of Sheikh Abdul Sattar Abu Risha. His brother [Achmad Fteikhan al Rishawi] gets high marks for continuing the process of organizing the tribes to become factors in good governance. The nature of the Marine and Army engagement with the tribes gave the tribes the breathing space they needed, got al Qaeda off their back, gave them the breathing space they needed to get themselves organized and ultimately begin to defend themselves, and that spread. And, as we would watch, for example, I would go see Sheikh Sattar, and he would have in his diwan, in his guesthouse, he'd have a guesthouse full of 40 or 50 sheikhs when I'd go to see him. And these guys would be from Diyala Province, Salah ad Din Province, Ninawa Province. They'd come from Baghdad, and all around the Sunni Triangle, these Awakening movements were starting, almost like franchises. And I'm sure if he hadn't been assassinated, Abdul Sattar would have eventually had them pay dues or something, because he was a consummate businessman as well as a counterinsurgent.

It started there, and I don't want to put words in General Petraeus's mouth, but I think he's been quoted in other places saying that what began in the Anbar Province spread throughout Iraq and emerged ultimately in the form of the Sons of Iraq. And this whole concept of the Sons of Iraq created neighborhood security that took some of the heat off the police and let the police get after their own counterinsurgency operations, which took some of the heat off the Iraqi army and let them do the large scale counterinsurgency that they needed to do. And so that's really how it got kicked off, and so in many respects now the Sahwa, which was the Sahwa al Anbar [and] is now the Sahwa al Iraq, and it's become a political party. It's much less about counterinsurgency operations now than it is about politics, both at a provincial and national level.

McWilliams: What are the things that the Marines did in al Anbar that Coalition forces in other parts of Iraq are doing now?

Allen: Well, I'm not sure necessarily that the Marines were doing it differently than the Army. I think the circumstances permitted what the Marines were doing to be more successful more quickly, if you follow what I'm saying. So what I want to be clear of is that I don't want to convey that the Army wasn't doing it right. What I would convey is that the outcomes can be different, based on the security environment.

What the Marines were doing, to get very specific, was from top to bottom, at least when I was there, we were organized and guided by a very clear commander's intent that we worked very hard to craft. . . . It was something to the effect of the commander's guidance for the conduct of counterinsurgency operations in Anbar. We created a whole series of objectives based along the lines of operations, and the commander's intent unified everything from the conversations I had down to what rifle company commanders were attempting to do with the local tribal elements. So we were unified from top to bottom.

Plus, we fought as a MAGTF [Marine air ground task force], and a MAGTF fights a single battle, and that is tactical superiority. So the combination of having a well thought out, easily understood commander's intent, and the fact that as a MAGTF (and I include the Army brigade in that MAGTF), we fought as a single battle throughout the entire width and breadth and depth of the province, which was a third of the country, [which] gave us the ability to take a huge chunk of the Iraqi terrain off the map as a place where al Qaeda could find safe haven and safe passage. When we were able to do that for a third of the country, the simple dynamic changed in Iraq.

McWilliams: When you look at Iraq as a whole, how does Anbar presently fit in that?

Allen: It's very quiet, which is just what you want. When I read the intelligence reporting or I talk to people that have been in there visiting, they echo all of that. And so what's happening in Anbar is what we want to have happen in any country that is emerging from an insurgency, and that is predictability of government, the establishment of the rule of law, the effectiveness of the security forces, [and] the development of economic opportunity. All of that is well underway in the Anbar Province because when you get up in the morning there, your first question isn't "am I going to live to see the sunset," your first question is "how do I get my sheep to market?"

And if that's the worst problem you've got that day, then things are okay in that part of the Arab world. It took longer for that to be the first question in other places, but throughout a great deal of Iraq, much of what occurred in Anbar is occurring also routinely now.

McWilliams: Sir, going back to Colonel MacFarland, you said he took a risk in engaging these local sheikhs. Was that on his own initiative?

Allen: Sure. Because General Rick Zilmer created an environment where he expected his regimental and brigade commanders to take initiative, it was. It was on his own initiative. The history is inaccurately painting that the Marines were unhappy with him for doing that. To my knowledge, that is in fact completely erroneous. That's not true. So I don't know where that comes from, but Sean MacFarland deserves a lot of credit for having reached out to Sheikh Sattar.

Now here's the problem. . . . It was difficult to contact the sheikhs when the security environment was so bad. If you were a sheikh and you got seen with Americans, the chances were very good you were going to pay for it in a very bad way. Your family was going to be assassinated, you were going to get killed, your flocks would be driven off. Something bad was going to happen to you. We talked about operating inside the tribes. You can't win an insurgency as long as you're operating outside the human terrain.

Once we were able to penetrate the tribes and be accepted and trusted by them, then we were able to then isolate al Qaeda and go after them and eliminate them, and that was our goal. So the problem was penetrating the tribes, and from roughly the latter part of the summer of '06 until our battle handover, that process was just really getting underway. That's where I credit Rick Zilmer and Dave Reist and Bob Neller because they continued to have very aggressive security operations throughout the province and, where possible, make contact with the tribes with the idea of creating relationships.

Part of the problem was [that] you couldn't find sheikhs to talk to, because of the reasons I just said. But sometimes you'd talk to sheikhs, and they weren't the right ones. You'll hear the term "fake sheikh." And some of these guys were fake sheikhs. The problem with Abdul Sattar was because others of his family had already been killed by al Qaeda, he was not really what you might consider the preeminent member in his family to be the paramount sheikh. That was the first thing. Second, the Albu Risha tribe isn't a particularly significant tribe. It pales in comparison with the lineage of the Albu Nimer or the Albu Mahal or the Albu Issa tribe, many of these other—Albu Fahd. I mean, these are famous tribes in the history of Araby. You don't hear anything about the Albu Risha tribe. So he's a guy who isn't necessarily the number one guy in his tribe, in a tribe that's kind of a second or a third tier tribe. So when Abu Risha comes to you and says, "I've got the ability to provide three battalion sized formations of tribal militia, right now, if you'll help us out with some projects to try to make life better for our poor people," that's a risk, because you're going to give him money, and you're not sure where that money's going to go, because it's difficult for you to get into that area, because of security, to ensure the projects are being taken care of.

Here's the other problem: a lot of the sheikhs that we were talking to, the lineal sheikhs, and remember I told you it's all about power? A lot of those sheikhs aren't going to give any credit to a guy like Abu Risha for being an organizer and a leader because, in giving that guy credit, in giving Abu Risha credit in the concept of patronage and zero sum with regards to power and honor and shame, when a sheikh of a large lineal tribe gives credit to a guy like Abu Risha for being successful, when that sheikh himself wasn't successful, he has just assumed shame and given up honor.

I'm not being theoretical here. I'm telling you the way it is, in terms of tribal dynamics. So the way these guys, in order not to make themselves look impotent or incompetent when the time comes to justify to their own tribes on how come Abu Risha is doing so well on behalf of the Coalition, is to say [that] the Coalition doesn't understand him. The Coalition doesn't understand that he's a murderer and smuggler and a criminal. They constantly denigrated him.

So the risk was for those people outside who didn't really understand what was going on with the tribes, and Sean MacFarland reaching to Abdul Sattar. The risk was the appearance that Colonel MacFarland was dealing with a common criminal and a murderer, and the truth was, guess what? All the sheikhs are like that. Now I'm not proposing that all the sheikhs are common criminals and murderers, but what I'm telling you is, the way they portray each other in this concept of honor and shame, you've got to be very, very careful about what you hear and what you believe when one sheikh starts talking about another sheikh.

First of all, Sean is a great student of history. He's also a great student of tactics, and he understood counterinsurgency ops, and he understood that people are the critical terrain. People are the center of gravity in an insurgency, and if you don't pay attention to the people, then you will always be surprised by what happens around you, especially in a tribal environment. If you don't leverage what the tribes bring you on the battlefield, then the tribes will always confuse you. As we used to say in the Anbar Province, the first lens you look through when you're considering what's happening in front of you is the lens of tribalism.

McWilliams: You mentioned Marines approached Anbar as being historically significant. Do you have any other observations on that, sir?

Allen: Sure. We studied the tribes. We truly prepared ourselves and prepared our minds for what we were going to encounter there, and not to take away from anyone else's efforts in previous conflicts, but for the moment—and I'll speak to II MEF, because I only know II MEF, really. From the moment we all came together as a team, we put our professional military education to work in shaping our minds, understanding that unless we went in fully understanding the tribalism, understanding the personalities that we were going to face, and the whole dynamics of this code of conduct associated with being a member of an Arab tribe in Mesopotamia, you were not going to fully grasp the opportunities in front of you.

So we trained, and we studied, and we spoke with members of tribes. We learned from Iraqis, we brought in sociologists, and we went over. This was an historic means of preparation, and we hit the ground running and immediately were able to capitalize on the great work that had been done by I MEF ahead of us.

2008
Transition to Iraqi Control
2009

Interview 17
Transition to Iraqi Control, Part I

Major General John F. Kelly

Commanding General
I Marine Expeditionary Force (Forward)
Multi National Force • West

February 2008 to February 2009

Major General John F. Kelly was deputy commanding general for I Marine Expeditionary Force and served as commanding general of Multi National Force West from February 2008 to February 2009, his third tour in Iraq. Previously, he served as assistant commanding general of 1st Marine Division during the drive to Baghdad in 2003. He subsequently led Task Force Tripoli to Tikrit, then supervised the division's security and stability operations in seven Shi'a provinces in southern Iraq during the summer of 2003. He returned to Iraq in 2004 in the same capacity when I Marine Expeditionary Force deployed to al Anbar Province.

When Major General Kelly returned to Iraq in 2008 as the commanding general of Multi National Force West, he focused on closing U.S. camps, downsizing Coalition forces, demilitarizing cities, and transferring control of al Anbar's governance and security to the Iraqis.

In this interview, Major General Kelly describes meeting with Iraqi sheikhs, police, and soldiers to gain their perspectives on the insurgency, al Qaeda, and the Sahwa, or Awakening. He details the Marines' role in the Awakening, particularly how Marines trained Iraqi police and soldiers, and also mentions erroneous accounts of the Awakening. Finally, he notes some of the elements in turning al Anbar Province's security over to the Iraqis.

Major General Kelly was interviewed by Colonel Gary W. Montgomery on 26 March 2009 at Camp Pendleton, California.

Colonel Gary W. Montgomery: What differences did you see from deployment to deployment, as far as on our side, or from the other side?

Major General John F. Kelly: ... After I left [September 2004], al Qaeda had come in strong at that point, you had [Abu Musab al] Zarqawi, and these were brutal, awful men. The price for working with us might have been that your eight year old daughter is brutally raped, and they send you the videotape, or she's raped and thrown into a bonfire. These kind of things were commonly reported.

When I came in for this last tour, I started to talk to sheikhs, and [Iraqi] policemen, [and Iraqi army officers and listened to] the stories they told. Many of the men that were now policemen were former insurgents. ...I could sit and talk to a lot of these men and ask, "How did it start?" And they'd all say, "Oh, my brother," or "my friend, let's not talk about those days." No, it'd be interesting, particularly [with] the army guys, to see what we did wrong, how did this thing start? And they'd say, "What did you do wrong? Everything.". . .

Everyone, when they would talk to me, sheikhs, policemen, army guys that we would deal with, [told me that] it all came to that April '03 "massacre," as they called it, [fighting between U.S. soldiers and Iraqis in Fallujah] was the point at which they were convinced we were bad people, "we" meaning the Coalition. We were anti Sunni, we were pro Shi'a, and they couldn't work with us because we had gunned down 77 people—this is them talking—and didn't apologize, wouldn't admit that we had done something wrong. Subordinate to that was the disbandment of the army and the fact that we didn't seem to be working very hard in Anbar to right some of these UN [United Nations] sanction type wrongs. . . .

As the insurgency started, let's call it outraged citizens getting guns to fight us, the so called "nationalists," because of the heavy handedness or whatever it was called, outraged citizens. And that insurgency then was taken over by al Qaeda, who came in with a willingness to die, a lot of money, a lot of organization. Over time, the common cause between the two groups that were fighting us turned into an al Qaeda kind of directed insurgency, but then the sheikhs again telling you that as al Qaeda began to try to establish their brand of lifestyle—extreme sharia law—and started to actually execute people, beating women who are uncovering their faces. If they saw someone smoking, they'd beat them.

As the sheikhs started to resist them—or not cooperate with them maybe is a better way to do it—they started trying to kill the sheikhs. More than one of the paramount senior sheikhs, the paramount dignified sheikhs, of which in Anbar Province there's 17 of them, these are the guys that when you meet with them don't ask you for anything. They don't ask you for the contracts. These are the top tier tribal leaders.

Kind of as a sidebar, one of the statuses that the Marine commander had on the ground—me now, [Richard T.] Rick Tryon before me, [Walter E.] Walt Gaskin before him, General [Richard C.] Zilmer—we were considered to be a paramount dignified sheikh of sheikhs of the Marine tribe, and that became the recognized, most powerful tribe in the province—the richest tribe, and the most militarily capable. So I would go to these sheikh engagements where sometimes there would be 200 sheikhs there, but my proper place was with the paramount dignified sheikhs. And if I spent too much time with one of the second [or] third tier sheikhs, one of my peers, if you would, would come over and direct me. "Okay, you're being very benevolent, but you're spending too much time with him," would be the message. "Come over here with the senior sheikhs."

As they relay the story, al Qaeda couldn't be reasoned with, there was only one other force there that might be willing to work with them, and that was us, the Army and the Marines that were in the province. . . .

What I find interesting is . . . the number of people who were taking credit for the Awakening—and not Iraqis, but U.S. military guys. . . . Before the history was written, revisionist history was already being written around individuals. There are colonels and even generals that are saying, "I was the one that started the Awakening. I dealt with the tribes." It's always fascinating to me when people want to take that much credit. But, in any event, when the Awakening did start, it was an amazing process, because suddenly you had a people that were fighting us, and in their mind fighting us for good reasons—the nationalists, or the righteous men, wronged kind of guys—they suddenly started working with us.

Montgomery: Was the Awakening something that we caused, or that we enabled?

Kelly: I wasn't there for it, but many conversations with the sheikhs lead me to believe strongly that al Qaeda caused it, and we enabled it. The people that had been fighting us, or trying to stand on the sidelines were between a rock and a hard place, one of the rocks was al Qaeda. They couldn't go to them and say, "Hey, listen, let's make an accommodation," because of course al Qaeda had a view of the caliphate and Iraq and extreme sharia law and all of that, so they couldn't turn to them. And then you had the hard place, the Coalition, but maybe that was sandstone. And we had always said, and General [James N.] Mattis actually coined the phrases "no better friend, no worse enemy, than a United States Marine," and "first, do no harm."

The sheikhs would tell me that in spite of the fact that we were killing you guys, either us or al Qaeda, in spite of the fact that we were rocketing you all the time, you were still trying to force us to work with you. Limited use of force, trying to work with them all the time, working with the governor, trying to repair stuff—all of this, even in the bad days, [kept the door open]. So they came to us, and we enabled them to continue this so called Awakening process.

They deserve a lot of credit. [But] to a degree, they did not fight al Qaeda. They no longer supported the fight, and helped us identify who al Qaeda was, where they were. There are individual sheikhs who would take down the one or two fighters and drop a headless body off at the main gate of one of the combat bases. And you cannot understate the effectiveness of the task force, the special operators who [went] after al Qaeda—the individual takedown of individual fighters. They took the network down at the leadership level. It cannot be understated how much work they did and continue to do, and they did the same thing, focusing on the Shi'a militia groups.

But to answer your question, I think al Qaeda caused it and we enabled it. In this last tour, I'm more than willing to give my *wasta*, as it's called, as the head of the Marine tribe, to the head of one of the other tribes, so that his people will hold him in high regard, because he's helping us help them, if you know what I mean. I used to talk in groups and give huge credit to sheikhs who were there, who fought al Qaeda, knowing full well the guy spent all of his time in Jordan. Still, he would pump up, and his people would become proud of him, and all that kind of thing. They rule with this issue of wasta and respect and all of that.

Many of these sheikhs were sent outside the country. We in America sometimes looked at the guys who left the country as cowards or something. Many of the tribes—these guys left the country, the tribes told them to go to Jordan and Syria, because they were the senior guys, and it's too messy—there's not a real process to select a new sheikh—so they sent these guys. They were the obvious targets of al Qaeda, al Qaeda was going after them, and the tribes for their own safety [sent them of the country]. . . .

Sheikh [Abdul] Sattar [Abu Risha] got an awful lot of the credit, but he's not a paramount dignified sheikh, nor is his brother normally considered one of the paramount sheikhs. . . .

Montgomery: But do you think that we could have won in Anbar if al Qaeda had been less heavy handed?

Kelly: . . . That's an interesting question. What if al Qaeda had never shown up? If al Qaeda had never shown up, and we were allowed to fight the fight we wanted to after Fallujah II, without the constant pressure to fight the insurgents militarily—at that point, it would have only been nationalist insurgents. I think we could have won. The Iraqis admit that they couldn't fight us. The things that the insurgents deal with with us was how fast we could react to them. They knew when they fought us, when they had an ambush, they had 40 seconds or less, because just a minute after that, we had gunships or we had, I was talking to some of them about how when they fought us, ambushed us, it seemed we were always trying to get around behind them, cut them off.

In this fight, the built up areas were the sanctuaries. In the Vietnam War, it was the jungle where they hid. In this war, it was Fallujah, Ramadi, Saqlawiyah. Get back to those built up areas, bury the gun or throw the gun in the loft, and then go back to being just a normal Iraqi. Many of them would comment to me that as soon as it started, you immediately started maneuvering to try to get in behind us. That's what we teach Marines. But within a few minutes, we had gunships [on scene]. So they understood that they couldn't beat us militarily.

Had we, the Marines and the Army units in Anbar, only had a military approach to the problem, we could be still banging away at each other today. But you had the "do no harm" stand, and the task force tracking down the bad guys. At the same time, us attempting to help, I think, was the war winning strategy. We just couldn't apply it until the population at least became somewhat supportive of us. . . .

Montgomery: Given that we've heard from various sources that insurgencies often last 10 years—it's not unusual—this one turned relatively quickly.

Kelly: . . . The advantage we had, of course, was our police, certainly by the time I got there, they were good enough to handle things. And the two army divisions that we trained in Anbar, starting back when General [John F.] Sattler was there, were very good. So the advantage we had was our security forces, so called ISF, Iraqi security forces, were appreciably better than anyone else in the country, and everyone acknowledged that.

And we, in this third tour, started to back away, because it became clear to me that we were stunting their growth. They'd gotten to this point, but as long as there were Marines working so close with them, they were never going to advance beyond that point, so we started to back away. We started to take Marines out of the police stations 24/7. We didn't stop engaging with them, but we started to back out. We went from 109 police stations occupied to 21, and we shifted the duties of the Marines and soldiers in the PTTs, the police transition teams, to training them to do police work, protect and defend kind of work, crime scene preservation and investigative techniques, this kind of thing. Did the same thing with the army.

And the reason we won in Anbar, in a lot of ways, we had very, very large military transition teams, MTTs, down in the division level, or division, brigade and battalion level. They were three times bigger than the requirement [set] by the RFF, by the request for forces. They were three times bigger. Why? I think it was General Sattler that said, "In order to train these guys, we've got to be with them 24/7. We've got to eat with them, play soccer with them, live with them, fight with them." We didn't know if we could trust them three and half, four years ago, so we made the transition teams big enough that if there was treachery, the transition teams could defend themselves until a grunt unit, QRF, quick reaction force, got to them.

By the time I got there, standing on the shoulders of every Marine, soldier, and sailor that had served there before me, started looking at the fact that we were stunting the continued professionalism and growth of the army because we had these very large transition teams. So we cut all of the transition teams pretty much when I got there down to the RFF levels. As an example, we had at the division level 37 in a MTT team. There was only a requirement for 11, so we cut it down to 11. And then a Marine colonel, pretty high quality guy, post command, maybe battalion commander, . . . as long as that colonel was the adviser, the head of the MTT team, he essentially was the commander of the division, and the two star Iraqi guy would defer to him so much that in reality, again, the two star Iraqi guy was not truly the commander. It was the colonel. Every decision, they'd look at the colonel and say, "Well, is this a good decision?"

So we also not only cut the MTT teams down to RFF size, but we went one rank lower, so the colonel became a lieutenant colonel, and obviously every rank one rank lower. And then frankly by the midpoint of my tour, we started to un MTT [remove advisors from] the battalions to where there was no MTT team with the battalion, and we maintained a MTT team significantly smaller at the brigade level and at the division level. When I left, we started to un MTT at the battalion level, and then change them from what they were, which is really a shadow command structure, to advisers, as opposed to, again, what they were, which was this shadow thing.

All of this is why we were so successful in training our police and our army units. They did very, very well in the fights, independent fights they got involved in. They were the ones that went down in Basrah in March of '08 [and] saved the day. They went to Sadr City and saved the day. They're in Diyala fighting now, they're in Baghdad. These are independent brigades that do very, very well. It shocked people in Baghdad when they watched how good the 1st [Iraqi Army] Division [was]. Most of the 1st Division left Anbar and went under Major General Tariq [Abdul Wahab Jassim] to Basrah. This is after the 14th Division mutinied, or melted away, or whatever—collapsed. And the next division they sent in was the 1st Division, trained in Anbar by the Marine Corps, and they were phenomenal.

The British commander called me and said, "How the hell did you guys do this?" He said, "We can't get them to leave the base, and they [the 1st Division] went right to work. They're in the city, they're fighting. How'd you get them to do that?" When units from these divisions flew out to Diyala, the American division commander called and said, "Where'd you get these guys?" And, just as importantly—more importantly—the Iraqi division, battalion, brigades that they fought with in those other places saw what was possible. And what was interesting, the 1st and 7th Division out of Anbar [is] 60 percent Shi'a and only 40 percent local Sunni boys. So you had a mixed division that was Iraqi [that was] very good in a couple of tough fights. And the prime minister [Nouri Kamil Mohammed Hassan al Maliki] recognized how important it was for the Iraqis to fight these fights. . . .

More than once I've been asked in interviews and whatnot, how much did the surge help or turn the tide in Anbar? Of course the reality is there were almost no surge forces in Anbar. When the surge came in, General [David H.] Petraeus put the surge forces where he thought he most needed them. . . . So you didn't have much in the way of surge forces out there, and really, in a lot of ways we were kind of left alone. The Marine commanders were kind of left alone.

Once the disastrous decision was made, I think, to go into Fallujah I, and of course an awful lot of people were involved in making us do Fallujah I ran for cover, and to this day, you can never find the guy that actually ordered it. You read [former Ambassador L. Paul] Bremer's book, and he's critical of the Marines and all that, but the point is that we were allowed to kind of do our own thing out there, which is consistent with our culture anyway.

But I was talking about the counterinsurgency manual. People have asked me, was it the counterinsurgency manual, that you finally had an updated counterinsurgency manual, so you could then execute and fight the war? And I said, "Well, I think the counterinsurgency manuals we had in the past were perfectly good, in my personal opinion." I think the counterinsurgency tactics, techniques, and procedures we learned from Vietnam and other counterinsurgencies were very valid. . . .

One of the ways we kept the nationalist insurgents that used to make a lot of noise about starting to fight us again when I was just past in Iraq was to convince them we were leaving. We would talk through some of the former Ba'athists, through some of the generals that had contacts with these mostly former army officers who were national 1920 Brigade, those guys. And I would do it personally, and all the commanders would say the same thing. We'd say, "Look, the number one item on your agenda is for the Coalition to leave. That is also the number one item on our agenda. So you're going to get what you want. In the meantime, we're trying to help, so don't fight us."

One of the reasons we closed Camp Fallujah [is that] Fallujah in this war, it will be the Mount Suribachi or the Hue City or the Tet Offensive, if you will. Fallujah will be the name that will always be remembered from this war. We had a Camp Fallujah. I needed to get smaller anyway. We were in the process of trying to guard ourselves, so we picked Camp Fallujah [in part because of the name]; the message was, the camps we needed the most in the bad days were closing because we were getting smaller.

Remember, when I got there, I had 38,000 U.S. military personnel under my command. When I left, I had 23,000. The Army left almost entirely, but the point is that I believe we convinced the nationalists that were getting a little bit frustrated, because the security situation got better. However, things weren't getting better fast enough, because the central government wasn't very quick to respond, and we convinced them we were going home. And I would get out there and tell them all the time. Look, I did radio shows. We put these in newspapers. I used to be 38 [thousand], now I'm 30, now I'm 25, now I'm 23, we're getting smaller. We closed Camp Fallujah with a lot of fanfare. It took us about a year to close it. We started an IO [information operations] campaign to tell the communities we're leaving, and we have to close these bases. We closed the base at al Qaim. We left Habbaniyah. And all of this was purposely advertised to convince a lot of these guys that . . . we're going home, we want to go home, this thing is all but over. Hang tough.

And we engaged an awful lot of senior former Ba'athists, and they had blood on their hands, but they were excluded from rehabilitation by the anti Ba'ath laws, but these weren't murderers. . . . We engaged with these guys. We worked on behalf of them to get their pensions. I think about 75 percent of them finally got their pensions from the central government. We won them on our side, and they had big influence with these young guys who were the former leaders of the nationalist insurgents. And the message was, just be patient, and they worked on our behalf to keep those guys patient.

Interview 18
Transition to Iraqi Control, Part II

Brigadier General Martin Post

Deputy Commanding General
I Marine Expeditionary Force (Forward)
Multi National Force • West

February 2008 to February 2009

Brigadier General Martin Post, a Marine aviator, was deputy commanding general for I Marine Expeditionary Force and served as deputy commanding general of Multi National Force West from February 2008 to February 2009. He was responsible for governance, economics, and reconstruction in al Anbar Province.

In this interview, Major General Post discusses the transition from II Marine Expeditionary Force to I Marine Expeditionary Force, work on the fuel and power supply, and efforts to improve governance and economic capacity. He describes the relationship with the State Department's provincial reconstruction teams and embedded provincial reconstruction teams and their joint efforts to improve the agriculture sector. He details helping the Iraqis develop budgets and describes improvements in security, the drop in kinetic violence, the transition to Iraq control, the success of Marine military and police training teams, the reduction of Coalition forces, and detainee releases.

Brigadier General Post was interviewed by Colonel Stephen E. Motsco on 18 March 2009 at Camp Pendleton, California.

Colonel Stephen E. Motsco: Can you describe your recent tour as the deputy commanding general of Multi National Force West?

Brigadier General Martin Post: ... Let me just preface the timing of what transpired. II MEF [II Marine Expeditionary Force] was there [in al Anbar Province] prior to us. II MEF really came out of the fight. When they got there, there was still some pretty significant fighting going on. That would have been in early '07 time frame. And then, come about the summer of '07, things started to improve. That was really kind of the back side of the Awakening, if you want to call it that, where the Sunni tribes came and were working with the Coalition forces in Anbar to fight al Qaeda.

One of the things that you really have to understand is the tribes *are* Anbar. There are tribes all throughout Iraq, but the tribes in Anbar, the Sunni tribes, are really the real deal. They pretty much run [things], from a day to day perspective. They are the connecting file here with the people. There's nothing that goes on inside Anbar Province that is not affiliated in some way, shape, or form through tribal connections or tribal law or so forth.

So one of the things that General John [R.] Allen did, who was the deputy CG [commanding general] for II MEF, he spent [a great deal] of time bringing back tribal leaders back into Anbar who [had] gone to Jordan. He spent a lot of time doing kind of shuttle diplomacy and went back and brought them back. And so, really, by the time we showed up, in January of 2008, for all intent and purposes, all the paramount sheikhs for the tribes were back in place. There were still onesies and twosies in Jordan, but, quite frankly, at that time those guys were never going to come back. And even though we did talk to a couple of them, they were kind of sitting pretty comfortable. They were truly more businessmen at this junction, turned into international businessmen, and I don't think, they may come back here in three or four years if Iraq continues to progress. So really, when you take a look at the tribe piece of this thing, the II MEF had brought all the tribes back, so I didn't have to really worry about that. I didn't have to worry about doing that type of engagement, because they were all there.

What we worked on . . . was really economics and the governance piece of this thing, continuing to try to ensure that process. I spent a lot of time, obviously, as you would expect, with the governor, with the provincial council, which was a body of about 49 folks that were kind of your legislative side of the state, which in this case was the Anbar Province. And so we, collectively, with the PRT [provincial reconstruction team], but really to start with—I'll kind of describe this—there was a transition while we were there. When we got there, it was kind of like the MNF West [Multi National Force West] was in charge, and the PRT followed . . . Even though the PRT had a role and responsibilities, because of the security situation, because of how this thing had transitioned, we kind of ran everything, if you would, in coordination and conjunction with a good relationship with the PRT.

There were four PRTs in Anbar. There was the provincial PRT, which was in Ramadi. You had an ePRT [embedded provincial reconstruction team] in Fallujah, another ePRT in Ramadi for the city of Ramadi proper, which was the capital, and then you had an ePRT in al Asad, which covered from Hit all the way out to the Syrian border, up the Euphrates River Valley.

We got in there, sat down and started taking a look at the state of affairs with respect to Anbar. It became real clear early on that there were two common denominators. One was on the infrastructure side—power and fuel. You weren't going to get anything done because of the current state of those two primary, key linchpins in restarting an economy. So the deal was, if we could increase the amount of fuel that's brought into the province, and at that point they were getting less than 10 million liters a month of all types of product, whether it be kerosene, gas, or what I call benzene, which is their gas. It was about a tenth of what they needed, what they required. They were getting about 20 percent of the power they needed in the province, off the national grid, because of the status of the national grid. So what that told you it would be is they were getting about four to six hours of power a day, off the national grid—average—across the province. And everybody depended upon generators for the rest of the time. Of course, you need fuel to run generators. And so you can see, again, it was this Catch 22 type deal with them.

So if you're talking about businesses, if you're talking about trying to get investors—all of the things that you want to do to try to get this economy turned around—always went back to fuel and power, right from the get go. The power situation was such that we weren't ever going to solve that problem, because that's about a 5 to 10 year problem. [For example,] a major power plant [is] being built in Anbar, by Haditha. . . . [But] they stopped work because the negotiations with contracts. . . . Haditha Dam [is] the big power producer for the province, [but] even though the Haditha Dam was pushing out power inside Anbar Province, they couldn't keep it all. They had to push it out and get their allocation back.

So at the end of the day, we knew that the power situation was going to be kind of a throwaway, so we really concentrated on fuel.

When we first got there, they were doing two fuel runs a month, up to the Baiji oil refinery, escorted by Marines, basically bringing back about 200 trucks a month, 250 sometimes, of the products— kerosene, diesel, and benzene, or gas, if you would. And of course, as I said, that was hardly enough to make anything work. I sat down with the governor, I said, "Listen, this isn't going to work. We need to come up with a better way." Plus, we said, "Us going out and escorting your fuel shipments, in the long run, we've got to get out of this. We're not going to do this forever for you." So there was a lot of negotiations that went on. We finally got them to come to the table and get a private contractor in to start moving fuel. It took a while to get this thing cranking. It was about a four or five month process. But, at the end of the day, when we left, they were getting about anywhere between 800 and 1,000 trucks a month, so it was about a four to five fold increase in fuel coming into the province, which was substantial.

The second piece of it was there was an oil refinery up near Haditha, called Haqlaniyah, or . . . "K3," that's the oil refinery. Obviously, the pipes from Baiji to K3 were mincemeat, so that wasn't going to work, so we sat down and figured out, hey, how can we get crude oil down to the refinery and start refining the product in the province proper? We decided, hey, maybe we can move it by train. There was a large train station right there, within about four klicks [kilometers] of the K3. I took a look at the mechanics of this thing, said it's feasible, and so over about a three month period, from nothing but dirt to a facility at a railroad [siding], where you could pull train cars in, offload the crew right there, put the pumps, put all the piping in and pump it all the way four klicks over to K3. Then it went through the whole iteration of restarting K3 refinery. The U.S. government spent about $4 million on that, and there was some Iraqi government money spent, not a lot, but the governor provided us some money. But at the end of the day, as that effort works and we got the refinery started, and actually, we started producing fuel right there in Anbar.

There's a subset here to this, because I told you about the power plant up by Haditha. There was a pipeline running from this K3 over to that power plant. That power plant ran off of heavy fuel oil, which is a by product of refining, and there was a pipeline built to that. So at the end of the day, when that power plant is completed, you have to have K3 running, because they're going to use the by product of heavy fuel oil to run their generators, to produce the power. So there was a connecting dot here in the long term for how you were going to get power, more power to the national grid. Also, another refinery running, putting more people to work and so forth. So that was probably one of the successes that when we walked away, from a fuel standpoint, where in some cases we were getting equivalency up over 1,000 trucks a month, when we started with less than 200 when we first got there.

When we first got there, everybody complained about fuel. When we left, there were never any complaints about having enough fuel. It was power. And of course the one thing that was increased because of what the fuel, all the local generators, they had more fuel. The moms were happy because there was maybe four or five or six hours of additional power a day being generated there by neighborhoods or your own local generator.

So those things, again, it gets back to the basic premise of when you're trying to recrank a country back up, with the infrastructure of a country. There was some war damage to infrastructure, but it was primarily superficial. When you get down to water, sewage, all the basic, fundamental things you need to run a society as we would think of it, most of it was dilapidated. It was in place, or in some cases just had not been maintained, so what we found ourselves is we had to go in and, in a lot of cases go in and start fixing that type of stuff.

As you would expect, [such efforts were] problematic because, again, Anbar Province is kind of unique. The eastern side of Anbar, Fallujah and Ramadi, was about 70 percent of the population— two cities. Of course, eastern Anbar is the smallest size. Then you go from Hit all the way out to the Euphrates, Syrian border, and then all the way down to Jordan. As you know, it's spread out pretty well, so now trying to go back into those cities, up toward Hit, Haditha, Rawah, Ana, al Qaim, and so forth and trying to look at those individual infrastructures and fix things that needed to get done. So really, what we did on that was we had our civil affairs dets [detachments] that were actually with the RCTs [regimental combat teams], and they worked hand in hand with the ePRTs. And so what you had was—I call it the tactical level stuff—they were down there looking at individual problems in individual cities, prioritizing with the local councils, trying to figure out what money they were getting from the Iraqi government to fix things. And what we would do is come in, either using DoD [Department of Defense] funds, CERP [commander's emergency relief program] or DoS [Department of State] funds, QRF funds—quick reaction funds. They would try to identify an issue and try to help fix something, some piece of infrastructure.

So it was slow going in some cases, but in other cases, because of how we could manipulate or how we could use DoD funds, especially CERP, is we could get things done pretty quick. Going through our process was fairly quick at the MEF, so repairing infrastructure, repairing schools, post offices, community centers, all the things that had to get done. A lot of that, quite frankly, is because Marines have lived in a lot of these facilities, or the Iraqi forces have lived in these cities during the fight. So what we did is, when we started getting this province back on its feet, all of a sudden, well, those buildings used to be part of running cities or towns. So now you had, once you pull them out, of course, they were, as you would expect, gutted, nothing there. So we went back in and put them back to really better than what they were previously, whether it be a schoolhouse, or a mayor's office, or a municipalities building, power, electricity, air conditioning, all the things that you would need so somebody could go in there and go to work.

So we spent [a lot] of time through 2008, all the way through Anbar, basically rebuilding that infrastructure that could sustain, as I would call it, kind of the leadership or the workforce to get the economy moving, to get the things up and running. So that was a balancing act, and of course the toughest challenge we had—and it was a learning process—was training the Iraqis how to plan and how to do, as you and I call it, O&M, operations and maintenance. We don't have the time or energy here this morning to go through the ministries in Baghdad, how all that worked, but needless to say, it's pretty chaotic, it's pretty top down, and quite frankly, the Iraqis would build something. They'd build it and that was it. They would not have budgets to go back in, like we would have a budget, to, okay, I've got to put X amount of dollars in there to keep the thing running, check filters, and go back and do all the things you would want to do.

So trying to have them understand that, well, that's a key piece. I could build the facility for you, but in six months, if you don't keep up with it, if you don't have trained technicians doing it, then in six months it'll break, and then you're going to walk away from it. Their weakest—from a provincial level, the governor of the provincial council and the director generals (the DGs) of all the different entities—their weakest thing was planning. You've got to remember, they were [used to] centralized planning, everything from Baghdad. They gave it to you, they executed it, and nobody—you never questioned Baghdad. So if they didn't give you the money to sustain it, it was like, well, tough.

[We're] trying to have them understand that, okay, if you're going to do this, then where is the follow through? I'll rebuild this school, get the DG of education for the city and the DG of education for the province, have them sit down and say, "Okay, where are the teachers? Where are the school supplies? Where are all the desks? Where are all the things that you need to stand this school up?" And once we started doing that, all of a sudden, the light bulbs started coming on with these folks. Okay, they got it. What we were trying to do was reengineer 40 years of mindset of how things work. . . .

The planning piece was the most difficult, and part and parcel of that was . . . the ability to build a budget. Again, previously, provinces were just given things. They never submitted a budget request, per se. Each ministry would go down through their director general into a province, minister of electricity, minister of oil, minister of health, minister of education. They would all have individual budgets, would come into the province, and those director generals would do what they needed to do in their health or education, disconnected really from what the governor or the provincial council was doing. So trying to get those two bodies to sit down and say, "Okay, let's look strategically at the province. What do we need to do to build a budget?"

So in 2008, an extraordinary amount of work was done, and we brought some comptrollers in, a couple of guys from Headquarters Marine Corps who do this for a living, actually from P&R, Programs and Resources, and we basically. We give [the Iraqis] an A for effort, but it was probably a C end product, but they built a budget. And [the comptrollers] went from city to city and sat down with each city council, and they said, "Okay, you prioritize what your issues are. You break it out by sector. What projects do you need?" And they went all through the province, brought all that back to Ramadi, racked and stacked them all, and then at the end of the day, they submitted that budget back there, and that was submitted in July of 2008. So that was the first time that a province had ever really that methodically had gone through and looked at it.

And again, first time, it wasn't perfect, how we would look at it from a Western eye. We'd kind of go, "Oh, I'm not liking this." But, at the end of the day, that worked. . . . They're going through those throes in Anbar right now in preparation for the 2010 budget. They're working now for that next iteration. So hopefully what will happen here is what they learned last year, what they're going to see for what they need for this year, build that dedicated planning, but a budget also built on a good planning foundation, and submit that to Baghdad.

And, hopefully, over time, they will slowly start to build their infrastructure back up to where it needs to be. Again, I go back to the basic fundamentals. I think three to five years, the power is going to be, there's obviously from a national grid perspective, there's going to be a substantial increase in power in the province and throughout Iraq. So what that will happen is, to me, [when that happens], it puts them as a second tier world country, because now they have power 24/7. [In the United States] it's a state of emergency if you don't have power for two hours, especially with our wives. But if you can imagine living on six to eight hours of power when it's 120 degrees out—tough living.

This equates back to who wants to go in and invest in Iraq? A lot of people said, "Oh, the only way to fix Iraq is to get investors to come in and do all this, and they'll make it happen." Yeah, but there are certain things that an investor wants to have. So if I'm going to go build a plant down in Georgia, I'm going to have water, I'm going to have power. I'm going to have all the things that are there. I go and just plug into them, quite frankly. It's not easy, but it's fundamentally there. If you're going to build a plant in Anbar Province, well, the first thing you've got is you're going to have to bring in four one megawatt generators because there's not enough power to run that plant. Oh, by the way, you have to have fuel to do that, and how are you going to [get that]? There's just a degree of difficulty that some people, quite frankly—and I'm talking about some very senior people in the U.S. government—never thought through.

But, having said that, we did spend a lot of time over in Jordan. We did spent a lot of time working with international businessmen. A lot of expats from Anbar went to Jordan, took a lot of money with them. They're willing to come back, and some have come back and, quite frankly, some of them are already investing in Anbar Province, which is good, which we didn't have to set up. They're entrepreneurs. If they see there's money to be made, guys will figure out how to do it. There are already capitalists running around, without a doubt, in Anbar, throughout Iraq. They're figuring out real quick if there is money to be had, people will figure out a way to provide a service, and they're making that work. So, as I look at it, there's going to be a steady increase. . . .

There was one constant in Anbar—agriculture. At one time, Anbar Province used to be kind of the bread basket, because the Euphrates River runs right through the middle of it. And, quite frankly, if you have water in the desert, anything grows. But what we found, like anything else, was the infrastructure of that had not been taken care of. [There was] a lack of education of how to maintain fields, how they do water management. It was very, very poor. Now, quite frankly, I will tell you that we happened to have a couple—go figure—a couple farmers, Reservists. One guy was a potato farmer from the state of Washington. He knew this stuff. The PRT obviously had some USAID [United States Agency for

International Development] guys in there, and also some ag experts from the States.

We sat down and took a look at what could we do in the agriculture sector. First thing is, well, it's like anything else. There's subsets. The first is the water. You've got to move the water, and then you've got to get it to the fields, and then you've got to—there's about eight steps here to make things work. Thirty five provincial level water pumping stations, three quarters of them weren't working. Okay, let me fix that. That's mechanic stuff, that's pumps and generators, so we did that, through the Iraqis—sat down with the Iraqis, mapped it all out. What do we have to get done? Where are they at? Even finding some of these damn things, by lat long grid, took us a while. But at the end of the day, we got all that squared away. Hundreds of miles of canals in Anbar, small, large, basically have to be maintained on a three to five year cycle or they just go up in reeds. And the reeds that grow in these damn things, it's like a piece of barbed wire. . . . And so what happened was they hadn't been maintained. So damn near every canal over there was choked with these large reeds. These things were probably 10, 12 feet high. So we spent an inordinate amount of money, an inordinate amount of time, working with the Iraqis, and the Iraqis used some of their resources also to go back and start clearing canals. . . .

I don't know what the final number was, but we cleared thousands of kilometers of canals, again, as part and parcel, so now you can get the water to the fields, and then to the local farmers. And then, working with the appropriate ag specialists, and we had some folks from Texas A&M come in; . . . they'd sit down with the local farmers, [from] trying to develop co ops to how they could go to an end to end process. Again, it goes back to 40 years of you were given seed by Baghdad, and you planted. The government bought your product, and it just repeated. No initiative, per se, open market where if you could try something different and go and basically take your product and sell it for the best price, because you always got the price. So, again, their mindset was, hey, if I can sell it, the government will buy it, and I'll be okay. Trying to step into a free market sector and, again, I'm not an economist or an agriculture specialist, but try and get them to understand. They got it.

Quite frankly, the younger generation over there gets it. The ones that are in their 20s and 30s, who haven't been so ingrained by the past, will turn this country around. The guys who are my age, in their 50s and 60s, who have been there, their whole life was driven by [the] top down [system], from Saddam [Hussein], here's how we do business, then, well, trying to break them [out of the past] and get them to see a different way. . . . From a governance and economic standpoint, what we try to do is, working with the governor, working with the provincial council, working with all the city mayors, try to develop a process, sector by sector, and again, have them establish priorities. It's tough for them to grasp. Hey, this is all broke. Well, okay, great. You've got 10 things that are broke, what's number 1 and what's number 10? Just like we do. That's the same thing that we do in the States, and sometimes you don't like it. So that was a process that we had to kind of ingrain in them, and they're figuring it out, and it'll be a slow, it'll be a continued, hopefully a positive trend over here in the next several years as they continue to work. . . .

I had not been to Anbar Province before. So I didn't have an expectation, whereas some guys who had been there, like General Kelly had been there previously, had seen the darker days, and gone back. It was a startling difference. . . . When II MEF left, II MEF had lost 90 Marines in combat operations in a year, in their year there. In the year we were there, we lost 22 in combat operations. We lost some other Marines in noncombat. But if that's the scale, that is some scale, 90 to 22. So we weren't fighting, and most of our casualties were IEDs [improvised explosive devices], losing Devil Dogs [troops] in vehicles, for the most part. Some onesies and twosies, a couple of other situations, but primarily in vehicles.

We very rarely ever started a shot first. We did offensive operations, we did some operations up in the desert. We ran a lot of guys down in the wadis and so forth, but at the end of the day, I think offensively, we didn't shoot any artillery the whole time we were there, not a single round. We did some illum[ination]. That was about the extent of it. I think we might have done four to five missions, with aircraft, when we actually got hold of some bad guys running around a desert. . . . But really, the offensive, kinetic operations, [while] we were there, really we mounted pretty much nothing. We were still being proactive, but it was just less and less and less, the entire year through 2008, which obviously was a good thing.

And again, it goes back to—you talk to the Iraqis—when we first got there, . . . security was still the number one priority—security, security, security. When we left, if you asked them what their problems were, the first five things weren't security. It was not enough power, we need to fix the schools. . . .

What we did when we first got there in April, . . . the MEF was at Camp Fallujah. I moved my G 9, our CMO [civil military operations], to Ramadi and collocated it with the PRT, for two reasons. One was, it needed to be there, because if we're going to do a single effort, you can't have two entities out there running around doing things, not connected. And we built a joint common plan with them that basically was signed by General Kelly and Mr. James [V.] Soriano, who was the PRT lead, saying basically, "These are our priorities, and this is what we're going to do," kind of the first step. And we worked that over the summer.

At the same time, and again, I'll give you a couple of the challenges that we saw going in. One challenge was we were going to have to shift the security file to the Iraqis, provincial PIC, provincial Iraqi control. We were supposed to do that; actually, we were supposed to do that in March April when we first got there. They weren't ready. We ended up doing it 1 September. It took about 60 days because of some political stuff in Baghdad on the Iraqi side, not necessarily on the Coalition side. That was a big deal, . . . and that was kind of a mindset change for them to say, okay, that's not our problem anymore. You've got a problem, that's yours to solve, whether it be the police, whether it be the Iraqi army. But that was a good step to kind of get their feet on the ground.

Then the next piece of this thing was the elections. Now, the elections were supposed to go in October. They got slid because of political maneuvering in Baghdad, but that was really the next iteration of where they kind of are really standing on their own two feet. And just when we left, and it was within days of us leaving, they had over 300,000 Sunnis vote in al Anbar Province, where they had 3,000 vote in the first election. These people were ready. They knew they screwed it up. In hindsight, you're always smarter. They didn't vote the first time around, so they looked at the elected officials who were running the province as, "You weren't elected." But it's like, well, hey, tough. The ones that voted, we're working. Somebody's got to do the job. So it'll be an interesting year. We were hoping to be there through the transition, where we started the new provincial council, the new governor, just to see all that work. And of course, II MEF is going through that right now as we speak, which is nothing but goodness.

At the same time, in the fall, and basically in October, we did something in Iraq that no other province had done, or no other MND [multinational division] or MNF [multinational force] had done. We basically put the PRT in the lead for all governance and economics, and several reasons for that, but really the fundamental reason was, at the end of the day—and this is probably my biggest complaint of how things ran in Iraq, proper—was you can't have two cooks in the kitchen. It's the fundamental view, there can't be two bosses. It doesn't work. So if you took a look at Baghdad, you had Department of State, you had the embassy. In the embassy, they had an economic section, and then they had the OPA, which is the Office of Provincial Authority, which the [call] still was in the embassy, who all the PRTs worked through. Yes, you had engineers, another organization called ITAO, which is Iraq transition [assistance] office, who worked—actually, it was a surrogate for the embassy, and they kind of did engineering type stuff. And then you had MNF West [Multi National Force West], you had MNF Iraq [Multi National Force Iraq], MNC I [Multi National Corps Iraq], Corps, and they all had their hands in reconstruction and that type of thing.

So if you took a look at how the U.S. government was doing this, it was [messed] up. You had all these different people, all great Americans, all wanting to do the right thing, but in my opinion, not a single guy or gal in charge who said, "This is the way we're going to go," and make it go. The challenges there were—which you would expect—is you had to work through multiple agencies in Baghdad to get things done. Okay, fine. You figured out who the players were, and you made it work. I won't go through the iteration on that. But what we decided to do was, hey, if we're going to talk the talk, then let's walk the walk. So what we did was, we went to the PRT and said, Jim [Soriano], "We're going to give you the lead on all these things. What talent do you want?" I had about, oh, 35, 40 folks working for me in the G 9, CMO. Actually, the number was higher than that, but there were a lot of enlisted kids driving and so forth, but really, the nuts and bolts guys that were doing the stuff. Jim was going to handle about 45 folks in the PRT ish ballpark, so I said, "What talent do you need from us?" And so they came up with about 15 folks, and I gave 15 Marines to the PRT, in different disciplines, with different expertise. And then they didn't work for me anymore. They worked for Jim Soriano, worked for the PRT.

[Notes that the new organizational structure "caused a hell of a lot of consternation in Baghdad," particularly when they told people, "Don't talk to us, talk to PRT. They've got this. They now are the lead for Anbar Province."]

The interesting thing is, when we went up and briefed this concept, the ambassador said, "This is the best thing I've seen. This is the way we ought to be doing business in Iraq," kind of the one guy in charge type thing. Candidly, if I was given the mission to go do this and start over again, knowing what I know, is I would have put the reconstruction czar under the DoD [Department of Defense], and I would have taken all the smart, appropriate DoS [Department of State] folks, whether it be the ag folks or all the different folks who were out there, and put them in one organization under DoD. Because, quite frankly, whether you like it or not, is the culture of DoD, we can get things done, where the culture of DoS, different culture, God love them to death. It just is what is what it is. . . .

The other thing we did during 2008, we started weaning them off of Coalition force capacity. For example, the governor never went anywhere without the Coalition force taking him, never went anywhere—to Baghdad, to a city, to go to work in the morning. And, candidly, as you well imagine, when he first got the job, they were fighting; he was fighting to get into work and fighting to go home every day, during the bad days. At some point we told the governor, in the late summer, "Governor, we're not going to do this anymore for you. You're going to go to work. You had your own PSD [personal security detail], [should have] trained your guys in your own PSD. If you want to go to Baghdad, governor, you've got to get yourself to Baghdad. Now, if there's something we need to go up there with specifically, sure, we'll fly in." And we did fly him a couple of times for key meetings and so forth.

So what we tried to do, under our watch over there, when we were dealing with the Iraqis, was to try to take a step back and say, "You guys start doing this.". . . We had to minimize our footprint. We had to get out of the cities, and that's where we go back into rehabbing all the things that we broke, and all the facilities we hadn't maintained, and go refurbish them and so forth as we pulled out.

The ECPs [entry control points] [were a] big deal. I mean, that's how you control the people going in and out of Fallujah. We turned the ECPs over to the Iraqis, [but] we waited until they asked us to do that. After the security arrangement, after we did provincial Iraqi control on 1 September, it was about two months later that they came to us and [said], "Hey, we're ready to take the ECPs.". . .

So our year, . . . we predominantly closed the deal on the security side, continued to do the training with the police, training with the border patrol, the border forces. The Iraqi army was really in pretty good shape. The commitment the Marine Corps had made to transition teams, TTs, years ago, paid off. I mean, the 1st and 7th Divisions were the best two divisions in the Iraqi army, and it showed, because they pulled them and went to Basrah. They went to Diyala, they went to Mosul with those divisions, and they kicked ass, operating unilaterally, with Marine Corps TTs with them.

Quite frankly, the biggest compliment the Marine Corps ever got was when they had that little dustup in Basrah, and they sent the 1st Division down there, and we sent our TTs with them. The British commander . . . said, "Hey, the only reason that Basrah didn't fall was because of the Marines." Now of course you can imagine the Army guys almost fell out of their chair. What he meant was, the 1st Division was so good, and having the Marine

TTs with them, they came in there, they were just astounded how good they were, because their division, the 14th Division, the one in Basrah, was the one that just fell apart, ran away. So the Marine Corps over the years spent an inordinate bill with TTs and [getting] the right people in there, and so the 1st and 7th Division were extraordinary divisions. . . . They were the best in Iraq. . . .

The police matured substantially in 2008, probably have a couple more years really to go, but they basically now have the confidence to manage the security, the civil capacity, civil governance, in the cities and making that work.

The last thing that we were working on to try to close the deal was the professionalism of the border forces. . . . We're trying to increase the resources and logistics of the border forces so they can be a better entity, if you would, for the whole makeup.

So, on the security side, when we basically turned it over to II MEF, [we] said, "Listen, they've got it.". . . I think in another month or two, they're going to be down to three maneuver battalions in Anbar Province from when we were there. It was 14 when we first got there. So, again, you can see, a lot of things had changed.

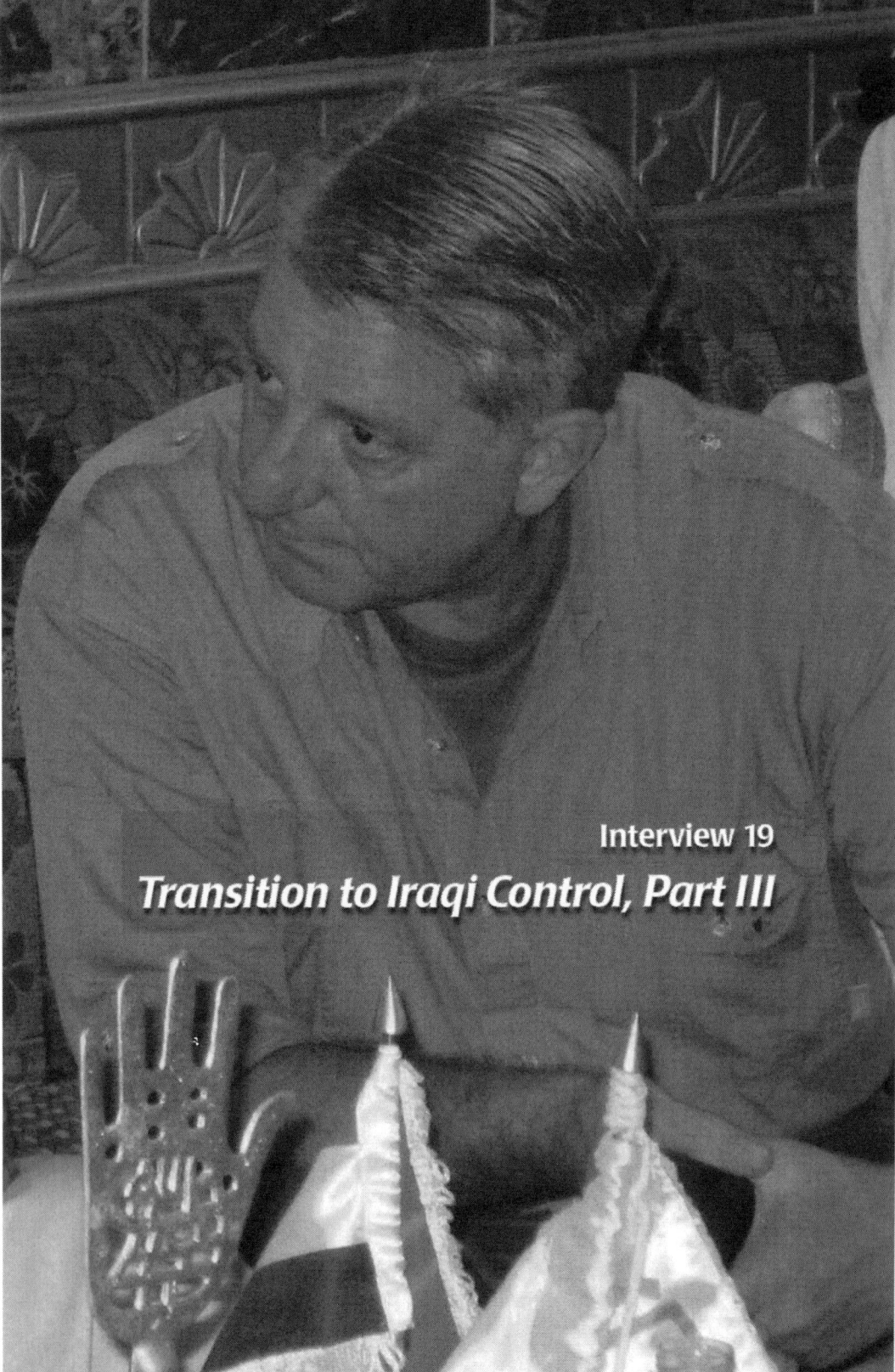

Interview 19
Transition to Iraqi Control, Part III

Mr. James V. Soriano

Provincial Reconstruction Team Leader
U.S. Department of State

September 2006 to Present (as of mid-2009)

Mr. James V. Soriano is a career U.S. Department of State Foreign Service officer with 25 years of experience. He has served in various capacities at the U.S. embassies in Yemen, Lebanon, Egypt, Jordan, and India. He had previously worked in Iraq in 2003 2004 as the senior Coalition civilian official in al Muthanna Province under the Coalition Provisional Authority. Soriano returned to Iraq in September 2006 as the leader of a 60 person provincial reconstruction team in al Anbar Province. He followed Mr. John Kael Weston, who worked closely with Marines in Iraq from 2004 through mid 2006.

As the provincial reconstruction team leader, Soriano worked with Multi National Force West building capacity in al Anbar's provincial government, private sector, and civil societies. In this interview, he details the team's structure and its relationships with Marines and Iraqis. He describes arriving in al Anbar during the height of the insurgency as the Awakening movement in Ramadi was beginning and explains how the Awakening progressed from an anti al Qaeda security movement into a political party.

Mr. Soriano was interviewed by Colonel Gary W. Montgomery and Chief Warrant Officer 4 Timothy S. McWilliams on 13 February 2009 at Camp Ramadi, Iraq.

Chief Warrant Officer-4 Timothy S. McWilliams: Please tell us a little bit about yourself and the provincial reconstruction teams [PRTs].

Mr. James V. Soriano: I arrived in Iraq in September of 2006, so I've been here in Anbar Province heading up the Provincial Reconstruction Team for the last two years and five months now. There are four PRTs in Anbar. Three of them are embedded at the regimental level [ePRTs], and the one I lead [provincial level within Ramadi], which is now about 60 people, combined military civilian, at the provincial level.

We are partnered with the MEF [Marine expeditionary force] headquarters. My counterpart is the deputy commanding general, [Brigadier General] John [E.] Wissler. This new MEF that just came in, II MEF, which just arrived just a few days ago, is the fourth MEF I've worked with, . . . so I've seen a lot of changes since September '06.

I arrived in the height of the insurgency [and] was initially stationed at Camp Blue Diamond in Ramadi. There was very little to do in Ramadi at that time because of the insurgency and the kinetics. So I moved myself over to Camp Fallujah, which is where the flagpole is [MNF W headquarters], and I sort of embedded myself, if I could put it that way, with the MEF staff until the spring of '07 [because] there was very little to do here in Ramadi.

I couldn't get out. We couldn't engage the provincial government. The purpose of a PRT, as you know, is capacity building. That's our job. And my Iraqi counterparts—I just told you about my Marine counterpart—is the governor [Mamoun Sami Rashid al Alwani], the provincial council chairman [Abu Abdul Salam], the provincial council, and then my staff engages the directors of the various departments—sewage, water, electricity, and so forth.

The PRT's activities rest on three legs, I would say. One would be capacity building with the provincial government. The other is encouraging the private sector. We've got some activities there. And the third would be civil society, trying to encourage civil society organizations, such as a farmers' co op we're trying to set up, and so on. We were active very recently, in the last several days, with having NGOs [nongovernmental organizations] do a voter awareness campaign during the recent provincial council election in January of '09.

As I said, when I first arrived, there was heavy fighting. The high point of the battle, if I recall correctly from the graphs, was November of '06. After November '06, the graph of monthly security incidents starts to trail down, and by the spring of '07, it falls out then. It just heads due south. At this time, the provincial council of Anbar fled Ramadi. Actually, it fled in March of '06, as I recall, before I arrived. There was a sustained attack on the government center, [a] 24 hour attack that Marines [who] were based there [had] to beat it off. But the council decided to pull up stakes, and they moved to the relative safety of Baghdad, where there were some secure areas for Sunnis. Even there, it was a touch and go situation for Sunnis. The council met ad hoc in Baghdad [but] did not disband. . . .

Only the governor kept normal office hours at the government center in Ramadi, in downtown Ramadi, surrounded by a company of Marines. When I first met him at his office, I think it was the last week of September of '06. There was a gun battle right outside on the street, RPGs [rocket propelled grenades] were going off, and a few months later, his office where we were having that meeting was destroyed by I guess a rocket or a mortar. That was December of '06. The government center was a shambles. It was a war zone, it was a battlefield. When I got there, we could run between buildings with full PPE [personal protective equipment] and crouching down and all of that. Today, we just walk around in shirtsleeves.

The council fled to Baghdad, where they met infrequently, and I would have to say that its only contact with Americans during those days was with a USAID [United States Agency for International Development] contractor called RTI, Research Triangle Institute, which was doing capacity building with provincial councils around the country. They have a campus in the IZ [international zone in Baghdad]. RTI and several of the leaders of the provincial council were regulars there, and, practically speaking, their early contact with Americans was through RTI through those dark days of the spring, summer, fall of '06. The council moved back to Ramadi slowly, in stages, in the spring of '07. The Marines flew them out by helicopter back to Ramadi. They landed at Blue Diamond, and we had a few meetings on Camp Blue Diamond. The Anbaris didn't like that. They didn't like the appearance of needing American military protection to meet the guys on the council. They did that in April, May, June of '07.

By July '07, they moved back to the government center in Ramadi and returned to their traditional seat of power. By August of '07, the ground floor of the government center, where the governor has his office, was repaired using CERP [Commander's Emergency Relief Program] funds. The upper floor was still a shambles. (It's a two story structure.) And [the governor] began to have normal business hours. They [Iraqis] started coming in looking for services in September, October of '07. Women and children were crawling all over the place, looking for assistance with their various petitions and needs with the government.

When I arrived, of course, the Awakening was an early phenomenon in September '06. I think it started in Anbar in about September 13th, '06, after some false starts earlier that year in '06, in which al Qaeda apparently beat back an earlier attempt by the Ramadi sheikhs to form an anti al Qaeda coalition.

Sheikhs cooperating with the Coalition was nothing new. It happened first of all in al Qaim, but that was a localized phenomenon. It didn't travel very far, and it was due mostly for economic reasons, because al Qaeda was encroaching upon their trans border smuggling business. In Ramadi, Sheikh Sattar Abu Risha and a group of like minded sheikhs got together, formed a coalition; earlier it was called the Anbar Salvation Council, [then] the Anbar Awakening Council. The latter phrase, Anbar Awakening Council, still exists and is a political party not associated with the Abu Rishas. It is associated with someone else who was a founding member. Many founding members, maybe two dozen or three dozen local sheikhs and notables.

Abu Risha, Sheikh Sattar, I saw him many times. I shared meals with him many times. He had the utmost contempt for the Iraqi Islamic Party and contempt for any political party that had a religious basis or a foundation. He became a media phenomenon almost immediately, and this was September '06. By November, October in '06, he was badgering the provincial council, which was in Baghdad, for seats for representation. The election for the provincial council took place in January of '05. It was widely boycotted. The mosques called for boycott, and you know the story—3,700 votes were cast in a huge province, and the IIP or Iraqi Islamic Party was the one that won the right to form the council and control.

By the fall of '06, that became intolerable to the Awakening sheikhs, Sattar and his fellow travelers there, and they felt that they stood and fought. The council fled. There was a sense of entitlement. There was a sense of contempt because they were religiously based. He went on TV many times. Sattar started a media campaign against corrupt government, absentee government, and all of the rest. [Iraqi Prime Minister Nouri Kamil Mohammed Hassan al] Maliki intervened in early November of '06. He sent Dr. Rafe al Essawi, who was a cabinet minister in those days, but today he's a deputy prime minister from Fallujah. He had him broker a deal, which was brokered at the Rasheed Hotel in Baghdad, in which the IIP, the governing party, agreed to expand the number of seats on the council from 40 to 48 and gave the additional seats to the Awakening. They had another person on the council that was sympathetic to them, so they had nine votes out of 48. That was the situation that existed, nine out of 48, throughout the next two years, until there was just an election a few days ago, basically.

Sattar certainly sent al Qaeda on the run. By winter of '06, early '07 I should say, it was clear that the battlefield had tipped in our favor, that his phenomenon did travel, as opposed to the early one in al Qaim that was imitated in other provinces. However, his leadership was basically localized to Ramadi. It never really got very much beyond Ramadi, and I think when we did the analysis of the last election, I think most of the votes that his group has gotten will come from Ramadi. There are probably several of the tribes that are sort of associated with him, and they probably gave him the bulk of the votes earned. It would be surprising to me if the Awakening sheikh—since [Sattar] was killed later—if his brother, Ahmad Abu Risha, was able to get a lot of votes outside of Ramadi. It's not a bad place to be, because Ramadi is the most populous city, has the most votes, so strategically, it's a well orchestrated political campaign. He was pretty much in a pretty good position because he got a lot of votes where most of the people live.

By the spring of '07, Sattar launched an attack and withdrawal kind of approach against the provincial council, turning up the heat, usually through a media campaign and complaints about corruption and malfeasance and so forth, always with the intention of getting more seats or increasing his power sharing agreement to his favor. The governor's position at this time was precarious. We all thought that Sattar was after the governor's chair, to get him kicked out. Mamoun Sami Rashid, as I just said earlier, was the only government official who actually maintained office hours during the dark days of '06, survived many assassination attempts. [He] thought that Sattar wanted him out. I was at an Iftar dinner, hosted by General Zilmer at Camp Fallujah. This would be October '06, at which Sattar and the governor were invited. And it was a very unpleasant dinner. . . .

As a compromise, the governor agreed to take on a deputy governor who would be named by Sattar Abu Risha. He was, as you know, supported by the 1st Brigade, 1st Armored Division, under then Colonel Sean [B.] MacFarland [USA], now General MacFarland, and then later, after March of '07, by the 1/3 BCT [1st Brigade Combat Team, 3d Infantry] with Colonel John [W.] Charlton [USA]. They parked an M1 Abrams tank right outside the front door of Sattar's compound and residence, right outside Camp Ramadi here, within eyesight for many months. It was taken away finally in October of '07.

So through the spring of '07, Sattar was keeping his pressure on. At that time, the deputy commanding general, General John [R.] Allen and I [went] to broker a cease fire of words, if you will, with the governor and Sattar Abu Risha and a lot of other sheikhs, a lot of shouting going on. And we sort of kept the lid on. Meanwhile, the battlefield was tipping into our favor throughout this period of time, and by the summer of '07, as I said, the provincial council returned to its normal seat of power and business returned to normal.

In September of '07, President [George W.] Bush visited and called on Prime Minister Maliki, the governor, and several sheikhs, including Sattar Abu Risha [at Al Asad air base]. Seven days later, Abu Risha was killed by a bomb planted on his compound, as he was apparently moving from his horse stable back to his residence. There was a roadside bomb, and I was downtown in Ramadi. I was at the government center, actually, and we heard the windows rattle, and we saw a plume of smoke and we didn't understand what it was until we got back to base. I went to the funeral. You can imagine who was there. General [Raymond T.] Odierno [USA] was there. At the time, he was the MNC I commander. Many hundreds, hundreds or thousands of mourners were there.

At this time, I had organized a visit to the United States for the so called Anbar eight, as I called them. This was the governor, the provincial council chairman, I wanted Sattar Abu Risha to join [us], and I got the provincial council chairman as well to agree with it, and he chose Mayor Latif [Obaid Ayadah of Ramadi]. So there were two members of the Awakening on that delegation, four from the IIP, and two independents. One was the governor and then his deputy governor. Governor Mamoun has IIP roots, but after he took office, I think in '05, he professed to govern in a nonpartisan way. The assassination created a vacancy on this delegation.*

This is an International Visitor [Leadership] Program. It was two weeks in the States. I accompanied them. General Allen accompanied them. We did a week in Washington. Sheikh Sattar's older brother, Ahmad Abu Risha, took over the wings of leadership of the Awakening and was added to the delegation. We called on the president in October or early November of '07, Secretary [Robert M.] Gates at DoD [Department of Defense], Secretary [of State Condoleezza] Rice. We did many calls to Capitol Hill. We flew down to Houston, Texas. We met the president's father [George H.W. Bush] down there and flew back up to Vermont. I think we were in Montpelier, and there was a National Guard unit that had served in Ramadi. . . . Throughout that visit, the behavior of all participants was, of course, in my presence, it was very proper, and polite. Perhaps behind my back, there was a lot of backbiting between them. . . .

---

*The eight members of the delegation were Mamoun Sami Rashid al-Alwani, provincial governor of al-Anbar Province; Dr. Abdulsalam Abdullah al-Ani, the provincial council chairman; Ahmad Bezia Fteikhan al-Rishawi, Satter Abu Risha's brother; Latif O. Ayada, mayor of Ramadi; Dr. Othman Hummadi, vice governor for planning; Dr. Ashour Hamid Saleh, a member of the provincial council and the Islamic Iraqi Party's top official in the province; Dr. Zekei Obaid Fayad, a provincial council member and the Islamic Iraqi Party leader in Fallujah; and Dr. Rafe al-Essawi, the minister of state for foreign affairs.

From New York, we went to Amman, Jordan, in November '07, and we had a week there for a workshop, organized by this USAID contractor I referred to a moment ago, RTI, and my staff. And the upshot of that workshop was to draft a provincial development strategy. We broke down into working groups, and the RTI guy paid the bills. It was over at the Marriot Hotel in Amman. They invited about 120 Anbaris, and about that many showed up. We had about 120, so that was the provincial council plus. And they invited—this is IIP, now; they're the ones who are giving us the guest list, the participants' list comes from the IIP, and they gave us a list of the Awakening folks to invite, too. It was supposed to be all inclusive, a joint effort, by Anbaris, to draft an economic vision statement of their own future in the immediate aftermath of an insurgency. The exercise was well worth it. The final product was kind of badly written, but the exercise of bringing people together was worth it. . . .

Ahmad Abu Risha transformed the Awakening from what was a counterinsurgency security organization, a wartime ally of us. Through the spring of '08, he transformed it into a political party, and that's when our relationship with him sort of changed. About April, May, they registered the Awakening as a political party. The tank in front of his house and the daily U.S. military engagement with him ceased. The tank was taken away I think in October '07, just before we went to the U.S. We just can't choose sides among political parties, the U.S. government can't, and certainly the U.S. military ought to stay out of such kind of activities. By the spring of '08, they changed the Awakening into a political party, registered it. He has offices in other provinces of dubious connection to his own organization.*

A lot of groups around the country call themselves Awakenings, and I tell visitors that there are a lot of awakenings in Iraq, but only one Awakening with a capital "A," and that's the one in Ramadi. The others are sort of awakenings localized. If they want to use that term, that's up to them. But the press also falls into the trap, as I've

---

* Since Satter Abu Risha's death, especially since Ahmad Abu Risha turned the Awakening into a political party, many of the original Awakening sheikhs have disengaged from the group.

written in my State Department reports, of characterizing Ahmad Abu Risha as the leader of the Sunni Awakening, giving the false impression that the Sunni Awakening is a monolithic thing. There's no such thing. And if there is such a thing, it's under the leadership of Ahmad Abu Risha, which there's no such thing. It's a double fallacy. . . .

Colonel Gary W. Montgomery: Was the Awakening something that had coordination, or was it just people being moved in the same direction by the sweep of events?

Soriano: I think the latter is a good way of describing it, tribes moving in the same direction because of the sweep of events, and I think I mentioned some time ago that there was an earlier alliance of tribes out of al Qaim with the Coalition, but it was localized, as I said. It didn't go beyond al Qaim. What made the Awakening of Ramadi more distinct was it was really the turning. In al Qaim, it did not really turn the battlefield, as such. The battle was still raging, and the worst was yet to come in terms of fighting.

The Awakening in Ramadi was somewhat different, and it had different characteristics. In al Qaim, I don't think the youths of the place moved forward to join the police force. Part of Sheikh Sattar's strategy was to encourage the youth of the place to join the police. When I arrived in the middle of '06, police recruitment drives would attract a dozen or so kids. By the spring of '07, there were more recruits than there were places at the academy to train them. Much of that was due to the change of attitude by the tribal sheikhs in the Ramadi area, which then spread. Youths of other tribes along the river began to join the police force, perhaps by the sweep of events that you just mentioned. But there was no monolithic movement. The Awakening was, is, and perhaps will be always a localized Ramadi phenomenon. The big tribe to the west is the Abu Nimer, and they are definitely not Awakening. They have an agenda, and they are our wartime allies as well. To the east of Fallujah, the city is least tribal, in many respects, and it's an area, as many people would say, of IIP sympathy, rather than the Awakening.

Montgomery: Is that more in political terms?

Soriano: Political terms, sympathies, yeah, looking for leadership. The idea of pan tribal politics really has to be examined. The dynamic of tribal politics implies that no one leader shall get too strong. But I think that's what's going on. Ahmad Abu Risha has reached that point. Tribal engagement is what the Marines did out here and the Army did out here in Anbar, and it was certainly a necessary tactic of the insurgency. And by tribal engagement, I mean a day to day meeting on a face to face basis at the battalion and the company level of localized sheikhs, using CERP [Commander's Emergency Relief Program] funds to lubricate a more productive relationship with those sheikhs and getting the sheikhs to get off the fence. Sheikhs are not leaders. Sheikhs are followers. Some would say sheikhs are cowards. They follow opinion. They do not lead opinion. Many of them fled to Jordan. Some of them were asked to go to Jordan by their own people, for their own safety.

It was a combination of four factors that led to the tipping of the battlefield in our favor. The first was a change of public opinion in '06 '07 in which there was a redefinition of the enemy. We were no longer seen as the enemy, but as a friend, and al Qaeda was no longer seen as a defender, but as an enemy. [The second] was a tribal engagement, the day to day tea drinking with a lot of local notables to get them to come off the fence and onto our side. The third was police recruitment, which is perhaps the most important factor of them all. There are now, what, 28,000 police in the province? When I arrived here, there were fewer than 6,000 on the rolls, but hardly any on the streets. And that filled the void. After the downfall of Saddam [Hussein], a void was created, and the bad guys floated in the void. And the fourth was the effectiveness of our combined operations, in all of its aspects, combined ISF [Iraqi security forces] and Coalition force operations, police operations, army operations, special teams that went after the bad guys and just eliminated them one by one. Those were important.

Even population control measures were part of that. I think the lesson learned there is the population in an insurgency will tolerate a certain amount of inconvenience, of population control measures, of barricades, entry points, and so forth, provided that the counterinsurgent also has to provide some measure of security at the end of the struggle. So he has to keep up his end of the bargain. You have to have a vehicle curfew for many hours a day. At the end of the day, if you want to put it that way, the security has to be restored. So those are I think the four big ones, the change of public opinion and the role of the mosque, by the way. It's something you don't even understand in public opinion. In '05, they were calling for insurrection. By '06, they were calling for moderation. By '09, they were telling the people to get out and vote. The change in public opinion, tribal engagement as a tool, police recruitment, and effectiveness of military operations.

Montgomery: You said that the sheikhs don't create public opinion, they follow it. But you also said that Sheikh Sattar had a strategy of getting the young men involved in the police force, which if it was his strategy, they were following him to some degree. I always had the impression that the tribes and the sheikhs were similar to feudalism, sort of a mutual contract. The sheikh helps gets jobs and benefits for the people who follow him, and in return, they do follow him, and it increases his influence. So it was sort of like feudalism without coercion.

Soriano: You're right. The point I wanted to make is that, by and large, tribal leaders are not leaders. They tend to be followers. I guess what I was trying to capture in that sentence is that most Iraqis hold tribal leaders in contempt, because of the feudal aspect that you just mentioned. It just reminds them of a way of life that is archaic in many respects. If you like a society where the destiny of a woman is decided before the time she's 14 years old, you'll love a tribal society like rural Iraq.

Montgomery: So is that why the rest of Iraq holds them out as the Wild West Anbar Province?

Soriano: Obviously, all of Iraq has some aspects of tribalism left, and the secret that is not said openly is that the people, when they go to the polls, prefer government by technocrats and not by tribal leaders. That's pretty clear. As a matter of fact, Ahmad Abu Risha, who did well at the polls, also has a party yoked to him and his coalition that is technocratic in nature and has links to the university.

The issue of tribal engagement [is] something I don't think the U.S. forces understood in '03 when we entered here, and perhaps we mistreated tribal leaders and didn't show them sufficient respect or understand their role. Tribal engagement had a very important role to play in turning the battle in our favor, by bringing [in] these fence sitters. "My God, the Americans are here. Let's jump on the bandwagon with them"—that didn't happen. It took some persuasion to get that to happen, and they—the tribal leaders—had to see that the battlefield was tipping in our favor, Sattar Abu Risha being the exception. And the reason why he stands out so much is because he is an exception. He was a leader. I can't take that away from the guy. But others, where he stands, there's 20, 30, 40 behind him that are fence sitters. Once we Americans discovered the the force multiplier effect of tribal engagement, we jumped all over it and ... tried to have other MNDs [multinational divisions] do what was done in Anbar to replicate the success we have here.

All of that is true historically, and the reason we did tribal engagement, as I said, is really to get the tribal leader to prevent his teenagers from planting bombs against American teenagers. Basically, that's what it pointed down to. Get your kids to stop planting IEDs for $200. Al Qaeda pays them whatever, and then they blow our kids up. That's true. We did get them to stop that, but tribal engagement by itself never explained why the first teenager planted the first bomb. If the counterinsurgent believes that the tribal leader is strong enough to influence his teenagers, why did the first teenager plant the first bomb? The answer is that the tribal system has been under stress for decades, for generations. The tribal way of life is being pulled apart by the forces of modernity and globalization, and even literacy. Making a woman read and write is a threat to a tribal way of life, to be quite honest with you. That was being torn apart.

The former regime runs into hiding, they're thrown out, a vacuum is created. We foolishly stand around with our hands in our pockets, and into that vacuum flow Islamic radicals. After that, chaos breaks out, and when you're in a situation like that, people really fell back on this primordial social structure of the tribe for protection. At that point, we went to the tribal leaders, and they said, "We need, first of all, security and protection."

Somebody has to write the study on the limits of tribal engagement. Marines get a full chapter in the next manual on counterinsurgency on tribal engagement. Their experience in Anbar Province is a textbook example of how to do it right. There's a limit to tribal engagement, and that is in the post conflict period. The logic of continuing to engage tribal leaders is opposite of that of capacity building for a legitimate structure of government, or a modern structure of government, I should say.

We've got RCT [regimental combat team] commanders in the field today who would love to get some CERP money and do a sweetheart deal with this sheikh and that sheikh to buy off their goodwill. CERP ought to be used by the commander for goodwill, sweetheart deals favoring this sheikh or that sheikh. But that act itself, the sweetheart deal, is an American version of the corruption that Iraqis themselves are fed up with. . . . But it's understandable. We do it to save lives, our own kids, okay? And there's nothing we can do, just to get out of here as fast as we can, find a way of exiting, spread around one last go around of play money to the sheikhs, if you will, say thank you very much, we've been here six, seven years, it's time for us to go home. . . .

The Marines got it. I mean, General [John F.] Kelly knew. He understood, he saw what had to be done, when it had to be done. You engage tribes, you beat the enemy. When the enemy is beaten, then you've got to do civil capacity. The tribes are still there. You still have to have some sort of engagement with them, but they're not necessarily the future. . . . What I saw in '06 was very impressive and was the model for other MNDs to follow. You guys found the key. You had a key, a force multiplier, with a little CERP money on that. There's nothing wrong with it. I'm not condemning that. That's fine, at a certain stage, when you're fighting a war. But, as time goes on, you've got to make adjustments.

Interview 20
Transition to Iraqi Control, Part IV

Ms. Carol J. Wilson

Al-Anbar Provincial Representative
United States Agency for International Development

August 2008 to August 2009

Ms. Carol J. Wilson arrived in al Anbar Province as the provincial representative for the United States Agency for International Development [USAID] in August 2008. After growing up on a farm in Iowa, she earned degrees from Iowa State University and the University of Virginia. She participated in international development as a Peace Corps volunteer before joining the U.S. Department of Agriculture, managing projects in India, Thailand, and Europe during her 10 years with that department. After serving more than 10 years with USAID, Ms. Wilson first went to Iraq in July 2006, working in the agency's Baghdad office to provide technical support and to design an agricultural program that would support the provincial reconstruction teams and help Iraqi farmers gain better access to overseas markets. Following that assignment, she went to Afghanistan for a year before returning to Iraq.

In this interview, Ms. Wilson describes the economic and agriculture programs that USAID has been providing to Iraqis to help revitalize their economic and agricultural sectors.

Ms. Wilson was interviewed by Colonel Gary W. Montgomery and Chief Warrant Officer 4 Timothy S. McWilliams on 13 February 2009 at Camp Ramadi, Iraq.

Chief Warrant Officer-4 Timothy S. McWilliams: Since last August [2008] when you arrived, can you give us an idea of the scope of work that you're doing?

Ms. Carol J. Wilson: As the USAID [United States Agency for International Development] rep, I started out at the embedded PRT [provincial reconstruction team]. . . . We have four projects here in Ramadi. One is the Community Stabilization Program. We have a micro plans institution here called al Taqaddum, which is part of a [Tejar] program. We have the Inma* program that is stimulating the mushroom factory and a little bit of other technical assistance here, and then we have what we call the Iraq Program, the Iraq Rapid Assistance Program [IRAP], which is designed to be a flexible grant program, similar to CERP [Commander's Emergency Response Project] funds, and we have access to funding on what we do, I guess immediate term type of assistance.

So it's my job just to oversee them, make sure that they do some oversight, just make sure that the project is going in the right way, provide some guidance to the team members on what type of programs or proposals they may develop, try to shape it so you don't have a negative impact. You may do a short term fix but have a negative impact on the long term, so we're trying to make sure that we don't do that inadvertently. There are times when we may make a decision that's strategic, and you say, "Well, we really do need to fix this right now." But I think that if you do that, you still need to know if there's going to be adverse effects in the long term, so you can take action to correct that.

Colonel Gary W. Montgomery: How do you determine that—if it will have an adverse impact in the long term?

Wilson: Some things we just know. Like, for example, giving out grant money to people, if you go in and it's right after a battle, and you want to get people back on their feet, it's a good thing. But if you keep continuing to give out that money, then you completely disrupt any financial system. Nobody will be looking at taking loans and looking at making longer term investments and making a business so they can pay it back, give back a loan. Instead, what you'll see now is people just coming to us, asking for money, just constantly wanting the money and thinking that we're just going to fix whatever it is that gets broken because we've been here fixing things for so long that they're just completely used to that, and probably thinking, "Why spend my own money, why take a loan, when I can get the Americans to pay for it?"

---

* Inma is an Arabic word that means growth.

So that's the sort of thing where we know that's what's going to happen. We've had experiences in other countries. We know that that's what's going to happen, but it's the amount of time that you do it. So that's where we're at now, trying to stop the grant programs and get it into more of a normal development assistance type of program, working with banking systems, working with financial institutions.

Getting people to pay for services, that's another example. People were wanting as part of the stabilization program, offering training programs to people, whether it be English, computer training, sewing, business training, whatever it may be. It may be well intentioned to provide the people with a stipend, transportation costs, etc., but what that does is then ruin any efforts of trying to make a business center or a training center sustainable by charging fees, because nobody's going to want to pay the fee, because they've always gotten that paid for. So that's the sort of thing we're trying to grapple with right now. They're just so used to getting things paid for that if we offer a class and just say you have to pay your own transportation, we have people who say, "No thank you. If you're not going to pay my transportation, I don't want to go." So then you have to say, "Well, then, why should we offer the class? If you're not willing to come and even bring yourself to it, let alone pay a fee for it, then why should we offer that class?"

McWilliams: You listed four programs. Could you describe those?

Wilson: Yes, the Community Stabilization Program, CSP, a lot of people here refer to it as IRD. IRD is our implementing program, International Relief and Development. The Community Stabilization Program was designed back in 2006. It got underway in 2007, and it was done in collaboration with the military as part of the counterinsurgency program. CSP has three areas they work on: infrastructure; economic growth and youth; and business development services. As part of the economic growth and youth program, they have some vocational training programs. All of it was really oriented toward employment generation, so it was getting people back to work. Even the infrastructure programs were about getting people back to work, and then the vocational training was to teach them the skills they may need for the infrastructure projects—masonry or bricklaying, masonry stuff, carpentry, other types of skills.

And then the business development services, what we did with our grants program, AID did support a grants program, but along with that, we included business development training. So the person would go through a training program on how to run a business, get the grant, and then three months later, they'd come back for a refresher course—after running the business for three months—on marketing and other ways to make your accounting practices, make your business more profitable. And so then they would do follow up visits and checks on the business. We would also do direct procurement, rather than just giving them the money directly, where if they had whatever type of store, then we would buy the product for them that they would then sell as part of the grant. So we tried not to just give away the money, in order to track where it went.

Montgomery: When you said community stabilization, what do you mean by that?

Wilson: The Community Stabilization Program was a civilian effort to come right along with the military [after violence or combat], often in collaboration with the civil affairs program. And oftentimes they would work together and divide up different areas, based on expertise, to work with that community to get it back on its feet again. So they were here in Ramadi working. They started here in I think it was early to mid 2007, and at first, the implementing, we had American staff that lived here on the base, and then as soon as it got secure enough, then they moved outside. I think they've said they've been out there a little over a year now, so that would have been actually probably late 2007 when they moved off the base and into town, into one of the villas. And then they established their office. I think they said it was 150 employees—Iraqi staff—they had working directly for them managing these different types of infrastructure and training programs. Overall, that program has been fairly large throughout the whole country. I think it's like $850 million. So I'm not talking about a small project when they're doing these sort of things.

They're reaching out to a lot of people. So, for example, one of the buildings we're doing here in Ramadi right now is the library, and that's a $2 million project.

To give you an idea of the scale of it, when I look at our IRD staff, I think they're very brave, because these were Americans that were working here, following directly after a military action, working with the communities, trying to get them back on their feet. And we're working, and they have their bodyguards and stuff, but they're unarmed. They're civilians. And to me, that's part of the success story. Right now, they're living in Ramadi, and they're moving around in armored vehicles, and they're guarded, but they're still moving around ... they're living in the city. We have five cities here in Anbar, so they were in Ramadi, Haditha, Habbaniyah, and al Qaim. So we've had Americans living in these cities probably the same amount of time as here in Ramadi. We have American staff out there. In some cases, I think like in Habbaniyah, though, they did live with the Marines on their base there, FOB [forward operating base].

Montgomery: I think the very fact that they're out in town now says a whole lot.

Wilson: I think so. . . . And they move around pretty freely. They're not wearing their vest and helmets [inaudible], and they're moving around, not having any problems. Their biggest concern is if the IP [Iraqi police] are just shooting off in the air, shooting their weapons around. So to me, that's where I look at it, as it definitely seems to me the time for the regular USAID type of programs to begin. You agree with our decision makers that the stabilization program needs to come to an end. It's now time for the next generation of programs, because our folks are definitely out there moving around.

McWilliams: So it's a building block approach?

Wilson: Exactly, and that's where we have other partners that have been nervous about coming up here, but I keep pointing to our IRD staffs and [say] look, they're here, living here, no problems.

Montgomery: Are you getting many NGOs [nongovernmental organizations] coming into the country?

Wilson: Well, IRD is an NGO. They're an international NGO. We have different types of whether they're for profit or not for profit. IRD is a not for profit institution. They're a large NGO that does a lot of implementation of USAID funded programs. They're here. CHF [Cooperative Housing Foundation] is another one that's an NGO, a large international NGO, but they're here, and they've been working in Anbar for quite some time. Their approach has been more under the radar screen, so while IRD was working very closely with the civil affairs units, CAP, Community Action Program, which has been implemented by CHF, was trying to work under the radar. So they would work with political staff, working with the communities, have no connection to American staff at all on the military. So they didn't meet with USAID people. They didn't meet with our military colleagues. They just definitely kept separate. And that's changing, too. That was another argument that we made, that's like Anbar is now secure enough, people are not under threat. They come out openly to meet with us, so there is no need for the CAP program to remain secret. We need to now know more about what's going on. They need to coordinate with us in advance, collaborate with us.

Montgomery: Oh, I see, it's a matter of how you calculate the allocation of funds and what you would expect from it.

Wilson: Yeah. And for a for profit contractor, usually the way we would work with them is at the direction of the government. It's in the government's interest, so if we're doing a project with them, we have more control over that. If we're working with a not for profit institution, we do what we would call a cooperative agreement, so that we have less oversight. It's more their program. It's more their implementation, more their decisions. We still have input into their work plan. They still have to meet government regulations and requirements, but we put more of the burden on the implementer to make some of those day to day decisions. Some people would say that there's more buy in that way, that since it's more their program, it's more in their interests to make sure that there's good results. But I've found that it also depends on the people. We have contractors that are working for us that care just as much about the results as a not for profit, so it just depends on the way we manage it, I guess.

Montgomery: Since they have less self interest in it, then would you say they're given more latitude?

Wilson: Yeah, I think that's pretty fair. A contractor would tend to go into a risky situation because they would take the risk because they want to make the profit. . . . We have Al Taqaddum, it's been three branches—there's one in Fallujah, one in Ramadi, and one in al Qaim. And they provide small loans to people, say between $3,000 and $4,000 is the average size of the loan. And then people repay that, and they pay a small fee. They try to avoid the interest rates here to try to make them more fitting in with the Islamic banking type of practices, but they'll charge a fee, and it's a sliding fee. So in some ways, it's almost similar to interest. You just pay it up front.

McWilliams: So that's available for anybody who needs to grow a business or start a business?

Wilson: Right. And then some of the issues are what types of collateral do people have? Do they always have access to collateral? What do they provide? And especially if it's a small business, then there are ways if they do have a legitimate business, and it makes it a lot easier to make the loan. They've given several loans for cars because people want to start driving taxis, so they turn that into a business. And that's if they have a good looking business plan, then a lot of times they'll take the risk. We have a really good repayment rate here. I think it's really high; it's like 90 percent for repayment. Some could argue in that case that they're not taking enough risks, they need to branch out and support more small businesses.

McWilliams: What other types of businesses are there?

Wilson: They've got taxis. I guess there have been a few women that have taken loans out for hairstyling, hairdressing types of businesses. Sewing seems to be popular. I'm not sure how many sewing centers there are that are profitable, but it sure seems to be popular. People talk about it a lot and want to set up sewing shops. I know of a couple of women that are running some larger ones, and they sew curtains for the hospitals and stuff like that, but they've gotten some loans from us, loans and grants actually, in a couple of cases. We've supported some agricultural type of loans, helping people buy equipment. We keep experimenting with seeds and fertilizer. That one's typically much more risky and harder to do. Even in the U.S., it's harder to do, but we're encouraging [that]. . . .

We've been trying to get the agriculture program, Inma, working more in Anbar. We've had a slow start in getting that program up and going and really reaching out into the provinces. They came out last year and reestablished a mushroom factory. [Mantha Kirbit had] a functioning mushroom factory before the war, and there's supposedly a good market for mushrooms, [but] part of the problem is transportation. Because of the heat and everything, they have to sell them daily. So he's working on cold storage facilities and trying to improve, get some cold storage trucks. . . . Once they get that, then they can actually reach the Baghdad market. . . . So it was helping him rehabilitate his facilities. They're pretty much just old and beat up. I don't think anything was really bombed out, but it was just pretty much neglected. And part of it was he wanted to get a larger sized business up and going because, again, it's employment generation that we're looking at. In addition, it just helps with the local market as well, which is very important.

McWilliams: And then your fourth program was the IRAP?

Wilson: Yeah. The IRAP program is a small grants program pretty much designed to assist the PRT technical officers in getting access to funding. I think the maximum was $200,000. They're going out with their civil affairs counterparts, and they see something that needs to be done. They didn't have access to the CERP funds so they could make a more immediate response. So it was a way for USAID [and the] State Department to be able to have access to that funding and be able to make a quick response.

We've used that to work along with the civil affairs units in some cases. If they're rehabilitating a school, maybe we'll buy furniture and books and outfit the school. In rehabilitating the library, we're also purchasing some furniture and some books for the library. In order to support the elections, we funded three NGOs that were then trained. They received all the training and got the certification, the cards and everything, and then they became trainers who went out and reached out to other NGOs, who then went and started letting people know this is—once we got the official ballots—here's the ballots, here's how to understand them, here's how you would go and vote. Not crossing the line, of course, and telling them who to vote for, but following the procedures. I think they said it was 30,000 people that were able to go and conduct their training or do the outreach programs. . . . So that was pretty successful.

McWilliams: What are some of the cultural challenges that you face here that you might not experience somewhere else? Are there unique challenges here?

Wilson: Yes. I think the biggest one, and frustration that we have, is being so disconnected from the community. Most places where we would work, and where we would have [US]AID programs, it's not as dangerous, usually. We're working in—crime notwithstanding; we do work in places like South Africa that have pretty high crime rates—but Guatemala, El Salvador, Honduras, Nicaragua, any of our Eastern European countries, we would be living, our officers would be living in the community in town. You'd get to know the neighbors. You're going to the restaurants. You essentially become a part of the community, so you're interacting with them, and you have a much closer understanding for the culture, for the language, because you'd be out there living and working in that, and you would have I guess an easier time of learning a language. Then also, [you are] just much closer to the project implementation as well because then you can see it first hand.

Here there's all kinds of rumors that go around, and I'll hear a variety of stories about whether people really think IRD was helpful or not. And some of that comes from the community that didn't get a project, so then they dislike IRD because they didn't get any—the contractor who didn't get the contract, so that he's going to complain about the work. Or they supported what they call the illegal councils, the councils that stayed versus the people that were part of the provincial council that left, or the city councils that left, and then they came back. So then you've got those divides in the political parties and so, "Oh, you're supporting that party, or that party." So if we were out there [as] a part of the community, then we would be interacting and seeing first hand, and we could talk about it, and we could talk to people.

Here, we're just so disconnected that we just hear the stories on occasion, and we don't really know where they're coming from. You kind of guess, but you don't really know. And then from a USAID perspective, we're really reliant on our implementing partner—for example, IRD—because they're out there. They're living out there. So I'm really reliant on getting information from them. Usually, it's part of my job to provide some oversight, monitoring of their work. Here I can do a little bit of it, but I can't do it the way we would normally do it.

McWilliams: Iraq was once referred to as a grain belt of the Middle East. Is there a possibility of returning to that?

Wilson: I think maybe in some very specific ways. I think it could be. I think they need to look harder at their irrigation systems and what they want to do, and sustainability of those irrigation systems. But putting up higher value crops, similar to in California, the high value—the broccoli, the tomatoes, cabbage, that sort of thing—versus wheat. If you look at it from that perspective, [wheat is] not economically supportable, in my opinion, for production here. So at the higher value, I think they could do better.

Montgomery: What's the shortcoming in irrigation systems?

Wilson: Some of that is looking at the recharge rates. In the U.S., with the [overall lock], for instance, we're depleting it. I don't know what the recharge rate is and whatnot, but the scientists will look at that. They would evaluate that. When I was in Afghanistan, that was definitely an issue, and what the geologists would tell me is it depends on if you're pulling out what they call "old water," or "ancient water," then you know it doesn't recharge quickly, and so you probably shouldn't be using that to irrigate. You have to be careful.

Montgomery: I thought it all just came right out of the river.

Wilson: Some of it. I think they are using probably some to irrigate, but usually they use a deep water well, and so then you're tapping down into those aquifers, the underground rivers. And that's where

I think they do need to take a look at that. USAID has been asked to rehabilitate some of the irrigation systems. So it was one of our requirements to do an environmental impact assessment. That's one of the things you check.

Because of the Oil for Food Program, it's been a long time since anybody's really undertaken real scientific studies here. That was one of the reasons for the significant decrease in agricultural production here was during the Oil for Food Program times, then they didn't get the inputs that they were used to getting as part of what Saddam [Hussein] used to give out, [which] was free seeds, and fertilizer, and tractors. It just got neglected, and during that time period, my understanding was that they lost some of their markets, and so it's just over a 10 year period of time, it's really hard to get that back.

McWilliams: Right. Now, are you talking al Anbar, or Iraq wide?

Wilson: I believe that's Iraqi wide. I know definitely it's had a significant impact here in Anbar, especially if you look at the markets. The farmers have lost those markets to other traders, and then once they get those traders that are used to working with them, and they know them, it's really hard to break back in. But I know it did impact all of Iraq.

Montgomery: What do you deal with in governance?

Wilson: In governance, we have a lot of different areas we're working on. Specifically, we're going to be working on training programs for the new provincial council and the new governor, and we will tailor make those programs to whatever the needs of the council members or the governor are, depending on who it is. If it's somebody who has no experience, we'll be able to give them the type of programs they need to get them up to speed. If it's somebody who we've been working with, and he's pretty well educated and understands it, then we can tailor make some programs if they have specific questions on some of the finer points.

The provincial powers law is pretty broad, and we definitely don't want to interpret it for anybody, but if somebody had questions on types of interpretation, then we could guide them to ways maybe in their own government where they could seek those types of clarifications, or give them examples of how we've tried to clarify them in the U.S. or even in another country, so that sort of thing. We're doing some work with civil society, trying to work with community groups since they're not used to working with their government and getting their needs supported, working with the community groups on how to advocate for changes in their community to the local government, to the municipal level government.

And then [we are] trying to train the municipal level government and the provincial government on how to listen to the constituents. What does that mean? Because working in a top down environment, they're just simply not used to taking that into account. Why ask? So we have to educate them [that] this is the way people will ask for things, and these are the appropriate ways that you can respond. . . . So somebody's just coming to—for example—coming to complain that the schools are dirty. Yes, you'll hire a cleaner, but then how do you impact the overall problem? Do you give more budget to the individual school? Are they going to be more top down? Are they going to just hire the cleaners and then go out and say, "Okay, you're going to clean the whole school." [We're] just giving them the type of options of the way they can respond.

Montgomery: Are they generally receptive to this, or do you have to overcome a sense of they've already got an idea of how things are going to work, in a way? Or "I'll go to the sheikh," that sort of thing?

Wilson: We hear a variety of things. I think that mostly what we're hearing is that the people want to be able to come to the government and have a representative government, rather than just relying on the sheikh, that they would like to have that. What's interesting is that we've been working with the ePRT [embedded provincial reconstruction team], working with the municipal government here. Mayor Latif [Obaid Ayada of Ramadi] and some of his advisers, especially at first, his adviser would come and say, "I've been to the schools. The schools are dirty. Coalition forces hired widows to clean the schools. We want you to hire more widows." Well, that's a good example of something that you need to start pushing the mayor and the DGs [director generals] of education on how to respond, rather than just asking us for the funding to do that. "That's something you need to do. That's how it works in America. Well, you've got to try it here, too." And so then, actually, they go off, and they'll make a report, and they'll come back and say, "Well, we were able to do this. We were able to get this fixed, we were able to do it."

So I think it's one of those things that I think they have it in their mind, "It can't be done," then they'll go do it, and it'll work. But then you have to keep reminding them, "Yes, it can be done," because then they'll come back to you again and say, "No, no, no, you can't do it." "Yeah, you can." So I think that is a bright spot. I think it is working by and large, but you've got to keep reminding them.

I've heard that story even on the larger scale with one of our budget guys who said that when they did go to Baghdad, when they did get the governor to go to Baghdad to fix a particular problem, it got fixed. But then if you're talking to the governor, he said, "Well, they don't listen to me. They won't do it." Well, that's where you pick your battles and you go push it. "Look, you had success before." Confidence building, I guess, hand holding [is what we're doing]. Some people would say maybe that's an example of it's time for us to back away—don't do it.

Everything I've heard from my USAID supervisors, I think they would agree with General [John F.] Kelly that it's been a very good and positive working relationship. I know that USAID has very much enjoyed also working with the Marines, and I guess feeling, I think in some ways it's sort of a [compatible] relationship. I know that the Marines are very action oriented and practical. USAID tends to try to be that way. We have our bureaucracy, but we're also project implementers. We go out, and we run programs. We may do it a little differently, but we're still program oriented.

Appendix

Acronyms & Abbreviations

Appendix

Acronyms and Abbreviations

I MEF	I Marine Expeditionary Force
II MEF	II Marine Expeditionary Force
ACE	Air Combat Element
ANGLICO	Air Naval Gunfire Liaison Company
AO	Area of Operation
AOR	Area of Responsibility
APC	Anbar People's Committee
AQI/AQIZ	Al Qaeda in Iraq
Arty LnO	Artillery Liaison Officer
ASR	Alternative Supply Route
BAT	Biometric Assessment Tool
BBC	British Broadcasting Corporation
BIAP	Baghdad International Airport
BCT	Brigade Combat Team
BTT	Border Transition Team
CA	Civil Affairs
CAG	Civil Affairs Group
CAP	Combined Action Platoon
Casevac	Casualty Evacuation
CBN	Chemical, Biological, and Nuclear Weapons
CentCom	U.S. Central Command, Tampa, FL
CERP	Commander's Emergency Relief Program
CFLCC	Coalition Forces Land Component Command
CG	Commanding General

CHF	Cooperative Housing Foundation
CJTF 7	Combined Joint Task Force 7
CLC	Concerned Local Citizens
CMO	Civil Military Operations
CMOC	Civil Military Operations Center
CNN	Cable News Network
CO	Commanding Officer
COA	Course of Action
COC	Combat Operations Center
COIN	Counterinsurgency
COP	Combat Outpost
CPA	Coalition Provisional Authority
CSP	Community Stabilization Program
CSS	Combat Service Support
DCG	Deputy Commanding General
Det	Detachment
DG	Director General
DoD	U.S. Department of Defense
DoS	U.S. Department of State
ECP	Entry Control Points
ECRA	Emergency Council for the Rescue of al Anbar
EOD	Explosive Ordnance Disposal
ePRT	Embedded Provincial Reconstruction Team
ERU	Emergency Response Unit
EWS	Expeditionary Warfare School, Quantico, VA
FAO	Foreign Area Officer
FLOT	Forward Line of Troops

FLT	Fallujah Liason Team
FOB	Forward Operating Base
FSSG	Force Service Support Group
GCC	Gulf Cooperation Council
GCE	Ground Combat Element
GDP	Gross Domestic Product
GOI	Government of Iraq
H&S	Headquarters & Support
HUMINT	Human Intelligence
HVI	High Value Individual
IA	Iraqi Army
IC	Intelligence Community
ICDC	Iraqi Civil Defense Corps
ID	Identification
IECI	Independent Election Committee of Iraq
IED	Improvised Explosive Device
IIP	Islamic Iraqi Party
IO	Information Operations
IP	Iraqi Police
IRAP	Iraq Rapid Assistance Program
IRD	International Relief and Development
ISF	Iraqi Security Forces
ISR	Intelligence, Surveillance, Reconnaissance
ITAO	Iraq Transition Assistance Office
IZ	International Zone, Baghdad ["Green Zone"]
JCC	Joint Coordination Center
JMD	Joint Manning Document
JSS	Joint Security Stations
JTAC	Joint Tactical Air Controller

KIA	Killed in Action
LAPD	Los Angeles Police Department
LD	Line of Departure
LNO	Liaison Officer
LOC	Line of Communication
LOO	Line of Operation
LRAD	Long Range Acoustic Device
MAGTF	Marine Air Ground Task Force
MARCENT	Marine Corps Central Command, Tampa, FL
MARDIV	Marine Division
MarForPac	Marine Forces Pacific
MCIA	Marine Corps Intelligence Activity
MEU	Marine Expeditionary Unit
MLG	Marine Logistics Unit
MML	Mohammed Mahmoud Latif
MNC I	Multi National Corps Iraq
MND	Multinational Division
MNF	Multinational Force
MNF I	Multi National Force Iraq
MNF W	Multi National Force West
MNF West	Multi National Force West
MOD	Minister of Defense
MOS	Military Occupational Specialty
MP	Military Police
MSR	Main Supply Route
MSI	Mutamar Sahwa al Iraq
MTT	Military Transition Team
NCO	Noncommissioned Officer
NGO	Nongovernmental Organization

NPR	National Public Radio
O&M	Operations and Maintenance
OGA	Other Government Agency
OIF I	Operation Iraqi Freedom I
OIF II	Operation Iraqi Freedom II
OODA	Observe, Orient, Decide, Act
OPA	Office of Provincial Authority
OP	Observation Posts
OpsO	Operations Officer
OVR	Operation Vigilant Resolve
P&R	Programs and Resources
PA	Public Address
PAO	Public Affairs Officer
PDOP	Provincial Director of Police
PFT	Physical Fitness Test
PIC	Provincial Iraqi Control
PGM	Precision Guided Missile
PJCC	Provisional Joint Coordination Center
PM	Prime Minister
PPE	Personal Protective Equipment
PRT	Provincial Reconstruction Team
PSD	Personal Security Detail
PsyOps	Psychological Operations
PTT	Police Transition Team
QRF	Quick Reaction Force or Quick Reaction Funds
R&S	Reconnaissance and Surveillance
RCT	Regimental Combat Team
RFF	Request for Forces
RIP	Relief in Place

RIPTOA	Relief in Place/Transfer of Authority
ROC	Required Operation Capacity
ROE	Rules of Engagement
RPG	Rocket Propelled Grenade
RTI	Research Triangle Institute
SAA	Sahwa al Anbar
SAI	Sahwa al Iraq
SASO	Stability and Support Operations
SeaBees	Construction Battalions (CBs)
SIGINT	Signals Intelligence
SecDef	Secretary of Defense
SOFA	Status of Forces Agreement
SOI	Sons of Iraq
SPTT	Special Police Transition Team
SVBIED	Suicide Vehicle Borne Improvised Explosive Device
TACON	Tactical Control
TECOM	Training and Education Command
TO	Table of Organization or Task Organization
TOA	Transfer of Authority
TPT	Tactical PsyOps [Psychological Operations] Team
TTP	Tactics, Techniques, and Procedures
UN	United Nations
USAID	United States Agency for International Development
VBIED	Vehicle Borne Improvised Explosive Device
WMD	Weapons of Mass Destuction
XO	Executive Officer

About the Editors

Chief Warrant Officer-4 Timothy S. McWilliams, U.S. Marine Corps Reserve, served in Fallujah in 2004 as a logistics officer. He joined the U.S. Marine Corps History Division in 2007 and has deployed to both Iraq and Afghanistan as a field historian. McWilliams has worked in the marketing and communications field and recently earned a master's degree in history from California State University, Chico.

Lieutenant Colonel Kurtis P. Wheeler, U.S. Marine Corps Reserve, deployed to Iraq during 2006 2007 as a field historian for the U.S. Marine Corps History Division and has also collected for the History Division in the Republic of Georgia. Commissioned in 1989, he served with 10th Marines in Operation Desert Storm and with the tank and civil affairs communities as a reserve officer. He holds bachelor's and master's degrees from Harvard University and is the history department chairman and teacher in Cazenovia, New York.

Printed in Great Britain
by Amazon.co.uk, Ltd.,
Marston Gate.